# THE ANNOTATED INNOCENCE OF
## FATHER BROWN

# THE
# ANNOTATED
## INNOCENCE
## OF
## FATHER BROWN

The Innocence of Father Brown
by
G. K. Chesterton

With Introduction and
Notes by
Martin Gardner

Oxford    New York
OXFORD UNIVERSITY PRESS
1987

Oxford University Press, Walton Street, Oxford OX2 6DP

Oxford    New York    Toronto
Delhi    Bombay    Calcutta    Madras    Karachi
Petaling Jaya    Singapore    Hong Kong    Tokyo
Nairobi    Dar es Salaam    Cape Town
Melbourne    Auckland

and associated companies in
Beirut    Berlin    Ibadan    Nicosia

Oxford is a trade mark of Oxford University Press

The Innocence of Father Brown was first published
in 1911 by Cassell and Company Ltd.

British Library Cataloguing in Publication Data
Chesterton, G. K.
[The innocence of Father Brown].
The annotated Innocence of Father Brown:
The innocence of Father Brown.
I. [The innocence of Father Brown] I. Title
II. Gardner, Martin, 1914–
823'.912[F]        PR4453.C4
ISBN 0-19-217748-6

Library of Congress Cataloging in Publication Data
Chesterton, G. K. (Gilbert Keith), 1874–1936.
The annotated Innocence of Father Brown.
Bibliography: p.    Includes index.
I. Gardner, Martin, 1914–    .  II. Title.
PR4453.C417   1987   823'.912   86–12830
ISBN 0-19-217748-6

Set by Promenade Graphics Ltd.
Printed in Great Britain by
Richard Clay Ltd.
Bungay, Suffolk

# CONTENTS

# INTRODUCTION

England's most famous fictional detective is, of course, Sherlock Holmes. So great was Conan Doyle's skill in story-telling that Holmes and Watson have become, in a sense, more 'real' than their creator. We know Holmes better than we know some of our friends, whereas Doyle has faded into a hazy simple-minded Spiritualist who seems to have no connection with Holmes.

The Baker Street Irregulars, an organization of Holmes enthusiasts, has grown steadily over the years, and there is now a vast literature of mock-serious scholarship devoted to the Holmes 'canon'. Several encyclopaedias are now available that list all the names and places in the canon. William Baring-Gould's *Annotated Sherlock Holmes* (New York: Clarkson Potter, 1967) brought together the results of more than half a century of research since Vincent Starrett's pioneering *Private Life of Sherlock Holmes* (New York: Macmillan, 1933).

Nothing like the Baker Street Irregulars has been formed around the Father Brown canon—five books of short stories plus several tales not in any of the books. I find this surprising. The little priest is by all odds the second most famous mystery-solver in English literature, and he has always had a devoted following, not just in England, but throughout the world. Moreover, Chesterton was as careless with his details as Dr Watson, and as many curious questions can be asked about the priest as about Holmes. What, for example, was Father Brown's first name? There are as many passages in the Father Brown books that concern matters familiar to Edwardian readers, but that are unintelligible today, as there are obscure references in the Holmes canon that were equally clear to Victorian readers.

*The Annotated Innocence of Father Brown* is my attempt to examine a Father Brown book—the first of five—with the same care, and in the same spirit, as Baring-Gould's *Annotated Sherlock Holmes*. The text is based on the earliest British edition (1911), in turn a reprinting of stories that appeared in two British periodicals, the *Storyteller* and *Cassell's Magazine*. The stories were heavily edited for the book with, one assumes, Chesterton's co-operation and approval. I have made no attempt in my notes to point out every word or phrase that was altered; that would have more than tripled the number of notes. I have limited such notes to spots where the original wording has special significance, or where a passage, sometimes an entire paragraph, was added or omitted. Many later editions of the book were carelessly proofed. My eighth edition of Cassell's *Father Brown Omnibus* (1956), for example, is still riddled with the printer's errors that occur in their first edition of the *Omnibus*, though not in the same company's first edition of *The Innocence*. There also are textual differences between the first British and the first American edition of *The Innocence*.

Father Brown stories obviously belong to the classical tradition of mysteries in which the reader is challenged to solve a puzzle. The story is a game between reader and writer. The author tries to play fair, yet at the same time surprise readers with a simple solution that they could have guessed but did not. Like so many Sherlockian plots, and those of Agatha Christie and other great masters of the puzzle genre, the plots of Father Brown tend to be enormously improbable. Indeed, improbable is an understatement. This should not, however, be grounds for dismissing the stories as unworthy. The proper attitude is to accept these semi-fantasies for what G.K. intended them to be—light-hearted comedies built around a puzzling crime. 'Mysterious murders', Chesterton once wrote, 'belong to the grand and joyful company of the things called jokes. The story is a fancy; an avowedly fictitious fiction. We may say if we like that it is a very artificial form of art; I should prefer to say that it is professedly a toy, a thing that children "pretend" with.'

You might be tempted to suppose that today's mystery fiction has abandoned fantasy for realism—taking plots away from what Raymond Chandler scornfully described as murder in the vicar's garden, and giving them back to the people who are really good at it. The modern 'hardboiled' detective story, as it has been called, with its emphasis on sex and violence, is often regarded as a shift from fantasy to tough realism. In some cases this is true, but it takes only a moment of reflection to realize that the hardboiled novel today has been pushed to extremes of improbability even greater than the extremes in Chesterton's tales.

Let us count some ways. When you watch a contemporary

2

television or motion-picture mystery you are likely to see more than half of the following tired motifs:

1. The detective goes to bed at least once with a buxom young woman involved in his case, while his loyal and equally gorgeous secretary, back in the office, is tirelessly checking data on the crime.

2. There will be at least one wild car chase in which the cars will narrowly miss killing twenty pedestrians. They will knock over street stands, damage parked cars, sometimes drive through a crowded playground. During the chase the cars will screech around corners and perform acrobatic leaps that outdo trained horses. The chase may end with a terrible car crash out of which passengers will emerge (they seem never to have used seat belts) in a slightly dazed condition just before the car explodes into flames.

3. The detective will chase a suspect over the roofs of tall buildings, the pair leaping twenty feet across chasms.

4. The detective will jump and crash through a closed window.

5. The detective will engage in at least one fist fight in which he will be hit repeatedly on the face by bare fists. In the real world such blows would shatter his jaw, break his nose, or knock out an eye. At the end of the fight the hero's clothes will be immaculate, though he may be breathing hard and have a slight cut on a cheek.

6. Faced with a locked door, the dectective will take a small tool from his pocket, jiggle it in the lock, and in two seconds the lock is picked. (Ask any locksmith how long it takes an expert to pick a cylinder lock.)

7. With one kick the detective will break open a sturdy hotel door.

8. Although the detective seems unusually bright, always alert to danger, at some point a bad guy will sneak up behind him and knock him out with a blow that would smash the skull of King Kong. A few minutes later the detective is reviving, rubbing the back of his head, perhaps dashing cold water on his face.

9. A guilty party will meet justice by being shot to death, or by falling off the top of a building or from a high spot in an empty warehouse through which he has been chased for ten minutes. The poor detective is too dumb to realize that since the bad guy

3

is known to have killed ten people to cover up his first murder, all he has to do is let the man get away and be picked up by the police.

We must understand, however, that our hero is angry and wants personal revenge. After all, the bad guy has just shot his new girl friend. It is all so sad. Will our hero ever forget the lady? Farewell my lovely. Let her sleep the big sleep. Back to walking the city's mean streets where who knows what evil lurks? The girl will be totally forgotten by next week's episode, but there will be another blonde bimbo to take her place. Meanwhile, that beautiful secretary, always faithful to her boss, will still be labouring in his dingy office. She loves her boss, but does he love her? We never know.

This is reality? Clearly it is fantasy as far out as anything in the Holmes or Father Brown canons. Indeed, after watching a few recent detective movies, or reading their book counterparts, turning to a Father Brown story seems like a return to reality. The fact is, some of the most criticized improbabilities in Chesterton's tales are more plausible than many events in modern mystery plots.

Real life detectives are seldom poor parish priests. True. But neither are they macho supermen. Raymond Chandler got away with hardboiled plots better than most writers because he injected humour and philosophy into his fiction and wrote believable dialogue, but don't imagine that a Chandler plot is more probable than a Father Brown plot. You get the illusion of reality, that suspension of disbelief, because Chandler, like Conan Doyle, was a skilful writer. No British cleric ever finds himself in a Father Brown plot, but then neither does any Los Angeles detective ever find himself in a Chandler plot. Even Chandler's slang is fake. Remember how everyone keeps calling Philip Marlowe a 'shamus'? I recall an interview with a professional Los Angeles police official who said he never heard a private detective called a shamus, in California or anywhere else.

Yes, Father Brown plots are almost fantasies, and if you don't like fantasy and can't enjoy a mystery story without explicit sex, extreme violence, and lots of four-letter words, then Father Brown is not for you. But there is much more to Father Brown stories than preposterous plots and weird ways of committing crimes. There is superb writing, marvellous descriptive scenes of both nature and city life, humour, and, above all, philosophical reflections. Sherlock Holmes stories are adventures without morals. Chesterton found it difficult to write a story, mystery or otherwise, that did not make a moral or metaphysical point. Sometimes the point is identified with Christian theology, although Chesterton was not a Catholic when he started his Father Brown series. As Anthony Boucher put it in an introduction to a selection of Father Brown tales, 'It took Father Brown eleven years to convert his creator.'* In this first of the Father Brown books there is surprisingly little rhetoric that is uniquely Catholic. With rare exceptions the metaphysical messages are worth pondering regardless of your beliefs, even if you are an atheist. It has often been said, and justly, that Chesterton was the first to perfect the metaphysical mystery. For me, at any rate, it is this aspect of his stories that lifts them above almost all other crime stories.

Chesterton admirers consider *The Innocence of Father Brown* the best of the canon's five books. I agree, but I think its superiority is sometimes exaggerated. It is true that Chesterton tired of Father Brown, as Conan Doyle did of Holmes, but then found himself obliged to continue the series because the public wanted to read more about Father Brown, and because it was a way of obtaining the money he needed to support his periodical *G.K.'s Weekly*. Although some later Father Brown tales can be called pot-boilers, in my opinion many of Chesterton's best stories are in the later books. The Holmes canon ends with *The Case Book of Sherlock Holmes*, stories so inferior that they seem written by a different hand. This is not true of Father Brown. Even the flimsiest tales in the final book contain something of interest. If in reading this book you are discovering Father Brown for the first time, you will not be disappointed to go on to the others.

It is only natural to compare Father Brown with his distinguished predecessor, Sherlock Holmes. First some parallels:

---

* Anthony Boucher, himself a Catholic, wrote two mystery novels and several short stories about Sister Ursula. She was one of a still growing company of priests, ministers, nuns, and rabbis to follow in Father Brown's footsteps. The latest member is Monsignor John Blackwood ('Blackie') Ryan, in Father Andrew Greeley's novel *Happy Are the Meek* (New York: Warner, 1985).

Both men were celibate. At least we can be sure Father Brown was, and there is no evidence Holmes ever had affairs with women. (It has been suggested that perhaps he did, but Watson was too discreet to tell us about them.)

Both men had an admiring friend—the good doctor Watson for Holmes, the reformed criminal Flambeau for Father Brown. Both Watson and Flambeau eventually married and settled down.

Both men had grey eyes.

Both men lived for a time in, of all places, Chicago. Holmes once found it necessary to be in Chicago under the name of Altamont, disguised as a spy for the Germans ('His Last Bow'). Father Brown was the chaplain of a prison in Chicago ('The Mistake of the Machine').

Both men spoke French. Holmes occasionally quoted French sentences. In 'The Wrong Shape', when Flambeau speaks French to Father Brown, the priest answers in the same language.

Both men were skilled in observing details not noticed by others, and in making shrewd deductions—in Father Brown's case, mostly psychological deductions—from what they saw or heard.

Both men altered as their creators continued to write about them and get a firmer grasp on their personalities. At one time Holmes professed not to know that the Earth goes around the Sun because it had no relation to his work. Later we find him quite knowledgeable about all sorts of things unconnected with crime. Father Brown, in subsequent books, is far from the clumsy, absent-minded curate of the first volume.

It was, of course, Chesterton's intention to make Father Brown's appearance as ordinary as possible, a simple-looking exterior that concealed an extraordinarily subtle mind. As Chesterton writes in the last chapter of his *Autobiography*:

In Father Brown, it was the chief feature to be featureless. The point of him was to appear pointless; and one might say that his conspicuous quality was not being conspicuous. His commonplace exterior was meant to contrast with his unsuspected vigilance and intelligence; and, that being so, of course I made his appearance shabby and shapeless, his face round and expressionless, his manners clumsy, and so on. (pp. 333–4)

None of these external traits was characteristic of Father John O'Connor, the actual priest whose intellectual qualities and knowledge of evil inspired Chesterton's Father Brown. G.K.'s description of how this came about, in the chapter from which I just quoted, is unforgettable. Chesterton and Father O'Connor, on a long walk across the Yorkshire moors, had fallen into a discussion about crime. Chesterton was astonished 'to find that this quiet and pleasant celibate had plumbed those abysses far deeper than I. I had not imagined that the world could hold such horrors' (pp. 337–8). Later that day, G.K. and the priest found themselves in conversation with two young Cambridge undergraduates. They were enormously impressed by Father O'Connor's knowledge of such things as Palestrina and Baroque architecture, but when the priest left the room one of them remarked:

'All the same, I don't believe his sort of life is the right one. It's all very well to like religious music and so on, when you're all shut up in a sort of cloister and don't know anything about the real evil in the world. But I don't believe that's the right ideal. I believe in a fellow coming out into the world, and facing the evil that's in it, and knowing something about the dangers and all that. It's a very beautiful thing to be innocent and ignorant; but I think it's a much finer thing not to be afraid of knowledge.'

To me, still almost shivering with the appallingly practical facts of which the priest had warned me, this comment came with such a colossal and crushing irony, that I nearly burst into a loud harsh laugh in the drawing-room. For I knew perfectly well that, as regards all the solid Satanism which the priest knew and warred against with all his life, these two Cambridge gentlemen (luckily for them) knew about as much of real evil as two babies in the same perambulator. (pp. 338–9)

'There sprang up in my mind', Chesterton continues, 'the vague idea of making some artistic use of these comic yet tragic cross-purposes, and constructing a comedy in which a priest should appear to know nothing and in fact know more about crime than the criminals.'

I afterwards summed up the special idea in the story called 'The Blue Cross', otherwise very slight and improbable, and continued it through the interminable series of tales with which I have afflicted the world. In short, I permitted myself the grave liberty of taking my friend and knocking him about; beating his hat and umbrella shapeless, untidying his clothes, punching his intelligent countenance into a condition of pudding-faced fatuity, and generally disguising Father O'Connor as Father Brown. The disguise, as I have said, was a deliberate piece of fiction, meant to bring out or accentuate the contrast that was the point of the comedy. There is also in the conception, as in nearly everything I have ever written, a good deal of inconsistency and inaccuracy on minor

7

points; not the least of such flaws being the general suggestion of Father Brown having nothing in particular to do, except to hang about in any household where there was likely to be a murder.

It was fifteen years after the incident of the two Cambridge students that Father O'Connor received Chesterton into the Church. Soon after Chesterton's death, Father O'Connor wrote a book about his friend, *Father Brown on Chesterton* (1937), in which you will find another account of Father Brown's origin.

For some reason, perhaps because of Chesterton's own bulk, or perhaps because Father Brown was likened in the first story to a 'Norfolk dumpling' (See Chapter 1, Note 6), many people tend to think of the priest as plump or dumpy. Actually, he was a small, slightly-built man with what G.K. calls a 'foolishly large head'. In 'The Eye of Apollo' he is called 'ugly'. His face is round, dull, and moon-like, with heavy expressionless features, and eyes 'as empty as the North Sea'. His hair is brown, his complexion swarthy, his nose stubby. Poor eyesight makes him squint when he reads without glasses, and he has a habit of blinking while lost in thought. When perplexed ('The Sign of the Sword') he sometimes bites a finger. He likes cigars and pipes, and occasionally drinks wine and beer. Unlike Holmes, he is always modest and self-effacing.

Father Brown moves around a lot from parish to parish, although we are told nothing about his parish work. Someone once said that the priest neglects his flock as much as Watson neglected his medical patients. In both cases, however, perhaps this is merely an illusion caused by the author, for obvious reasons, restricting his narratives solely to episodes involving crimes.

Although both detectives employ observation and deductive reasoning, the priest has no use for the magnifying glass, for analysing footprints and tobacco ash, or any other of the scientific techniques employed by Holmes, and to an even greater degree by later British sleuths such as Dr Thorndike. The main secret of the priest's success is intuition. A famous passage in 'The Secret of Father Brown', in which the priest explains his secret, is worth quoting in full:

'I'm afraid', said the American in tones that were still doubtful, and keeping his eye on the priest rather as if he were a wild animal, 'that

8

you'd have to explain a lot to me, before I knew what you were talking about. The science of detection—'

Father Brown snapped his fingers with the same animated annoyance. 'That's it,' he cried 'that's just where we part company. Science is a grand thing when you can get it; in its real sense one of the grandest words in the world. But what do these men mean, nine times out of ten, when they use it nowadays? When they say detection is a science? When they say criminology is a science? They mean getting *outside* a man and studying him as if he were a gigantic insect; in what they would call a dry impartial light; in what I should call a dead and dehumanised light. They mean getting a long way off him, as if he were a distant prehistoric monster; staring at the shape of his "criminal skull" as if it were a sort of eerie growth like the horn of a rhinoceros's nose. When the scientist talks about a type, he never means himself, but always his neighbour; probably his poorer neighbour. I don't deny the dry light may sometimes do good; though in one sense it's the very reverse of science. So far from being knowledge, it's actually suppression of what we know. It's treating a friend as a stranger, and pretending that something familiar is really remote and mysterious. It's like saying that a man has a proboscis between the eyes, or that he falls down in a fit of insensibility once every twenty-four hours. Well, what you call "the secret" is exactly the opposite. I don't try to get outside the man. I try to get inside the murderer . . . Indeed it's much more than that, don't you see? I *am* inside a man. I am always inside a man, moving his arms and legs; but I wait till I know I am inside a murderer, thinking his thoughts, wrestling with his passions; till I have bent myself into the posture of his hunched and peering hatred; till I see the world with his bloodshot and squinting eyes, looking between the blinkers of his half-witted concentration; looking up the short and sharp perspective of a straight road to a pool of blood. Till I am really a murderer.'

'Oh,' said Mr Chace, regarding him with a long grim face, and added: 'And that is what you call a religious exercise.'

'Yes,' said Father Brown. 'That is what I call a religious exercise.'

Holmes had pity for the victims of crimes and an impulse to right wrongs, but we have the impression that he was a detective mainly because he enjoyed the sport. We seldom feel this about Father Brown. Of course he likes to play the game, but it is always subordinate to a religious motive. As W. H. Auden once put it, the priest 'investigates murders, not for his own sake, nor even for the sake of the innocent, but for the sake of the murderer who can save his soul if he will confess and repent'.

Chesterton's Flambeau is as different from Father Brown as

Don Quixote differs from Sancho, or Holmes from Watson. The priest is short, Flambeau is unusually tall. Although Father Brown at times displays more agility and strength than we credit him with, he is far from the acrobat Flambeau is. In an essay on 'The Innocence of the Criminal' (*Fancies Versus Fads*), Chesterton describes a certain kind of swindler as 'a sort of comic acrobat, a knockout comedian who does as many things as possible on his head'.

It is a good description of Flambeau. Like Robin Hood and a thousand other thief–heroes in literature, Flambeau is the good criminal who never murders or seriously injures anyone. All he cares about is playing his game with the police—catch me if you can. He violates laws not so much to earn a living, or like Robin Hood to take conspicuous waste from the wealthy who do not deserve it, but just to keep the game going. Both he and Father Brown are street-wise in their knowledge of crime, yet both in a way are innocent. By having Flambeau reform, and for a time even work as a detective, he promotes Flambeau to the ranks of such famous fictional ex-thieves as Raffles and Jimmy Valentine, and hundreds of other reformed crooks who became the heroes of endless later mystery stories, movies, and television shows.

Much more could be said in this introduction about Father Brown and Flambeau if it were not a book of 200 footnotes. As it is, I shall leave to my notes all further comments on the pair.

A word about Chesterton's other mysteries. His greatest novel, *The Man Who Was Thursday* (published three years before the first Father Brown book) can be considered a mystery, but it is much more a metaphysical fantasy, an allegory woven around a wild adventure involving anarchists and policemen, than it is a conventional mystery novel. Some of the stories in G.K.'s first book of fiction, *The Club of Queer Trades*, may be called mysteries, but again, they are not mysteries of the conventional whodunit sort. However, there are four books of classical detective stories by Chesterton, almost forgotten today, that contain splendid tales. *The Man Who Knew Too Much* features a detective named Horne Fisher. *Four Faultless Felons* consists of four short novels, each about what seems to be a crime but actually is an act of goodness.

*The Poet and the Lunatics*, in which crimes are solved by poet–artist Gabriel Gale, is my personal favourite. I think the tales in this much neglected volume represent Chesterton at his best. And finally there is his last book of mysteries, *The Paradoxes of Mr Pond*, in which each story takes off from a paradoxical remark by Pond that cries out for explanation. If you enjoy Father Brown and have not looked into the above titles, you have treats in store. Many of these tales, in my opinion, are superior to many of the later Father Brown stories.

As for Chesterton himself, so many excellent biographies are available and still being written that I shall be brief. He was born in London in 1874, and died at Beaconsfield in 1936. At seventeen he left school to study commercial art, and though he never tired of sketching—he illustrated several of his own books as well as books by others—he quickly discovered that his major talent was writing. Enormously prolific, his more than a hundred volumes include essays, literary criticism, biography, fantastic novels, short stories, history, poetry, plays, and vigorous defences of Christian dogmas. His greatest work of apologetics, *Orthodoxy*, was published in 1908, when he and his wife were Anglo-Catholics. Fourteen years went by before Chesterton (followed two years later by his wife) converted to Roman Catholicism.

Politically, G.K. had little respect for either capitalism or socialism, defending a populist view which he and his friends called distributism—a strong democracy combined with pro-grammes to redistribute wealth more justly. Much of Chesterton's later energies and money were spent on *G.K.'s Weekly* in which distributist opinions were aired and debated. His friendship with Hilaire Belloc, another tireless crusader for the Catholic faith, led George Bernard Shaw to nickname the pair 'the Chesterbelloc'. Chesterton wrote rapidly, often careless with facts (it was said that his book on Robert Browning contained only two dates, both wrong), but his flashing, sword-play style was noted for its gusto, humour, and vivid poetic phrasing.

Although I am not a Catholic (I am a creedless philosophical theist), anyone familiar with my confessional *The Whys of a Philosophical Scrivener* (New York: Morrow, 1983) will understand how I can admire the heart of Chesterton's theology more than the secular philosophies of G.K.'s most famous antagonists, Shaw and H.G. Wells. Above all, I share with Chesterton and his little priest an attitude of astonishment, humility, and gratitude over the wild fact that a universe exists, and that somehow you and I are allowed to be part of its transcendent, incomprehensible plan.

Let me close with two guesses. As the decades flip by, I believe that Chesterton's stature as writer and thinker will grow,* whereas Conan Doyle's will continue to diminish. Of course the chronicles of Dr Watson will be read as long as civilization lasts, but what does Sherlock Holmes have to do with his gullible creator? My second guess is that this will be true also of the Father Brown books. I believe they will be relished long after most of today's popular mysteries, perhaps also most of Chesterton's polemical writings, have been forgotten.

---

* It is worth noting here a comment made by the Latin American writer Jorge Luis Borges during a lecture on 'The Detective Story' (reprinted in the 'Detection Issue' of the Canadian periodical *Descant*, Winter 1985/86). He referred to Chesterton as 'Poe's great disciple' and went on to say, 'Chesterton said that there had never been detective stories better than those of Poe, but Chesterton himself seems to me better than Poe.'

# To
# WALDO AND MILDRED D'AVIGDOR*

---

* Waldo Percy Henry d'Avigdor (1877–1947) and his wife, the former Mildred Wain, were both friends of Chesterton before they met and married. G.K.'s older friendship with Waldo went back to his boyhood when they were students at St. Paul's School, a school for boys in the Hammersmith borough of London. It had been founded in the early 1500s and attended by such notables as Milton and Pepys.

Gilbert and Waldo were among the dozen or so members of a small but energetic club that G.K. and his friends established. They called it the Junior Debating Society although, as Chesterton says in his *Autobiography*, if there was a Senior Debating Society none of them had heard of it. The club published a periodical called *The Debater* in which appeared some of Chesterton's earliest prose and verse.

About a third of the members, including Waldo and his brother, were Jewish. Years later Chesterton described Waldo as a person who 'masks with complete fashionable triviality a Hebraic immutability of passion tried in a more ironical and bitter service than his Father Jacob'. (Maisie Ward, *Gilbert Keith Chesterton*, p. 103).

Another JDC member, Edmund Clerihew Bentley, was Gilbert's best boyhood friend. Chesterton's *Greybeards at Play* and *The Man Who Was Thursday* have verse dedications to Bentley, and Bentley returned the honour by dedicating *Trent's Last Case* to Chesterton, a novel that G.K. calls (in his *Autobiography*, p. 55) 'the best detective story of modern times'. It was Bentley's middle name, Clerihew, that became attached to a whimsical form of verse which he invented, many examples of which were published in books with illustrations by Chesterton and others.

The JDC anthem, sung to the tune of *Clementine*, is worth quoting:

> I'm a member, I'm a member, member of the JDC.
> I belong to it forever. Don't you wish that you were me?

While Chesterton was studying art at the Slade School, he and a music student named Mildred Wain became lifelong friends. In *Return to Chesterton*, Miss Ward reprints part of a poem G.K. wrote to Mildred titled 'Our Lady of Wain', in which he describes her as a combination of Puck and Cecilia. It was from Mildred that G.K. first heard the strange name of Blogg, the surname of Mildred's friend Frances and the woman G.K. would soon marry. 'He thought it was a funny name,' Chesterton wrote much later about

13

himself. 'Had he been told that he would ever pronounce it with the accents of tears and passion he would have said, in his pride, that the name was not suitable for that purpose.' Chesterton surely had Blogg in mind when he has Father Brown say (in 'The Scandal of Father Brown', the title story of the last Father Brown book): 'You see, you are so incurably romantic that your whole case was founded on the idea that a man looking like a young god, couldn't be called Potter. Believe me, names are not so appropriately distributed.'

One of H.G. Wells's early stories, 'Miss Winchelsea's Heart', is about an English woman who falls in love with a young man she meets in Rome. She turns down his marriage proposal solely because his last name is Snooks. Chesterton was not so foolish.

Miss Ward (in *Return to Chesterton*) reports several amusing anecdotes about G.K. that she heard from Mildred. On one occasion, when Chesterton was arguing a point over breakfast in a restaurant, he banged his fist on the edge of his plate, tipping two poached eggs into his lap. All he said to the waitress was, 'Will you please bring me two more poached eggs. I seem to have lost the others.' On another occasion, during a party to celebrate Mildred's engagement to Waldo, Chesterton got into an argument with her sister Anne. It was late and Anne fell asleep. Gilbert failed to notice this, said Mildred, because he kept answering his own questions.

When Chesterton became engaged to Frances Blogg, he wrote the following charming letter about it to Mildred. (I quote from Miss Ward's biography):

DEAR MILDRED,

On rising this morning, I carefully washed my boots in hot water and blacked my face. Then assuming my coat with graceful ease and with the tails in front, I descended to breakfast, where I gaily poured the coffee on the sardines and put my hat on the fire to boil. These activities will give you some idea of my frame of mind. My family, observing me leave the house by way of the chimney, and take the fender with me under one arm, thought I must have something on my mind. So I had.

My friend, I am engaged. I am only telling it at present to my real friends: but there is no doubt about it. The next question that arises is—whom am I engaged to? I have investigated this problem with some care, and, as far as I can make out, the best authorities point to Frances Blogg. There can I think be no reasonable doubt that she is the lady. It is as well to have these minor matters clear in one's mind.

I am very much too happy to write much; but I thought you might remember my existence sufficiently to be interested in the incident.

Waldo has been of so much help to me in this and in everything, and I am so much interested in you for his sake and your own, that I am encouraged to hope our friendship may subsist. If ever I have done anything rude or silly, it was quite inadvertent. I have always wished to please you.

After his marriage, Waldo d'Avigdor joined the Alliance Insurance Company, Wigmore Street Branch, in 1896, and worked there until his retirement in 1928 for reasons of health. He died in 1947, survived by his wife.

# The Blue Cross*

BETWEEN the silver ribbon of morning and the green glittering ribbon of sea, the boat touched Harwich and let loose a swarm of folk like flies, among whom the man we must follow was by no means conspicuous—nor wished to be. There was nothing notable about him, except a slight contrast between the holiday gaiety of his clothes and the official gravity of his face. His clothes included a slight, pale grey jacket, a white waistcoat, and a silver straw hat with a grey-blue ribbon. His lean face was dark by contrast, and ended in a curt black beard that looked Spanish and suggested an Elizabethan ruff. He was smoking a cigarette with the seriousness of an idler. There was nothing about him to indicate the fact that the grey jacket covered a loaded revolver, that the white waistcoat covered a police card, or that the straw hat covered one of the most powerful intellects in Europe. For this was Valentin himself, the head of the Paris police and the most famous investigator of the world; and he was coming from Brussels to London to make the greatest arrest of the century.

---

* Flambeau, the French 'colossus of crime', tries to steal from Father Brown a silver cross set with blue sapphires. The story first appeared in the *Storyteller* (September 1910).

According to Maisie Ward (*Return to Chesterton*), 'The Blue Cross' was written when Chesterton and his wife were visiting Lucian Oldershaw, a boyhood friend of G.K. who had become his brother-in-law. (Chesterton married Frances Blogg and Oldershaw married her sister Ethel.) Searching Oldershaw's house for a detective story he hadn't read, and not finding one, G.K. decided to write one himself.

The editor of the *Storyteller* introduced the magazine's Father Brown series as follows: 'These stories are undoubtedly the most extraordinary work Mr Chesterton has yet penned, and show this clever writer in quite a new vein. Father Brown is a character destined to be long remembered in fiction.'

Flambeau[1] was in England. The police of three countries had tracked the great criminal at last from Ghent to Brussels, from Brussels to the Hook of Holland;[2] and it was conjectured that he would take some advantage of the unfamiliarity and confusion of the Eucharistic Congress, then taking place in London. Probably he would travel as some minor clerk or secretary connected with it; but, of course, Valentin could not be certain; nobody could be certain about Flambeau.

It is many years now since this colossus of crime suddenly ceased, keeping the world in a turmoil; and when he ceased, as they said after the death of Roland, there was a great quiet upon the earth. But in his best days (I mean, of course, his worst) Flambeau was a figure as statuesque and international as the Kaiser. Almost every morning the daily paper announced that he had escaped the consequences of one extraordinary crime by committing another. He was a Gascon of gigantic stature and bodily daring; and the wildest tales were told of his outbursts of athletic humour; how he turned the *juge d'instruction*[3] upside down and stood him on his head, 'to clear his mind'; how he ran down

1. This French word for torch suggests the man's flamboyant personality and career. In 'The Queer Feet' we are told by Father Brown that Flambeau is not his real name, but not until the last Father Brown book (in the story 'The Secret of Father Brown') do we learn that his real family name is Duroc, a name suggesting the durable Rock of Peter, on which Chesterton believed the Catholic Church to have been founded. For Flambeau's first name, see 'The Eye of Apollo', Note 1.

2. The Hook of Holland, *Hoek van Holland*, is a small port city on the west coast of The Netherlands where an artificial channel for the river Maas connects Rotterdam with the North Sea. Coming from Brussels, Flambeau would have embarked from the Hook of Holland to cross the North Sea, land at Harwich, and from there go by train to London.

3. *Juge d'instruction* is the examining magistrate, though more active in investigating cases than his British or American counterpart. Standing on one's head to clear the mind was one of Chesterton's favourite notions. He liked the artist's practice of looking back through the legs to see a landscape's shapes and colours from a fresh perspective. Gabriel Gale, the poet–detective in Chesterton's collection *The Poet and the Lunatics*, frequently stood on his head so he could view the world as Peter must have viewed it when (according to legend) he was crucified head downward, 'seeing in death the beautiful vision of his boyhood . . . the landscape as it really is: with the stars like flowers, and the clouds like hills, and all men hanging on the mercy of God'.

the Rue de Rivoli with a policeman under each arm. It is due to him to say that his fantastic physical strength was generally employed in such bloodless though undignified scenes; his real crimes were chiefly those of ingenious and wholesale robbery. But each of his thefts was almost a new sin, and would make a story by itself. It was he who ran the great Tyrolean Dairy Company in London, with no dairies, no cows, no carts, no milk, but with some thousand subscribers. These he served by the simple operation of moving the little milk-cans outside people's doors to the doors of his own customers. It was he who had kept up an unaccountable and close correspondence with a young lady whose whole letter-bag was intercepted, by the extraordinary trick of photographing his messages infinitesimally small upon the slides of a microscope. A sweeping simplicity, however, marked many of his experiments. It is said that he once repainted all the numbers in a street in the dead of night merely to divert one traveller into a trap. It is quite certain that he invented a portable pillar-box, which he put up at corners in quiet suburbs on the chance of strangers dropping postal orders into it.[4] Lastly, he was known to be a startling acrobat; despite his huge figure, he could leap like a grasshopper and melt into the tree-tops like a monkey. Hence the great Valentin, when he set out to find Flambeau, was perfectly well aware that his adventures would not end when he had found him.

But how was he to find him? On this the great Valentin's ideas were still in process of settlement.

There was one thing which Flambeau, with all his dexterity of disguise, could not cover, and that was his singular height. If Valentin's quick eye had caught a tall apple-woman, a tall grenadier, or even a tolerably tall duchess, he might have arrested them on the spot. But all along his train there was nobody that could be a disguised Flambeau, any more than a cat could be a disguised giraffe. About the people on the boat he had already satisfied himself; and the people picked up at Harwich or on the journey limited themselves with certainty to six. There was a short railway official travelling up to the terminus, three fairly

---

4. Flambeau's flimflams are amusing, but of course totally impractical. We know at once we are not in the real world but in a Chestertonian England with its special mix of realism, humour, and fantasy.

short market gardeners picked up two stations afterwards, one very short widow lady going up from a small Essex town, and a very short Roman Catholic priest going up from a small Essex village.[5] When it came to the last case, Valentin gave it up and almost laughed. The little priest was so much the essence of those Eastern flats; he had a face as round and dull as a Norfolk dumpling;[6] he had eyes as empty as the North Sea;[7] he had several brown paper parcels, which he was quite incapable of collecting. The Eucharistic Congress had doubtless sucked out of their local stagnation many such creatures, blind and helpless, like moles disinterred. Valentin was a sceptic in the severe style of France, and could have no love for priests.[8] But he could have pity for them, and this one might have provoked pity in anybody. He had a large, shabby umbrella, which constantly fell on the floor. He did not seem to know which was the right end of his return ticket. He explained with a moon-calf simplicity to everybody in the carriage that he had to be careful, because he had something made of real silver 'with blue stones' in one of his brown-paper parcels. His quaint blending of Essex flatness with saintly simplicity continuously amused the Frenchman till the priest arrived (somehow) at Stratford[9] with all his parcels, and came back for

---

**5.** The village of Cobhole, as we learn in the next story. In 'God of the Gongs' (*The Wisdom of Father Brown*) the priest makes a return visit to his former Cobhole parish.

**6.** 'Norfolk dumpling' is a common expression for an inhabitant or native of Norfolk.

**7.** The metaphor would occur naturally to Valentin, who has just crossed the North Sea, but what a marvellous metaphor it is! The sea looks empty on the surface, but beneath the waves it teems with fantastic life and dark mystery. Father Brown's face is often described as 'expressionless'. We are told in 'The Purple Wig' (*The Wisdom of Father Brown*) that he has a snub nose. His head is frequently called large, and in 'The Scandal of Father Brown' (in the book of the same title) he is said to have the 'heavy' features of a peasant, with a complexion dark enough for him to be mistaken for a Mexican, Indian, or black. On the colour of Father Brown's eyes—grey—see Note 10 of Chapter 3.

**8.** In the next story we discover how passionately Valentin hated the Roman Catholic Church.

**9.** Stratford is a railway station east of London. In the *Storyteller*, and in the British first edition of the book, it is called Tottenham, a Middlesex residential suburb.

his umbrella. When he did the last, Valentin even had the good nature to warn him not to take care of the silver by telling everybody about it.[10] But to whomever he talked, Valentin kept his eye open for someone else; he looked out steadily for anyone, rich or poor, male or female, who was well up to six feet; for Flambeau was four inches above it.

He alighted at Liverpool Street,[11] however, quite conscientiously secure that he had not missed the criminal so far. He then went to Scotland Yard[12] to regularise his position and arrange for help in case of need; he then lit another cigarette and went for a long stroll in the streets of London. As he was walking in the streets and squares beyond Victoria, he paused suddenly and stood. It was a quaint, quiet square, very typical of London, full of an accidental stillness. The tall, flat houses round looked at once prosperous and uninhabited; the square of shrubbery in the centre looked as deserted as a green Pacific islet. One of the four sides was much higher than the rest, like a daïs; and the line of this side was broken by one of London's admirable accidents—a restaurant that looked as if it had strayed from Soho.[13] It was an unreasonably attractive object, with dwarf plants in pots and long, striped blinds of lemon yellow and white. It stood specially high above the street, and in the usual patchwork way of London, a flight of steps from the street ran up to meet the front door almost as a fire-escape might run up to a first-floor window. Valentin stood and smoked in front of the yellow-white blinds and considered them long.

The most incredible thing about miracles is that they happen.

---

10. In view of Father Brown's vast knowledge of crime and human nature, it seems unlikely he would chatter to strangers about the value of the silver cross he was carrying. It is tempting to suppose that the priest was deliberately provoking a theft, but there is no evidence of this. In his eagerness to make Father Brown appear innocent, Chesterton exaggerated his naïvety. As the stories proceed, and G.K. better understands the character of his priest, Father Brown becomes much less naïve and clumsy.

11. Liverpool Street railway station is in the City (east central London).

12. Scotland Yard, as all Englishmen and all Sherlockians outside England know, is simply the name of the London Metropolitan Police headquarters.

13. Soho is a central London district famous for its Italian and French restaurants, and for its many writers and artists.

A few clouds in heaven do come together into the staring shape of one human eye. A tree does stand up in the landscape of a doubtful journey in the exact and elaborate shape of a note of interrogation.[14] I have seen both these things myself within the last few days. Nelson does die in the instant of victory; and a man named Williams does quite accidentally murder a man named Williamson; it sounds like a sort of infanticide. In short, there is in life an element of elfin coincidence which people reckoning on the prosaic may perpetually miss. As it has been well expressed in the paradox of Poe,[15] wisdom should reckon on the unforeseen.

Aristide Valentin was unfathomably French; and the French intelligence is intelligence specially and solely. He was not 'a thinking machine';[16] for that is a brainless phrase of modern fatalism and materialism. A machine only *is* a machine because it

---

**14.** Startling coincidences can happen in so many countless ways that the wonder is that we fail to recognize more of them. It is probable, said Aristotle, that the improbable will often occur. Although Chesterton believed firmly in divine miracles, he was free of the superstition that trivial coincidences are examples of what Jung called synchronicity—paranormal patterns that somehow violate normal laws of probability.

'Life is full of a ceaseless shower of small coincidences'; G.K. opens his essay on 'Five Hundred and Fifty-Five' (*Alarms and Discursions*) 'too small to be worth mentioning except for a special purpose, often too trifling even to be noticed, any more than we notice one snowflake falling on another.' Chesterton goes on to cite examples, including this one: 'A man named Williams did walk into a strange house and murder a man named Williamson; it sounds like a sort of infanticide.' I do not know whether G.K. wrote this sentence before or after the similar sentence in 'The Blue Cross', but the wording suggests that he had in mind an actual crime.

**15.** I have not found a passage in which Poe speaks explicitly of the need to expect the unforeseen. Perhaps Chesterton had in mind Poe's comments about remarkable coincidences that open his story 'The Mystery of Marie Roget'.

**16.** The reference is to a series of ingenious and bizarre mystery tales, popular at the time, about a Professor Augustus F. X. Van Dusen who was so good at solving crimes by pure reasoning that he was known as 'the thinking machine'. The author, Jacques Futrelle, was an American journalist who died at the age of 37 in the sinking of the *Titanic*, just a year after the publication of *The Innocence of Father Brown*. Futrelle's stories were collected in *The Thinking Machine* (1907) and *The Thinking Machine on the Case* (1908). Two anthologies of these tales, edited by Everett Bleiler, are available as Dover paperbacks.

cannot think. But he was a thinking man, and a plain man at the same time. All his wonderful successes, that looked like conjuring, had been gained by plodding logic, by clear and commonplace French thought. The French electrify the world not by starting any paradox, they electrify it by carrying out a truism. They carry a truism so far—as in the French Revolution. But exactly because Valentin understood reason, he understood the limits of reason. Only a man who knows nothing of motors talks of motoring without petrol; only a man who knows nothing of reason talks of reasoning without strong, undisputed first principles. Here he had no strong first principles. Flambeau had been missed at Harwich; and if he was in London at all, he might be anything from a tall tramp on Wimbledon Common[17] to a tall toast-master at the Hôtel Métropole.[18] In such a naked state of nescience, Valentin had a view and a method of his own.

In such cases he reckoned on the unforeseen. In such cases, when he could not follow the train of the reasonable, he coldly and carefully followed the train of the unreasonable. Instead of going to the right places—banks, police stations, rendezvous—he systematically went to the wrong places; knocked at every empty house, turned down every *cul de sac*, went up every lane blocked with rubbish, went round every crescent that led him uselessly out of the way.[19] He defended this crazy course quite logically.

17. Wimbledon Common: the recreational grounds of Wimbledon, comprising 1,100 acres of unenclosed land. Wimbledon is a residential suburb south-west of London, whose distinguished residents have included William Wilberforce, Charles James Fox, Frederick Marrgat, the novelist, and John Murray, the publisher.

It is best known today, of course, as the site of international tennis matches.

18. When the Hôtel Métropole opened in London in 1885, on Northumberland Avenue south of Charing Cross, it was considered one of the world's most elegant hotels. The British government bought it in 1936 to serve as a residence for government officials in nearby Whitehall.

19. Allowing chance to break the monotony of planned behaviour was one of Chesterton's favourite stratagems. He liked to enter a railway station, buy a ticket to an unfamiliar town with a name that appealed to him, then wander home from there as circumstances dictated. His essay 'Ballade of a Town' (*Tremendous Trifles*) tells of the sudden glamour a city in Belgium acquired the instant G.K. realized he had accidentally left a train at the wrong station and was in a place where he was not supposed to be.    [*cont. over*]

He said that if one had a clue this was the worst way; but if one had no clue at all it was the best, because there was just the chance that any oddity that caught the eye of the pursuer might be the same that had caught the eye of the pursued. Somewhere a man must begin, and it had better be just where another man might stop. Something about that flight of steps up to the shop, something about the quietude and quaintness of the restaurant, roused all the detective's rare romantic fancy and made him resolve to strike at random. He went up the steps, and sitting down at a table by the window, asked for a cup of black coffee.

It was half-way through the morning, and he had not break-fasted; the slight litter of other breakfasts stood about on the table to remind him of his hunger; and adding a poached egg to his order, he proceeded musingly to shake some white sugar into his coffee, thinking all the time about Flambeau. He remembered how Flambeau had escaped, once by a pair of nail scissors, and once by a house on fire; once by having to pay for an unstamped letter, and once by getting people to look through a telescope at a comet that might destroy the world. He thought his detective brain as good as the criminal's, which was true. But he fully rea-lised the disadvantage. 'The criminal is the creative artist; the detective only the critic,'[20] he said with a sour smile, and lifted his coffee cup to his lips slowly, and put it down very quickly. He had put salt in it.

---

In his autobiography Chesterton tells how he and his wife planned their second honeymoon by not planning it. First they boarded a passing omni-bus. When they saw a railway station they got off and bought tickets for the next train leaving. It took them to a town called Slough. From there they walked haphazardly through the countryside until they stopped at an inn and learned for the first time they were in Beaconsfield. They liked the town so much that they later bought a home there.

There are many games in which random moves are essential for playing one's best strategy. In his game of 'catch the criminal' Valentin is following the sage advice of the Cheshire Cat when it told Alice that if she had no par-ticular goal it didn't matter which way she went. Of course the intersection of Valentin's random walk with that of Father Brown and Flambeau is wildly improbable, an event Chesterton tried to make seem more plausible by his remarks on coincidences.

**20.** Valentin's admiration for the creative criminal was surely in part responsible for his own bungling attempt at crime in the next chapter.

He looked at the vessel from which the silvery powder had come; it was certainly a sugar-basin; as unmistakably meant for sugar as a champagne-bottle for champagne. He wondered why they should keep salt in it. He looked to see if there were any more orthodox vessels. Yes; there were two salt-cellars quite full. Perhaps there was some speciality in the condiment in the salt-cellars. He tasted it; it was sugar. Then he looked round at the restaurant with a refreshed air of interest, to see if there were any other traces of that singular artistic taste which puts the sugar in the salt-cellars and the salt in the sugar-basin. Except for an odd splash of some dark fluid on one of the white-papered walls, the whole place appeared neat, cheerful and ordinary. He rang the bell for the waiter.

When that official hurried up, fuzzy-haired and somewhat blear-eyed at that early hour, the detective (who was not without an appreciation of the simpler forms of humour) asked him to taste the sugar and see if it was up to the high reputation of the hotel. The result was that the waiter yawned suddenly and woke up.

'Do you play this delicate joke on your customers every morning?' inquired Valentin. 'Does changing the salt and sugar never pall on you as a jest?'

The waiter, when this irony grew clearer, stammeringly assured him that the establishment had certainly no such intention; it must be a most curious mistake. He picked up the sugar-basin and looked at it; he picked up the salt-cellar and looked at that, his face growing more and more bewildered. At last he abruptly excused himself, and hurrying away, returned in a few seconds with the proprietor. The proprietor also examined the sugar-basin and then the salt-cellar; the proprietor also looked bewildered.

Suddenly the waiter seemed to grow inarticulate with a rush of words.

'I zink,' he stuttered eagerly, 'I zink it is those two clergymen.'

'What two clergymen?'

'The two clergymen,' said the waiter, 'that threw soup at the wall.'

'Threw soup at the wall?' repeated Valentin, feeling sure this must be some singular Italian metaphor.

'Yes, yes,' said the attendant excitedly, and pointing at the

23

dark splash on the white paper; 'threw it over there on the wall.'

Valentin looked his query at the proprietor, who came to his rescue with fuller reports.

'Yes, sir,' he said, 'it's quite true, though I don't suppose it has anything to do with the sugar and salt. Two clergymen came in and drank soup[21] here very early, as soon as the shutters were taken down. They were both very quiet, respectable people; one of them paid the bill and went out; the other, who seemed a slower coach altogether, was some minutes longer getting his things together. But he went at last. Only, the instant before he stepped into the street he deliberately picked up his cup, which he had only half emptied, and threw the soup slap on the wall. I was in the back room myself, and so was the waiter; so I could only rush out in time to find the wall splashed and the shop empty. It don't do any particular damage, but it was confounded cheek; and I tried to catch the men in the street. They were too far off though; I only noticed they went round the next corner into Carstairs Street.'[22]

The detective was on his feet, hat settled and stick in hand. He had already decided that in the universal darkness of his mind he could only follow the first odd finger that pointed; and this finger was odd enough. Paying his bill and clashing the glass doors behind him, he was soon swinging round into the other street.

It was fortunate that even in such fevered moments his eye was cool and quick. Something in a shop-front went by him like a mere flash; yet he went back to look at it. The shop was a popular greengrocer and fruiterer's, an array of goods set out in the open air and plainly ticketed with their names and prices. In the two most prominent compartments were two heaps, of oranges and of nuts respectively. On the heap of nuts lay a scrap of cardboard, on which was written in bold, blue chalk, 'Best tangerine oranges, two a penny.' On the oranges was the equally clear and exact description, 'Finest Brazil nuts, 4d. a lb.' M. Valentin

---

21. The word 'soup', here and a few sentences later, is not in the text of the first magazine printing. It is called bovril. Bovril was the trade name for a popular instant beef soup introduced in England in the late nineteenth century.

22. There is a town called Carstairs in Scotland, but no such street in London.

looked at these two placards and fancied he had met this highly subtle form of humour before, and that somewhat recently. He drew the attention of the red-faced fruiterer, who was looking rather sullenly up and down the street, to this inaccuracy in his advertisements. The fruiterer said nothing, but sharply put each card into its proper place. The detective, leaning elegantly on his walking-cane, continued to scrutinise the shop. At last he said, 'Pray excuse my apparent irrelevance, my good sir, but I should like to ask you a question in experimental psychology and the association of ideas.'

The red-faced shopman regarded him with an eye of menace; but he continued gaily, swinging his cane, 'Why,' he pursued, 'why are two tickets wrongly placed in a greengrocer's shop like a shovel hat[23] that has come to London for a holiday? Or, in case I do not make myself clear, what is the mystical association which connects the idea of nuts marked as oranges with the idea of two clergymen, one tall and the other short?'

The eyes of the tradesman stood out of his head like a snail's; he really seemed for an instant likely to fling himself upon the stranger. At last he stammered angrily: 'I don't know what you 'ave to do with it, but if you're one of their friends, you can tell 'em from me that I'll knock their silly 'eads off, parsons or no parsons, if they upset my apples again.'

'Indeed?' asked the detective with great sympathy. 'Did they upset your apples?'

---

**23.** Many clergymen in Edwardian England wore a style of black hat with a shallow crown and a broad circular brim that occasionally turned up at the sides but always projected in front and back like a shovel. The hats were called shovels, and clergymen were derisively called shovel hats, similar to the way construction workers in the United States are now called hard hats. Both Father Brown and his companion were wearing shovel hats, as we soon learn. The hat, and a shabby umbrella, became almost as characteristic of Father Brown's appearance, in illustrations and films, as Sherlock Holmes's deer-stalker hat and pipe. In 'The Scandal of Father Brown', the title story in the last book of the canon, the priest's hat is said to look like 'a large black mushroom'.

> Lord Chancellors were cheap as sprats,
> And Bishops in their shovel hats
> Were plentiful as tabby cats——
>   In point of fact, too many.
>   W.S. Gilbert, *The Gondoliers*, Act 2

'One of 'em did,' said the heated shopman; 'rolled 'em all over the street. I'd 'ave caught the fool but for havin' to pick 'em up.'

'Which way did these parsons go?' asked Valentin.

'Up that second road on the left-hand side, and then across the square,' said the other promptly.

'Thanks,' replied Valentin, and vanished like a fairy. On the other side of the second square he found a policeman, and said: 'This is urgent, constable; have you seen two clergymen in shovel hats?'

The policeman began to chuckle heavily. 'I 'ave, sir; and if you arst me, one of 'em was drunk. He stood in the middle of the road that bewildered that——'

'Which way did they go?' snapped Valentin.

'They took one of them yellow buses over there,' answered the man; 'them that go to Hampstead.'[24]

Valentin produced his official card and said very rapidly: 'Call up two of your men to come with me in pursuit,' and crossed the road with such contagious energy that the ponderous policeman was moved to almost agile obedience. In a minute and a half the French detective was joined on the opposite pavement by an inspector and a man in plain clothes.

'Well, sir,' began the former, with smiling importance, 'and what may——?'

Valentin pointed suddenly with his cane. 'I'll tell you on the top of that omnibus,' he said, and was darting and dodging across the tangle of the traffic. When all three sank panting on the top seats of the yellow vehicle, the inspector said: 'We could go four times as quick in a taxi.'

'Quite true,' replied their leader placidly, 'if we only had an idea of where we were going.'

'Well, where *are* you going?' asked the other, staring.

---

24. Hampstead—a London suburb on a hill north-west of Regent's Park—is noted for its high concentration of writers, artists, and actors. Wilkie Collins, whose *Moonstone* was the first great detective novel, was born in Hampstead. John Keats lived there, and Dr Johnson, Robert Louis Stevenson, John Galsworthy, and later H. G. Wells. Among the artists of Hampstead were Constable, Turner, Gainsborough, Hogarth, Reynolds, and the Pre-Raphaelites. Residents of Hampstead are central characters in several Sherlock Holmes tales.

Valentin smoked frowningly for a few seconds; then, removing his cigarette, he said: 'If you *know* what a man's doing, get in front of him; but if you want to guess what he's doing, keep behind him. Stray when he strays; stop when he stops; travel as slowly as he. Then you may see what he saw and may act as he acted. All we can do is to keep our eyes skinned for a queer thing.'

'What sort of queer thing do you mean?' asked the inspector.

'Any sort of queer thing,' answered Valentin, and relapsed into obstinate silence.

The yellow omnibus crawled up the northern roads for what seemed like hours on end; the great detective would not explain further, and perhaps his assistants felt a silent and growing doubt of his errand. Perhaps, also, they felt a silent and growing desire for lunch, for the hours crept long past the normal luncheon hour, and the long roads of the North London suburbs seemed to shoot out into length after length like an infernal telescope. It was one of those journeys on which a man perpetually feels that now at last he must have come to the end of the universe, and then finds he has only come to the beginning of Tufnell Park.[25] London died away in draggled taverns and dreary scrubs, and then was unaccountably born again in blazing high streets and blatant hotels. It was like passing through thirteen separate vulgar cities all just touching each other. But though the winter twilight was already threatening the road ahead of them, the Parisian detective still sat silent and watchful, eyeing the frontage of the streets that slid by on either side. By the time they had left Camden Town[26] behind, the policemen were nearly asleep; at least, they gave something like a jump as Valentin leapt erect, struck a hand on each man's shoulder, and shouted to the driver to stop.

They tumbled down the steps into the road without realising why they had been dislodged; when they looked round for enlightenment they found Valentin triumphantly pointing his finger towards a window on the left side of the road. It was a large

**25.** At the time Chesterton wrote, Tufnell Park was a small region of villas in upper Holloway, in London's northern borough of Islington. It is now occupied by apartment buildings, although the layout remains much as it was in Victorian times.

**26.** Camden Town is a section of London just north-east of Regent's Park, at the centre of the borough of St. Pancras.

window, forming part of the long façade of a gilt and palatial public-house; it was the part reserved for respectable dining, and labelled 'Restaurant.' This window, like all the rest along the frontage of the hotel, was of frosted and figured glass; but in the middle of it was a big, black smash, like a star in the ice.

'Our cue at last,' cried Valentin, waving his stick; 'the place with the broken window.'

'What window? What cue?' asked his principal assistant. 'Why, what proof is there that this has anything to do with them?'

Valentin almost broke his bamboo stick with rage.

'Proof!' he cried. 'Good God! the man is looking for proof! Why, of course, the chances are twenty to one that it has *nothing* to do with them. But what else can we do? Don't you see we must either follow one wild possibility or else go home to bed?' He banged his way into the restaurant, followed by his companions, and they were soon seated at a late luncheon at a little table, and looking at the star of smashed glass from the inside. Not that it was very informative to them even then.

'Got your window broken, I see,' said Valentin to the waiter as he paid the bill.

'Yes, sir,' answered the attendant, bending busily over the change, to which Valentin silently added an enormous tip. The waiter straightened himself with mild but unmistakable animation.

'Ah, yes, sir,' he said. 'Very odd thing, that, sir.'

'Indeed? Tell us about it,' said the detective with careless curiosity.

'Well, two gents in black came in,' said the waiter; 'two of those foreign parsons that are running about. They had a cheap and quiet little lunch, and one of them paid for it and went out. The other was just going out to join him when I looked at my change again and found he'd paid me more than three times too much. "Here," I says to the chap who was nearly out of the door, "you've paid too much." "Oh," he says, very cool, "have we?" "Yes," I says, and picks up the bill to show him. Well, that was a knock-out.'

'What do you mean?' asked his interlocutor.

'Well, I'd have sworn on seven Bibles that I'd put 4s. on that bill. But now I saw I'd put 14s., as plain as paint.'

'Well?' cried Valentin, moving slowly, but with burning eyes, 'and then?'

'The parson at the door he says all serene, "Sorry to confuse your accounts, but it'll pay for the window." "What window?" I says. "The one I'm going to break," he says, and smashed that blessed pane with his umbrella.'

All three inquirers made an exclamation; and the inspector said under his breath, 'Are we after escaped lunatics?' The waiter went on with some relish for the ridiculous story:

'I was so knocked silly for a second, I couldn't do anything. The man marched out of the place and joined his friend just round the corner. Then they went so quick up Bullock Street that I couldn't catch them, though I ran round the bars to do it.'

'Bullock Street,'[27] said the detective, and shot up that thoroughfare as quickly as the strange couple he pursued.

Their journey now took them through bare brick ways like tunnels; streets with few lights and even with few windows; streets that seemed built out of the blank backs of everything and everywhere. Dusk was deepening, and it was not easy even for the London policemen to guess in what exact direction they were treading. The inspector, however, was pretty certain that they would eventually strike some part of Hampstead Heath.[28] Abruptly one bulging and gas-lit window broke the blue twilight like a bull's-eye lantern;[29] and Valentin stopped an instant before a little garish sweetstuff shop. After an instant's hesitation he went in; he stood amid the gaudy colours of the confectionery with entire gravity and bought thirteen chocolate cigars with a certain care. He was clearly preparing an opening; but he did not need one.

---

**27.** Like Carstairs Street (Note 22), Bullock Street was invented by Chesterton.

**28.** This enormous open space of heathland covers 800 acres north of Hampstead. 'Here we paid off our cab,' writes Watson in 'The Adventure of Charles Augustus Milverton' (*The Return of Sherlock Holmes*), 'and with our great coats buttoned up, for it was bitterly cold, and the wind seemed to blow through us, we walked along the edge of the heath.' Later in the same story Holmes and Watson run two miles across the heath to escape from pursuers.

**29.** A bull's-eye lantern has a convex lens to create a beam of light.

An angular, elderly young woman[30] in the shop had regarded his elegant appearance with a merely automatic inquiry; but when she saw the door behind him blocked with the blue uniform of the inspector, her eyes seemed to wake up.

'Oh,' she said 'if you've come about that parcel, I've sent it off already.'

'Parcel!' repeated Valentin; and it was his turn to look inquiring.

'I mean the parcel the gentleman left—the clergyman gentleman.'

'For goodness' sake,' said Valentin, leaning forward with his first real confession of eagerness, 'for Heaven's sake tell us what happened exactly.'

'Well,' said the woman a little doubtfully, 'the clergymen came in about half an hour ago and bought some peppermints and talked a bit, and then went off towards the Heath. But a second after, one of them runs back into the shop and says, "Have I left a parcel?" Well, I looked everywhere and couldn't see one; so he says, "Never mind; but if it should turn up, please post it to this address," and he left me the address and a shilling for my trouble. And sure enough, though I thought I'd looked everywhere, I found he'd left a brown-paper parcel, so I posted it to the place he said. I can't remember the address now; it was somewhere in Westminster. But as the thing seemed so important, I thought perhaps the police had come about it.'

'So they have,' said Valentin shortly. 'Is Hampstead Heath near here?'

'Straight on for fifteen minutes,' said the woman, 'and you'll come right out in the open.' Valentin sprang out of the shop and began to run. The other detectives followed him at a reluctant trot.

The street they threaded was so narrow and shut in by

---

**30.** The adjective *angular* was applied in England to persons who were bony, awkward, stiff in manner, and lacking in social graces. 'I am an angular man,' was a phrase that Grewgious, a barrister in Dickens's unfinished *Mystery of Edwin Drood*, never tired of saying. Does 'elderly young woman' mean a young woman who seems older than she actually is? The two adjectives are hyphenated as 'elderly-young' in the story's first magazine appearance.

shadows that when they came out unexpectedly into the void common and vast sky they were startled to find the evening still so light and clear. A perfect dome of peacock-green sank into gold amid the blackening trees and the dark violet distances. The glowing green tint was just deep enough to pick out in points of crystal one or two stars. All that was left of the daylight lay in a golden glitter across the edge of Hampstead and that popular hollow which is called the Vale of Health.[31] The holiday makers who roam this region had not wholly dispersed; a few couples sat shapelessly on benches; and here and there a distant girl still shrieked in one of the swings. The glory of heaven deepened and darkened around the sublime vulgarity of man;[32] and standing on the slope and looking across the valley, Valentin beheld the thing which he sought.

Among the black and breaking groups in that distance was one especially black which did not break—a group of two figures clerically clad. Though they seemed as small as insects, Valentin could see that one of them was much smaller than the other. Though the other had a student's stoop and an inconspicuous manner, he could see that the man was well over six feet high. He shut his teeth and went forward, whirling his stick impatiently. By the time he had substantially diminished the distance and magnified the two black figures as in a vast microscope, he had perceived something else; something which startled him, and yet which he had somehow expected. Whoever was the tall priest, there could be no doubt about the identity of the short one. It was his friend of the Harwich train, the stumpy little *curé* of Essex whom he had warned about his brown-paper parcels.

Now, so far as this went, everything fitted in finally and

---

31. At the western corner of Hampstead Heath, in a small valley below Spaniard's Road, is one of England's most curious hamlets: the Vale of Health. Originally it was a pestilential swamp called Hatches Bottom where a parish poor-house was located. The swamp was drained in 1800 and the name changed to the Vale of Health. Its most famous resident was the poet James Leigh Hunt, whose friends Keats and Shelley often came there to visit him. D. H. Lawrence and Edgar Wallace were among the writers who later lived there for a time.

32. This is one of those arresting, beautifully worded sentences that make it worthwhile to read slowly and carefully even the least important of Chesterton's stories.

rationally enough. Valentin had learned by his inquiries that morning that a Father Brown[33] from Essex was bringing up a silver cross with sapphires, a relic of considerable value, to show some of the foreign priests at the congress. This undoubtedly was the 'silver with blue stones'; and Father Brown undoubtedly was the little greenhorn in the train. Now there was nothing wonderful about the fact that what Valentin had found out Flambeau had also found out; Flambeau found out everything. Also there was nothing wonderful in the fact that when Flambeau heard of a sapphire cross he should try to steal it; that was the most natural thing in all natural history. And most certainly there was nothing wonderful about the fact that Flambeau should have it all his own way with such a silly sheep as the man with the umbrella and the parcels. He was the sort of man whom anybody could lead on a string to the North Pole; it was not surprising that an actor like Flambeau, dressed as another priest, could lead him to Hampstead Heath. So far the crime seemed clear enough; and while the detective pitied the priest for his helplessness, he almost despised Flambeau for condescending to so gullible a victim. But when Valentin thought of all that had happened in between, of all that had led him to his triumph, he racked his brains for the

---

**33.** This is the first mention of the priest's name. Chesterton's love of colours is reflected in his frequent use of colour names for fictional characters. He had earlier used Brown in 'The Tremendous Adventures of Major Brown' (*The Club of Queer Trades*). By giving it to the priest he reinforces the image of Father Brown as someone who outwardly seems as ordinary as the cheap brown paper in which his valuable cross is wrapped.

In his essay 'A Piece of Chalk' (*Tremendous Trifles*) Chesterton speaks of his fondness for drawing with coloured chalk on brown paper:

I then tried to explain the rather delicate logical shade, that I not only liked brown paper, but liked the quality of brownness in paper, just as I liked the quality of brownness in October woods, or in beer, or in the peat-streams of the North. Brown paper represents the primal twilight of the first toil of creation, and with a bright-coloured chalk or two you can pick out points of fire in it, sparks of gold, and blood-red, and sea-green, like the first fierce stars that sprang out of divine darkness.

'One of the wise and awful truths which this brown-paper art reveals', Chesterton says later in the same essay, 'is this, that white is a colour.' In similar fashion the dull brownness of Father Brown's appearance serves to intensify the white clarity of his wisdom and goodness.

For the mystery of Father Brown's first name, see Notes 2 and 9 in Chapters 10 and 11 respectively.

smallest rhyme or reason in it. What had the stealing of a blue-and-silver cross from a priest from Essex to do with chucking soup at wall-paper? What had it to do with calling nuts oranges, or with paying for windows first and breaking them afterwards? He had come to the end of his chase; yet somehow he had missed the middle of it. When he failed (which was seldom), he had usually grasped the clue, but nevertheless missed the criminal. Here he had grasped the criminal, but still he could not grasp the clue.

The two figures that they followed were crawling like black flies across the huge green contour of a hill. They were evidently sunk in conversation, and perhaps did not notice where they were going; but they were certainly going to the wilder and more silent heights of the Heath. As their pursuers gained on them, the former had to use the undignified attitudes of the deer-stalker, to crouch behind clumps of trees and even to crawl prostrate in deep grass. By these ungainly ingenuities the hunters even came close enough to the quarry to hear the murmur of the discussion, but no word could be distinguished except the word 'reason' recurring frequently in a high and almost childish voice. Once over an abrupt dip of land and a dense tangle of thickets, the detectives actually lost the two figures they were following. They did not find the trail again for an agonising ten minutes, and then it led round the brow of a great dome of hill overlooking an amphitheatre of rich and desolate sunset scenery. Under a tree in this commanding yet neglected spot was an old ramshackle wooden seat. On this seat sat the two priests still in serious speech together. The gorgeous green and gold still clung to the darkening horizon; but the dome above was turning slowly from peacock-green to peacock-blue, and the stars detached themselves more and more like solid jewels. Mutely motioning to his followers, Valentin contrived to creep up behind the big branching tree, and, standing there in deathly silence, heard the words of the strange priests for the first time.

After he had listened for a minute and a half, he was gripped by a devilish doubt. Perhaps he had dragged the two English policemen to the wastes of a nocturnal heath on an errand no saner than seeking figs on its thistles. For the two priests were talking exactly like priests, piously, with learning and leisure, about the most aerial enigmas of theology. The little Essex priest spoke the more simply, with his round face turned to the strengthening stars; the other talked with his head bowed, as if he were not even worthy to look at them. But no more innocently clerical conversation could have been heard in any white Italian cloister or black Spanish cathedral.

The first he heard was the tail of one of Father Brown's sentences, which ended: ' . . . what they really meant in the Middle Ages by the heavens being incorruptible.'

The taller priest nodded his bowed head and said:

'Ah, yes, these modern infidels appeal to their reason; but who can look at those millions of worlds and not feel that there may well be wonderful universes above us where reason is utterly unreasonable?'

'No,' said the other priest; 'reason is always reasonable, even in the last limbo, in the lost borderland of things. I know that people charge the Church with lowering reason, but it is just the other way. Alone on earth, the Church makes reason really supreme. Alone on earth, the Church affirms that God himself is bound by reason.'

The other priest raised his austere face to the spangled sky and said:

'Yet who knows if in that infinite universe——?'

'Only infinite physically,' said the little priest, turning sharply in his seat, 'not infinite in the sense of escaping from the laws of truth.'[34]

---

**34.** Father Brown is here a loyal disciple of Thomas Aquinas. There is one thing even God cannot do, the saint maintained, and that is to make true something logically contradictory. In today's philosophical language, any logically possible world can in some sense 'exist', and a few eccentric philosophers go to the extreme of insisting that every possible world is as 'real' as the 'actual world' we happen to be in. But a universe where, in the tall man's words, 'reason is utterly unreasonable' cannot exist in *any* sense, not even in the mind of God. For example, there cannot be a world in which $2 + 2 = 5$, or where valleys exist apart from mountains, or where a creature can be both completely a man and completely a horse, or where the past can be made different from what it was.

Rather than say there are things God cannot do, Aquinas recommended, it is better to say that certain things cannot be done. As a modern philosopher would put it, the statement 'A triangle has three angles' is analytic—it is true in virtue of what we take its words to mean. To deny its truth by saying 'A triangle does not have three sides' or 'A triangle has seven sides' is

Valentin behind his tree was tearing his finger-nails with silent fury. He seemed almost to hear the sniggers of the English detectives whom he had brought so far on a fantastic guess only to listen to the metaphysical gossip of two mild old parsons. In his impatience he lost the equally elaborate answer of the tall cleric, and when he listened again it was again Father Brown who was speaking:

'Reason and justice grip the remotest and the loneliest star. Look at those stars. Don't they look as if they were single diamonds and sapphires? Well, you can imagine any mad botany or geology you please. Think of forests of adamant with leaves of brilliants. Think the moon is a blue moon, a single elephantine sapphire. But don't fancy that all that frantic astronomy would make the smallest difference to the reason and justice of conduct. On plains of opal, under cliffs cut out of pearl, you would still find a notice-board, "Thou shalt not steal." '

Valentin was just in the act of rising from his rigid and crouching attitude and creeping away as softly as might be, felled by the one great folly of his life. But something in the very silence of the tall priest made him stop until the latter spoke. When at last he did speak, he said simply, his head bowed and his hands on his knees:

'Well, I still think that other worlds may perhaps rise higher than our reason. The mystery of heaven is unfathomable, and I for one can only bow my head.'

Then, with brow yet bent and without changing by the faintest shade his attitude or voice, he added:

'Just hand over that sapphire cross of yours, will you? We're all alone here, and I could pull you to pieces like a straw doll.'

The utterly unaltered voice and attitude added a strange violence to that shocking change of speech. But the guarder of the relic only seemed to turn his head by the smallest section of the compass. He seemed still to have a somewhat foolish face turned

---

to utter meaningless sounds. For a memorable defence of this see 'The Ethics of Elfland' (*Orthodoxy*) where Chesterton draws the eternally useful distinction between the possible laws of a fantasy world and impossible laws that violate the rules of a formal logic. 'We believe that a Bean-stalk climbed up to Heaven; but that does not at all confuse our convictions on the philosophical question of how many beans make five.'

to the stars. Perhaps he had not understood. Or, perhaps, he had understood and sat rigid with terror.

'Yes,' said the tall priest, in the same low voice and in the same still posture, 'yes, I am Flambeau.'

Then, after a pause, he said:

'Come, will you give me that cross?'

'No,' said the other, and the monosyllable had an odd sound.

Flambeau suddenly flung off all his pontifical pretensions. The great robber leaned back in his seat and laughed low but long.

'No,' he cried, 'you won't give it me, you proud prelate. You won't give it me, you little celibate simpleton. Shall I tell you why you won't give it me? Because I've got it already in my own breast-pocket.'

The small man from Essex turned what seemed to be a dazed face in the dusk, and said, with the timid eagerness of 'The Private Secretary':[35]

---

35. *The Private Secretary* was a three-act farce about the Reverend Robert Spaulding, an Anglican priest who had once been a private secretary. It presented a 'too amiable view of a clergyman' commented Chesterton in Chapter 5 of his *George Bernard Shaw*. The play was written by the English comedy actor Sir Charles Henry Hawtrey (1858–1923), who based it on *Der Bibliothekar*, an earlier German farce by Gustav von Moser. It opened in London in 1884 with the famous actor Sir Herbert Beerbohm Tree (half-brother of Max Beerbohm) playing the title role.

The farce was enormously popular, and so often revived that it became a rival of *Charley's Aunt*. The first great success of the comedian William Sydney Penley was when he replaced Tree. Penley became so identified with this role, says the *Oxford Companion to the Theatre*, that he was often said to have been the first to play the part. Later, he became similarly identified with the leading role of *Charley's Aunt*.

*The Private Secretary* was published in London and New York in 1907 by Samuel French, and reissued in a revised version when the farce was revived in London in 1954. Here is how the 1932 catalogue of Samuel French described the comedy:

Mr Marsland, by letter, engages as his secretary the Rev. Robert Spaulding, meekest of the meek, whose hair is parted down the center, whose trousers are four inches above his shoes, who wears goloshes, who is very limp, and who suffers from a chronic cold. For various reasons, Harry, Marsland's nephew, wishes his friend, Douglas Cattermole, to pass himself off as the secretary. The reverend gentleman arrives to fulfill his duties, and the young men have their work cut out to disabuse the minds of the elder people. This is one of the funniest and at the same time the cleanest farce-comedy ever written, which is why it has enjoyed its immense vogue among the better class of amateurs.

'Are—are you sure?'

Flambeau yelled with delight.

'Really, you're as good as a three-act farce,' he cried. 'Yes, you turnip, I am quite sure. I had the sense to make a duplicate of the right parcel, and now, my friend, you've got the duplicate and I've got the jewels. An old dodge, Father Brown—a very old dodge.'

'Yes,' said Father Brown, and passed his hand through his hair with the same strange vagueness of manner. 'Yes, I've heard of it before.'

The colossus of crime leaned over to the little rustic priest with a sort of sudden interest.

'*You* have heard of it?' he asked. 'Where have *you* heard of it?'

'Well, I mustn't tell you his name, of course,' said the little man simply. 'He was a penitent, you know. He had lived prosperously for about twenty years entirely on duplicate brownpaper parcels. And so, you see, when I began to suspect you, I thought of this poor chap's way of doing it at once.'

'Began to suspect me?' repeated the outlaw with increased intensity. 'Did you really have the gumption to suspect me just because I brought you up to this bare part of the heath?'

'No, no,' said Brown with an air of apology. 'You see, I suspected you when we first met. It's that little bulge up the sleeve where you people have the spiked bracelet.'[36]

'How in Tartarus,' cried Flambeau, 'did you ever hear of the spiked bracelet?'

'Oh, one's little flock, you know!' said Father Brown, arching his eyebrows rather blankly. 'When I was a curate in Hartlepool,[37] there were three of them with spiked bracelets. So, as I suspected you from the first, don't you see, I made sure that the cross should go safe, anyhow. I'm afraid I watched you, you know. So at last I saw you change the parcels. Then, don't you see, I changed them back again. And then I left the right one behind.'

---

36. So far as I can find out 'spiked bracelet' is a term G.K. invented. Since Flambeau used the device for exchanging a small parcel by way of a large sleeve, it must have been a mechanism similar to what crooked gamblers call a holdout. It is used for secretly switching playing cards in the course of a game.

37. Hartlepool is an eastern seaport town in the county of Durham.

'Left it behind?' repeated Flambeau, and for the first time there was another note in this voice beside his triumph.

'Well, it was like this,' said the little priest, speaking in the same unaffected way. 'I went back to that sweet-shop and asked if I'd left a parcel, and gave them a particular address if it turned up. Well, I knew I hadn't; but when I went away again I did. So, instead of running after me with that valuable parcel, they have sent it flying to a friend of mine in Westminster.' Then he added rather sadly: 'I learnt that, too, from a poor fellow in Hartlepool. He used to do it with handbags he stole at railway stations, but he's in a monastery now. Oh, one gets to know, you know,' he added, rubbing his head again with the same sort of desperate apology. 'We can't help being priests. People come and tell us these things.'

Flambeau tore a brown-paper parcel out of his inner pocket and rent it in pieces. There was nothing but paper and sticks of lead inside it. He sprang to his feet with a gigantic gesture, and cried:

'I don't believe you. I don't believe a bumpkin like you could manage all that. I believe you've still got the stuff on you, and if you don't give it up—why, we're all alone, and I'll take it by force!'

'No,' said Father Brown simply, and stood up also, 'you won't take it by force. First, because I really haven't still got it. And, second, because we are not alone'.

Flambeau stopped in his stride forward.

'Behind that tree,' said Father Brown, pointing, 'are two strong policemen and the greatest detective alive. How did they come here, do you ask? Why, I brought them, of course! How did I do it? Why, I'll tell you if you like! Lord bless you, we have to know twenty such things when we work among the criminal classes! Well, I wasn't sure you were a thief, and it would never do to make a scandal against one of our own clergy. So I just tested you to see if anything would make you show yourself. A man generally makes a small scene if he finds salt in his coffee; if he doesn't, he has some reason for keeping quiet. I changed the salt and sugar, and *you* kept quiet. A man generally objects if his bill is three times too big. If he pays it, he has some motive for passing unnoticed. I altered your bill, and *you* paid it.'

The world seemed waiting for Flambeau to leap like a tiger.

But he was held back as by a spell; he was stunned with the utmost curiosity.

'Well,' went on Father Brown, with lumbering lucidity, 'as you wouldn't leave any tracks for the police, of course somebody had to. At every place we went to, I took care to do something that would get us talked about for the rest of the day. I didn't do much harm—a splashed wall, spilt apples, a broken window; but I saved the cross, as the cross will always be saved. It is at Westminster by now. I rather wonder you didn't stop it with the Donkey's Whistle.'

'With the what?' asked Flambeau.

'I'm glad you've never heard of it,' said the priest, making a face. 'It's a foul thing. I'm sure you're too good a man for a Whistler. I couldn't have countered it even with the Spots[38] myself; I'm not strong enough in the legs.'

'What on earth are you talking about?' asked the other.

'Well, I did think you'd know the Spots,' said Father Brown, agreeably surprised. 'Oh, you can't have gone so very wrong yet!'

'How in blazes do you know all these horrors?' cried Flambeau.

The shadow of a smile crossed the round, simple face of his clerical opponent.

'Oh, by being a celibate simpleton, I suppose,' he said. 'Has it never struck you that a man who does next to nothing but hear men's real sins is not likely to be wholly unaware of human evil? But, as a matter of fact, another part of my trade, too, made me sure you weren't a priest.'

'What?' asked the thief, almost gaping.

'You attacked reason,' said Father Brown. 'It's bad theology.'

And even as he turned away to collect his property, the three policemen came out from under the twilight trees. Flambeau was an artist and a sportsman. He stepped back and swept Valentin a great bow.

'Do not bow to me, *mon ami*,' said Valentin, with silver clearness. 'Let us both bow to our master.'

---

**38.** Spots and Donkey Whistle: more made-up terms, though no doubt there were many curious dodges with equally colourful names in the criminal argot of the day.

And they both stood an instant uncovered, while the little Essex priest blinked about for his umbrella.

AFTERWORD

In this first of the Father Brown stories the priest sees through Flambeau's disguise because he does not talk like a priest. It is interesting to note that in the last Father Brown story that Chesterton wrote, 'The Vampire of the Village', Father Brown recognizes another false priest because he talks *too much* like a priest.

Father John O'Connor, the Irish priest who inspired the character of Father Brown, had this to say about 'The Blue Cross' in his book *Father Brown on Chesterton*:

The flat hat is true to life, but it perished in its prime, for it was wrong as wrong for my style of architecture. The large and cheap umbrella was my defence against wearing an overcoat, and the sapphire cross figuring in the first of the stories must have been a reminiscence of my boast that I had just bought five sapphires for five shillings. One was very deep, so it must have been of good water. Brown paper parcels! I carried them whenever I could, having no sense of style in deportment.

# The Secret Garden*

ARISTIDE VALENTIN, Chief of the Paris Police, was late for his dinner, and some of his guests began to arrive before him. These
were, however, reassured by his confidential servant, Ivan, the
old man with a scar, and a face almost as grey as his moustaches,
who always sat at a table in the entrance hall—a hall hung with
weapons. Valentin's house was perhaps as peculiar and celebrated as its master. It was an old house, with high walls and
tall poplars almost overhanging the Seine; but the oddity—and
perhaps the police value—of its architecture was this: that there
was no ultimate exit at all except through this front door, which
was guarded by Ivan and the armoury. The garden was large
and elaborate, and there were many exits from the house into the
garden. But there was no exit from the garden into the world outside; all round it ran a tall, smooth, unscalable wall with special
spikes at the top; no bad garden, perhaps, for a man to reflect in
whom some hundred criminals had sworn to kill.

As Ivan explained to the guests, their host had telephoned that
he was detained for ten minutes. He was, in truth, making some
last arrangements about executions and such ugly things; and
though these duties were rootedly repulsive to him, he always
performed them with precision. Ruthless in the pursuit of criminals, he was very mild about their punishment. Since he had
been supreme over French—and largely over European—police
methods, his great influence had been honourably used for the
mitigation of sentences and the purification of prisons. He was
one of the great humanitarian French freethinkers; and the only

---

* Father Brown solves the mystery of a decapitated corpse in the garden
of Aristide Valentin, chief of the Paris police. The story first appeared in the
*Storyteller* (October 1910). Announcing the story in the previous issue, the
editor called it 'the finest detective story I have ever published'.

thing wrong with them is that they make mercy even colder than justice.

When Valentin arrived he was already dressed in black clothes and the red rosette—an elegant figure, his dark beard already streaked with grey. He went straight through his house to his study, which opened on the grounds behind. The garden door of it was open, and after he had carefully locked his box in its official place, he stood for a few seconds at the open door looking out upon the garden. A sharp moon was fighting with the flying rags and tatters of a storm, and Valentin regarded it with a wistfulness unusual in such scientific natures as his. Perhaps such scientific natures have some psychic prevision of the most tremendous problem of their lives. From any such occult mood, at least, he quickly recovered, for he knew he was late, and that his guests had already begun to arrive. A glance at his drawing-room when he entered it was enough to make certain that his principal guest was not there, at any rate. He saw all the other pillars of the little party; he saw Lord Galloway, the English Ambassador—a choleric old man with a russet face like an apple, wearing the blue ribbon of the Garter. He saw Lady Galloway, slim and threadlike, with silver hair and a face sensitive and superior. He saw her daughter, Lady Margaret Graham, a pale and pretty girl with an elfish face and copper-coloured hair.[1] He saw the Duchess of Mont St. Michel, black-eyed and opulent, and with her her two daughters, black-eyed and opulent also. He saw Dr Simon, a typical French scientist, with glasses, a pointed brown beard, and a forehead barred with those parallel wrinkles

---

1. So many people with reddish hair, especially women, appear in Chesterton's fiction that it once gave rise to the myth that as a youth he had been in love with a woman who had red hair. This groundless speculation was laid to rest by Maisie Ward in the introduction to her biography *Gilbert Keith Chesterton*. G.K. liked women with red hair partly because his mother's hair was auburn, but mainly because he loved the dramatic quality of red—provided there was not too much of it. Chesterton's men and women often have red hair for the same reason that his skies often display red sunsets.

Red is the most joyful and dreadful thing in the physical universe; it is the fiercest note, it is the highest light, it is the place where the walls of this world of ours wear thinnest and something beyond burns through. It glows in the blood which sustains and in the fire which destroys us, in the roses of our romance and in the awful cup of our religion. It stands for all passionate happiness, as in faith or in first love.

Chesterton, 'The Red Town' (*Alarms and Discursions*)

which are the penalty of superciliousness, since they come through constantly elevating the eyebrows. He saw Father Brown, of Cobhole,[2] in Essex, whom he had recently met in England. He saw—perhaps with more interest than any of those—a tall man in uniform, who had bowed to the Galloways without receiving any very hearty acknowledgment, and who now advanced alone to pay his respects to his host. This was Commandant O'Brien, of the French Foreign Legion. He was a slim yet somewhat swaggering figure, clean-shaven, dark haired, and blue-eyed, and, as seemed natural in an officer of that famous regiment of victorious failures and successful suicides, he had an air at once dashing and melancholy. He was by birth an Irish gentleman, and in boyhood had known the Galloways—especially Margaret Graham. He had left his country after some crash of debts, and now expressed his complete freedom from British etiquette by swinging about in uniform, sabre and spurs. When he bowed to the Ambassador's family, Lord and Lady Galloway bent stiffly, and Lady Margaret looked away.

But for whatever old causes such people might be interested in each other, their distinguished host was not specially interested in them. No one of them at least was in his eyes the guest of the evening. Valentin was expecting, for special reasons, a man of world-wide fame, whose friendship he had secured during some of his great detective tours and triumphs in the United States. He was expecting Julius K. Brayne, that multimillionaire whose colossal and even crushing endowments of small religions have occasioned so much easy sport and easier solemnity for the American and English papers. Nobody could quite make out whether Mr Brayne was an atheist or a Mormon or a Christian Scientist; but he was ready to pour money into any intellectual vessel, so long as it was an untried vessel. One of his hobbies was to wait for the American Shakespeare—a hobby more patient than angling. He admired Walt Whitman, but thought that Luke P. Tanner, of Paris, Pa.,[3] was more 'progressive' than Whitman

---

2. Cobhole is an invented name. Chesterton may have been playing on the name Cobham, a village in Kent.

3. There are almost twenty towns in the US named Paris, but there has never been a Paris in Pennsylvania. Nor has there been, so far as I know, an American poet named Luke Tanner.

any day. He liked anything that he thought 'progressive.' He though Valentin 'progressive,' thereby doing him a grave injustice.

The solid appearance of Julius K. Brayne in the room was as decisive as a dinner bell. He had this great quality, which very few of us can claim, that his presence was as big as his absence. He was a huge fellow, as fat as he was tall, clad in complete evening black, without so much relief as a watch-chain or a ring. His hair was white and well brushed back like a German's; his face was red, fierce and cherubic, with one dark tuft under the lower lip that threw up that otherwise infantile visage with an effect theatrical and even Mephistophelean. Not long, however, did that *salon* merely stare at the celebrated American; his lateness had already become a domestic problem, and he was sent with all speed into the dining-room with Lady Galloway upon his arm.

Except on one point the Galloways were genial and casual enough. So long as Lady Margaret did not take the arm of that adventurer O'Brien, her father was quite satisfied; and she had not done so, she had decorously gone in with Dr Simon. Nevertheless, old Lord Galloway was restless and almost rude. He was diplomatic enough during dinner, but when, over the cigars, three of the younger men—Simon the doctor, Brown the priest, and the detrimental O'Brien, the exile in a foreign uniform—all melted away to mix with the ladies or smoke in the conservatory, then the English diplomatist grew very undiplomatic indeed. He was stung every sixty seconds with the thought that the scamp O'Brien might be signalling to Margaret somehow; he did not attempt to imagine how. He was left over the coffee with Brayne, the hoary Yankee who believed in all religions, and Valentin, the grizzled Frenchman who believed in none. They could argue with each other, but neither could appeal to him. After a time this 'progressive' logomachy had reached a crisis of tedium; Lord Galloway got up also and sought the drawing-room. He lost his way in long passages for some six or eight minutes: till he heard the high-pitched, didactic voice of the doctor, and then the dull voice of the priest, followed by general laughter.[4] They also, he

---

4. In the original magazine text this sentence reads: 'As he went towards it he could hear along passages the high-pitched, didactic voice of the doctor, and then the dull voice of the priest, followed by violent laughter.'

thought with a curse, were probably arguing about 'science and religion.' But the instant he opened the *salon* door he saw only one thing—he saw what was not there. He saw that Commandant O'Brien was absent, and that Lady Margaret was absent too.

Rising impatiently from the drawing-room, as he had from the dining-room, he stamped along the passage once more. His notion of protecting his daughter from the Irish-Algerian ne'er-do-well had become something central and even mad in his mind. As he went towards the back of the house, where was Valentin's study, he was surprised to meet his daughter, who swept past with a white, scornful face, which was a second enigma. If she had been with O'Brien, where was O'Brien? If she had not been with O'Brien, where had she been? With a sort of senile and passionate suspicion he groped his way to the dark back parts of the mansion, and eventually found a servants' entrance that opened on to the garden. The moon with her scimitar had now ripped up and rolled away all the storm-wrack. The argent light lit up all four corners of the garden. A tall figure in blue was striding across the lawn towards the study door; a glint of moonlit silver on his facings picked him out as Commandant O'Brien.

He vanished through the French windows into the house, leaving Lord Galloway in an indescribable temper, at once virulent and vague. The blue-and-silver garden, like a scene in a theatre, seemed to taunt him with all that tyrannic tenderness against which his worldly authority was at war. The length and grace of the Irishman's stride enraged him as if he were a rival instead of a father; the moonlight maddened him. He was trapped as if by magic into a garden of troubadours, a Watteau fairyland;[5] and, willing to shake off such amorous imbecilities by speech, he stepped briskly after his enemy. As he did so he tripped over some tree or stone in the grass; looked down at it first with irritation and then a second time with curiosity. The next instant the moon and the tall poplars looked at an unusual sight—an elderly

---

5. Jean Antoine Watteau (1684–1721) was a Parisian painter celebrated for his romantic scenes of elegantly dressed young men and women in colourful French gardens.

45

English diplomatist running hard and crying or bellowing as he ran.

His hoarse shouts brought a pale face to the study door, the beaming glasses and worried brow of Dr Simon, who heard the nobleman's first clear words. Lord Galloway was crying: 'A corpse in the grass—a blood-stained corpse.' O'Brien at least had gone utterly from his mind.

'We must tell Valentin at once,' said the doctor, when the other had brokenly described all that he had dared to examine. 'It is fortunate that he is here'; and even as he spoke the great detective entered the study, attracted by the cry. It was almost amusing to note his typical transformation; he had come with the common concern of a host and a gentleman, fearing that some guest or servant was ill. When he was told the gory fact, he turned with all his gravity instantly bright and business-like; for this, however abrupt and awful, was his business.

'Strange, gentlemen,' he said as they hurried out into the garden, 'that I should have hunted mysteries all over the earth, and now one comes and settles in my own back-yard. But where is the place?' They crossed the lawn less easily, as a slight mist had begun to rise from the river; but under the guidance of the shaken Galloway they found the body sunken in deep grass—the body of a very tall and broad-shouldered man. He lay face downwards, so they could only see that his big shoulders were clad in black cloth, and that his big head was bald, except for a wisp or two of brown hair that clung to his skull like wet seaweed. A scarlet serpent of blood crawled from under his fallen face.

'At least,' said Simon, with a deep and singular intonation, 'he is none of our party.'

'Examine him, doctor,' cried Valentin rather sharply. 'He may not be dead.'

The doctor bent down. 'He is not quite cold, but I am afraid he is dead enough,' he answered. 'Just help me to lift him up.'

They lifted him carefully an inch from the ground, and all doubts as to his being really dead were settled at once and frightfully. The head fell away. It had been entirely sundered from the body; whoever had cut his throat had managed to sever the neck as well. Even Valentin was slightly shocked. 'He must have been as strong as a gorilla,' he muttered.

Not without a shiver, though he was used to anatomical abortions, Dr Simon lifted the head. It was slightly slashed about the neck and jaw, but the face was substantially unhurt. It was a ponderous, yellow face, at once sunken and swollen, with a hawk-like nose and heavy lids—the face of a wicked Roman emperor, with, perhaps, a distant touch of a Chinese emperor. All present seemed to look at it with the coldest eye of ignorance. Nothing else could be noted about the man except that, as they had lifted his body, they had seen underneath it the white gleam of a shirtfront defaced with a red gleam of blood. As Dr Simon said, the man had never been of their party. But he might very well have been trying to join it, for he had come dressed for such an occasion.

Valentin went down on his hands and knees and examined with his closest professional attention the grass and ground for some twenty yards round the body, in which he was assisted less skilfully by the doctor, and quite vaguely by the English lord. Nothing rewarded their grovellings except a few twigs, snapped or chopped into very small lengths, which Valentin lifted for an instant's examination and then tossed away.

'Twigs,' he said gravely; 'twigs, and a total stranger with his head cut off; that is all there is on this lawn.'

There was an almost creepy stillness, and then the unnerved Galloway called out sharply:

'Who's that? Who's that over there by the garden wall?'

A small figure with a foolishly large head drew waveringly near them in the moonlit haze; it looked for an instant like a goblin, but turned out to be the harmless little priest whom they had left in the drawing-room.

'I say,' he said meekly, 'there are no gates to this garden, do you know.'

Valentin's black brows had come together somewhat crossly, as they did on principle at the sight of the cassock. But he was far too just a man to deny the relevance of the remark. 'You are right,' he said. 'Before we find out how he came to be killed, we may have to find out how he came to be here. Now listen to me, gentlemen. If it can be done without prejudice to my position and duty, we shall all agree that certain distinguished names might well be kept out of this. There are ladies, gentlemen, and there is a foreign ambassador. If we must mark it down as a crime, then it must be followed up as a crime. But till then I can use my own

47

discretion. I am the head of the police; I am so public that I can afford to be private. Please Heaven, I will clear every one of my own guests before I call in my men to look for anybody else. Gentlemen, upon your honour, you will none of you leave the house till to-morrow at noon; there are bedrooms for all. Simon, I think you know where to find my man, Ivan, in the front hall; he is a confidential man. Tell him to leave another servant on guard and come to me at once. Lord Galloway, you are certainly the best person to tell the ladies what has happened, and prevent a panic. They also must stay. Father Brown and I will remain with the body.'

When this spirit of the captain spoke in Valentin he was obeyed like a bugle. Dr Simon went through to the armoury and routed out Ivan, the public detective's private detective. Galloway went to the drawing-room and told the terrible news tactfully enough, so that by the time the company assembled there the ladies were already startled and already soothed. Meanwhile the good priest and the good atheist stood at the head and foot of the dead man motionless in the moonlight, like symbolic statues of their two philosophies of death.

Ivan, the confidential man with the scar and the moustaches, came out of the house like a cannon ball, and came racing across the lawn to Valentin like a dog to his master. His livid face was quite lively with the glow of this domestic detective story, and it was with almost unpleasant eagerness that he asked his master's permission to examine the remains.

'Yes; look, if you like, Ivan,' said Valentin, 'but don't be long. We must go in and thrash this out in the house.'

Ivan lifted the head, and then almost let it drop.

'Why,' he gasped, 'it's—no, it isn't; it can't be. Do you know this man, sir?'

'No,' said Valentin indifferently; 'we had better go inside.'

Between them they carried the corpse to a sofa in the study, and then all made their way to the drawing-room.

The detective sat down at a desk quietly, and even with hesitation; but his eye was the iron eye of a judge at assize.[6] He made a few rapid notes upon paper in front of him, and then said shortly: 'Is everybody here?'

---

6. 'At assize' means sitting in a court session.

'Not Mr Brayne,' said the Duchess of Mont St. Michel, looking round.

'No,' said Lord Galloway in a hoarse, harsh voice. 'And not Mr Neil O'Brien, I fancy. I saw that gentleman walking in the garden when the corpse was still warm.'

'Ivan,' said the detective, 'go and fetch Commandant O'Brien and Mr Brayne. Mr Brayne, I know, is finishing a cigar in the dining-room; Commandant O'Brien, I think, is walking up and down the conservatory. I am not sure.'

The faithful attendant flashed from the room, and before anyone could stir or speak Valentin went on with the same soldierly swiftness of exposition.

'Everyone here knows that a dead man has been found in the garden, his head cut clean from his body. Dr Simon, you have examined it. Do you think that to cut a man's throat like that would need great force? Or, perhaps, only a very sharp knife?'

'I should say that it could not be done with a knife at all,' said the pale doctor.

'Have you any thought,' resumed Valentin, 'of a tool with which it could be done?'

'Speaking within modern probabilities, I really haven't,' said the doctor, arching his painful brows. 'It's not easy to hack a neck through even clumsily, and this was a very clean cut. It could be done with a battle-axe or an old headsman's axe, or an old two-handed sword.'

'But, good heavens!' cried the Duchess, almost in hysterics, 'there aren't any two-handed swords and battle-axes round here.'

Valentin was still busy with the paper in front of him. 'Tell me,' he said, still writing rapidly, 'could it have been done with a long French cavalry sabre?'

A low knocking came at the door, which, for some unreasonable reason, curdled everyone's blood like the knocking in Macbeth. Amid that frozen silence Dr Simon managed to say: 'A sabre—yes, I suppose it could.'

'Thank you,' said Valentin. 'Come in, Ivan.'

The confidential Ivan opened the door and ushered in Commandant Neil O'Brien, whom he had found at last pacing the garden again.

The Irish officer stood up disordered and defiant on the threshold. 'What do you want with me?' he cried.

'Please sit down,' said Valentin in pleasant, level tones. 'Why, you aren't wearing your sword. Where is it?'

'I left it on the library table,' said O'Brien, his brogue deepening in his disturbed mood. 'It was a nuisance, it was getting——'

'Ivan,' said Valentin, 'please go and get the Commandant's sword from the library.' Then, as the servant vanished, 'Lord Galloway says he saw you leaving the garden just before he found the corpse. What were you doing in the garden?'

The Commandant flung himself recklessly into a chair. 'Oh,' he cried in pure Irish, 'admirin' the moon. Communing with Nature, me boy.'[7]

A heavy silence sank and endured, and at the end of it came again that trivial and terrible knocking. Ivan reappeared, carrying an empty steel scabbard. 'This is all I can find,' he said.

'Put it on the table,' said Valentin, without looking up.

There was an inhuman silence in the room, like that sea of inhuman silence round the dock of the condemned murderer. The Duchess's weak exclamations had long ago died away. Lord Galloway's swollen hatred was satisfied and even sobered. The voice that came was quite unexpected.

'I think I can tell you,' cried Lady Margaret, in that clear, quivering voice with which a courageous woman speaks publicly. 'I can tell you what Mr O'Brien was doing in the garden, since he is bound to silence. He was asking me to marry him. I refused; I said in my family circumstances I could give him nothing but my respect. He was a little angry at that; he did not seem to think much of my respect. I wonder,' she added, with rather a wan smile, 'if he will care at all for it now. For I offer it him now. I will swear anywhere that he never did a thing like this.'

Lord Galloway had edged up to his daughter, and was intimidating her in what he imagined to be an undertone. 'Hold your tongue, Maggie,' he said in a thunderous whisper. 'Why should you shield the fellow? Where's his sword? Where's his confounded cavalry——'

He stopped because of the singular stare with which his

7. In the *Storyteller* and in the British and US first editions, *boy* is spelled *bhoy*.

daughter was regarding him, a look that was indeed a lurid mag-
net for the whole group.

'You old fool!' she said, in a low voice without pretence of
piety, 'what do you suppose you are trying to prove? I tell you
this man was innocent while with me. But if he wasn't innocent,
he was still with me. If he murdered a man in the garden, who
was it who must have seen—who must at least have known? Do
you hate Neil so much as to put your own daughter——'

Lady Galloway screamed. Everyone else sat tingling at the
touch of those satanic tragedies that have been between lovers
before now. They saw the proud, white face of the Scotch aristocrat and her lover, the Irish adventurer, like old portraits in a
dark house. The long silence was full of formless historical
memories of murdered husbands and poisonous paramours.

In the centre of this morbid silence an innocent voice said:
'Was it a very long cigar?'

The change of thought was so sharp that they had to look
round to see who had spoken.

'I mean,' said little Father Brown, from the corner of the room,
'I mean that cigar Mr Brayne is finishing. It seems nearly as long
as a walking-stick.'

Despite the irrelevance there was assent as well as irritation in
Valentin's face as he lifted his head.

'Quite right,' he remarked sharply. 'Ivan, go and see about Mr
Brayne again, and bring him here at once.'

The instant the factotum had closed the door, Valentin
addressed the girl with an entirely new earnestness.

'Lady Margaret,' he said, 'we all feel, I am sure, both gratitude and admiration for your act in rising above your lower dignity and explaining the Commandant's conduct. But there is a
hiatus still. Lord Galloway, I understand, met you passing from
the study to the drawing-room, and it was only some minutes
afterwards that he found the garden and the Commandant still
walking there.'

'You have to remember,' replied Margaret, with a faint irony
in her voice, 'that I had just refused him, so we should scarcely
have come back arm in arm. He is a gentleman, anyhow; and he
loitered behind—and so got charged with murder.'

'In those few moments,' said Valentin gravely, 'he might
really——'

The knock came again, and Ivan put in his scarred face.

'Beg pardon, sir,' he said, 'but Mr Brayne has left the house.'

'Left!' cried Valentin, and rose for the first time to his feet.

'Gone. Scooted. Evaporated,' replied Ivan, in humorous French. 'His hat and coat are gone, too, and I'll tell you something to cap it all. I ran outside the house to find any traces of him, and I found one, and a big trace, too.'

'What do you mean?' asked Valentin.

'I'll show you,' said his servant, and reappeared with a flashing naked cavalry sabre, streaked with blood about the point and edge. Everyone in the room eyed it as if it were a thunderbolt; but the experienced Ivan went on quite quietly:

'I found this,' he said, 'flung among the bushes fifty yards up the road to Paris. In other words, I found it just where your respectable Mr Brayne threw it when he ran away.'

There was again a silence, but of a new sort. Valentin took the sabre, examined it, reflected with unaffected concentration of thought, and then turned a respectful face to O'Brien. 'Commandant,' he said, 'we trust you will always produce this weapon if it is wanted for police examination. Meanwhile,' he added, slapping the steel back in the ringing scabbard, 'let me return you your sword.'[8]

At the military symbolism of the action the audience could hardly refrain from applause.

For Neil O'Brien, indeed, that gesture was the turning-point of existence. By the time he was wandering in the mysterious garden again in the colours of the morning the tragic futility of his ordinary mien had fallen from him; he was a man with many reasons for happiness. Lord Galloway was a gentleman, and had offered him an apology. Lady Margaret was something better

---

**8.** Swords and sword play are common in Chesterton's fiction, notably in his novels *The Ball and the Cross* and *The Napoleon of Notting Hill*, and in such short stories as 'The Sword of Wood', 'The Five of Swords', and several stories in this book. He wrote a poem called 'A Song of Swords'. Note that in this tale even the moon has the shape of a scimitar.

Chesterton owned a walking stick which concealed a sword. He carried it, he liked to say, in case he ever needed it to save a lady in distress. While dictating he often drew his sword to fence with the cushions. Father O'Connor, in *Father Brown on Chesterton*, recalls seeing G.K. in his garden making 'deadly passes with the sword-stick at the dahlias'.

than a lady, a woman at least, and had perhaps given him something better than an apology, as they drifted among the old flower-beds before breakfast. The whole company was more lighthearted and humane, for though the riddle of the death remained, the load of suspicion was lifted off them all, and sent flying off to Paris with the strange millionaire—a man they hardly knew. The devil was cast out of the house—he had cast himself out.

Still, the riddle remained; and when O'Brien threw himself on a garden seat beside Dr Simon, that keenly scientific person at once resumed it. He did not get much talk out of O'Brien, whose thoughts were on pleasanter things.

'I can't say it interests me much,' said the Irishman frankly, 'especially as it seems pretty plain now. Apparently Brayne hated this stranger for some reason; lured him into the garden, and killed him with my sword. Then he fled to the city, tossing the sword away as he went. By the way, Ivan tells me the dead man had a Yankee dollar in his pocket. So he was a countryman of Brayne's, and that seems to clinch it. I don't see any difficulties about the business.'

'There are five colossal difficulties,' said the doctor quietly; 'like high walls within walls. Don't mistake me. I don't doubt that Brayne did it; his flight, I fancy, proves that. But as to how he did it. First difficulty: Why should a man kill another man with a great hulking sabre, when he can almost kill him with a pocket knife and put it back in his pocket? Second difficulty: Why was there no noise or outcry? Does a man commonly see another come up waving a scimitar and offer no remarks? Third difficulty: A servant watched the front door all the evening; and a rat cannot get into Valentin's garden anywhere. How did the dead man get into the garden? Fourth difficulty: Given the same conditions, how did Brayne get out of the garden?'

'And the fifth,' said Neil, with eyes fixed on the English priest who was coming slowly up the path.

'Is a trifle, I suppose,' said the doctor, 'but I think an odd one. When I first saw how the head had been slashed, I supposed the assassin had struck more than once. But on examination I found many cuts across the truncated section; in other words, they were struck *after* the head was off. Did Brayne hate his foe so fiendishly that he stood sabring his body in the moonlight?'

53

'Horrible!' said O'Brien, and shuddered.

The little priest, Brown, had arrived while they were talking, and had waited, with characteristic shyness, till they had finished. Then he said awkwardly:

'I say, I'm sorry to interrupt. But I was sent to tell you the news!'

'News?' repeated Simon, and stared at him rather painfully through his glasses.

'Yes, I'm sorry,' said Father Brown mildly. 'There's been another murder, you know.'

Both men on the seat sprang up, leaving it rocking.

'And, what's stranger still,' continued the priest, with his dull eyes on the rhododendrons, 'it's the same disgusting sort; it's another beheading. They found the second head actually bleeding into the river, a few yards along Brayne's road to Paris; so they suppose that he——'

'Great Heaven!' cried O'Brien. 'Is Brayne a monomaniac?'

'There are American vendettas,' said the priest impassively. Then he added: 'They want you to come to the library and see it.'

Commandant O'Brien followed the others towards the inquest, feeling decidedly sick. As a soldier, he loathed all this secretive carnage; where were these extravagant amputations going to stop? First one head was hacked off, and then another; in this case (he told himself bitterly) it was not true that two heads were better than one. As he crossed the study he almost staggered at a shocking coincidence. Upon Valentin's table lay the coloured picture of yet a third bleeding head; and it was the head of Valentin himself. A second glance showed him it was only a Nationalist paper, called *The Guillotine*, which every week showed one of its political opponents with rolling eyes and writhing features just after execution; for Valentin was an anti-clerical of some note. But O'Brien was an Irishman, with a kind of chastity even in his sins; and his gorge rose against that great brutality of the intellect which belongs only to France. He felt Paris as a whole, from the grotesques on the Gothic churches to the gross caricatures in the newspapers. He remembered the gigantic jests of the Revolution. He saw the whole city as one ugly energy, from the sanguinary sketch lying on Valentin's table up to where, above a mountain and forest of gargoyles, the great devil grins on Notre Dame.

The library was long, low, and dark; what light entered it shot from under low blinds and had still some of the ruddy tinge of morning. Valentin and his servant Ivan were waiting for them at the upper end of a long, slightly-sloping desk, on which lay the mortal remains, looking enormous in the twilight. The big black figure and yellow face of the man found in the garden confronted them essentially unchanged. The second head, which had been fished from among the river reeds that morning, lay streaming and dripping beside it: Valentin's men were still seeking to recover the rest of this second corpse, which was supposed to be afloat. Father Brown, who did not seem to share O'Brien's sensibilities in the least, went up to the second head and examined it with his blinking care. It was little more than a mop of wet white hair, fringed with silver fire in the red and level morning light; the face, which seemed of an ugly, empurpled and perhaps criminal type, had been much battered against trees or stones as it tossed in the water.

'Good morning, Commandant O'Brien,' said Valentin, with quiet cordiality. 'You have heard of Brayne's last experiment in butchery, I suppose?'

Father Brown was still bending over the head with white hair, and he said, without looking up:

'I suppose it is quite certain that Brayne cut off this head, too.'

'Well, it seems common sense,' said Valentin, with his hands in his pockets. 'Killed in the same way as the other. Found within a few yards of the other. And sliced by the same weapon which we know he carried away.'

'Yes, yes; I know,' replied Father Brown submissively. 'Yet, you know, I doubt whether Brayne could have cut off this head.'

'Why not?' inquired Dr Simon, with a rational stare.

'Well, doctor,' said the priest, looking up blinking, 'can a man cut off his own head? I don't know.'

O'Brien felt an insane universe crashing about his ears; but the doctor sprang forward with impetuous practicality and pushed back the wet white hair.

'Oh, there's no doubt it's Brayne,' said the priest quietly. 'He had exactly that chip in the left ear.'

The detective, who had been regarding the priest with steady and glittering eyes, opened his clenched mouth and said sharply: 'You seem to know a lot about him, Father Brown.'

'I do,' said the little man simply. 'I've been about with him for some weeks. He was thinking of joining our church.'

The star of the fanatic sprang into Valentin's eyes; he strode towards the priest with clenched hands. 'And, perhaps,' he cried, with a blasting sneer, 'perhaps he was also thinking of leaving all his money to your church.'

'Perhaps he was,' said Brown stolidly; 'it is possible.'

'In that case,' cried Valentin, with a dreadful smile, 'you may indeed know a great deal about him. About his life and about his——'

Commandant O'Brien laid a hand on Valentin's arm. 'Drop that slanderous rubbish, Valentin,' he said, 'or there may be more swords yet.'

But Valentin (under the steady, humble gaze of the priest) had already recovered himself. 'Well,' he said shortly, 'people's private opinions can wait. You gentlemen are still bound by your promise to stay; you must enforce it on yourselves—and on each other. Ivan here will tell you anything more you want to know; I must get to business and write to the authorities. We can't keep this quiet any longer. I shall be writing in my study if there is any more news.'

'Is there any more news, Ivan?' asked Dr Simon, as the chief of police strode out of the room.

'Only one more thing, I think, sir,' said Ivan, wrinkling up his grey old face, 'but that's important, too, in its way. There's that old buffer[9] you found on the lawn,' and he pointed without pretence of reverence at the big black body with the yellow head. 'We've found out who he is, anyhow.'

'Indeed!' cried the astonished doctor, 'and who is he?'

'His name was Arnold Becker,' said the under-detective, 'though he went by many aliases. He was a wandering sort of scamp, and is known to have been in America; so that was where Brayne got his knife into him. We didn't have much to do with him ourselves, for he worked mostly in Germany. We've communicated, of course, with the German police. But, oddly enough, there was a twin brother of his, named Louis Becker, whom we

---

**9.** 'Old buffer' simply means a chap or fellow—'usually expressing a slight degree of contempt' (*Oxford English Dictionary*).

had a great deal to do with. In fact, we found it necessary to guillotine him only yesterday. Well, it's a rum thing, gentlemen, but when I saw that fellow flat on the lawn I had the greatest jump of my life. If I hadn't seen Louis Becker guillotined with my own eyes, I'd have sworn it was Louis Becker lying there in the grass. Then, of course, I remembered his twin brother in Germany, and following up the clue——'

The explanatory Ivan stopped, for the excellent reason that nobody was listening to him. The Commandant and the doctor were both staring at Father Brown, who had sprung stiffly to his feet, and was holding his temples tight like a man in sudden and violent pain.

'Stop, stop, stop!' he cried; 'stop talking a minute, for I see half. Will God give me strength? Will my brain make the one jump and see all? Heaven help me! I used to be fairly good at thinking. I could paraphrase any page in Aquinas once. Will my head split—or will it see? I see half—I only see half.'

He buried his head in his hands, and stood in a sort of rigid torture of thought or prayer, while the other three could only go on staring at this last prodigy of their wild twelve hours.

When Father Brown's hands fell they showed a face quite fresh and serious, like a child's. He heaved a huge sigh, and said: 'Let us get this said and done with as quickly as possible. Look here, this will be the quickest way to convince you all of the truth.' He turned to the doctor. 'Dr Simon,' he said, 'you have a strong head-piece, and I heard you this morning asking the five hardest questions about this business. Well, if you will ask them again, I will answer them.'

Simon's pince-nez dropped from his nose in his doubt and wonder, but he answered at once. 'Well, the first question, you know, is why a man should kill another with a clumsy sabre at all when a man can kill with a bodkin?'

'A man cannot behead with a bodkin,' said Brown calmly, 'and for *this* murder beheading was absolutely necessary.'

'Why?' asked O'Brien, with interest.

'And the next question?' asked Father Brown.

'Well, why didn't the man cry out or anything?' asked the doctor; 'sabres in gardens are certainly unusual.'

'Twigs,' said the priest gloomily, and turned to the window which looked on the scene of death. 'No one saw the point of the twigs. Why should they lie on that lawn (look at it) so far from any tree? They were not snapped off; they were chopped off. The murderer occupied his enemy with some tricks with the sabre, showing how he could cut a branch in mid-air, or whatnot. Then, while his enemy bent down to see the result, a silent slash, and the head fell.'

'Well,' said the doctor slowly, 'that seems plausible enough. But my next two questions will stump anyone.'

The priest still stood looking critically out of the window and waited.

'You know how all the garden was sealed up like an air-tight chamber,' went on the doctor. 'Well, how did the strange man get into the garden?'

Without turning round, the little priest answered: 'There never was any strange man in the garden.'

There was a silence, and then a sudden cackle of almost childish laughter relieved the strain. The absurdity of Brown's remark moved Ivan to open taunts.

'Oh!' he cried, 'then we didn't lug a great fat corpse on to a sofa last night? He hadn't got into the garden, I suppose?'

'Got into the garden?' repeated Brown reflectively. 'No, not entirely.'

'Hang it all,' cried Simon, 'a man gets into a garden, or he doesn't.'

'Not necessarily,' said the priest, with a faint smile. 'What is the next question, doctor?'

'I fancy you're ill,' exclaimed Dr Simon sharply; 'but I'll ask the next question if you like. How did Brayne get out of the garden?'

'He didn't get out of the garden,' said the priest, still looking out of the window.

'Didn't get out of the garden?' exploded Simon.

'Not completely,' said Father Brown.

Simon shook his fists in a frenzy of French logic. 'A man gets out of a garden, or he doesn't,' he cried.[10]

---

10. The doctor has been trying to defend a traditional law of logic called the 'excluded middle' which states that an assertion is either true or not true. The law obviously applies only to a formal two-valued logic, or to sharply defined dichotomies that permit no third possibility. An integer, for

'Not always,' said Father Brown.

Dr Simon sprang to his feet impatiently. 'I have no time to spare on such senseless talk,' he cried angrily. 'If you can't understand a man being on one side of a wall or the other, I won't trouble you further.'

'Doctor,' said the cleric very gently, 'we have always got on very pleasantly together. If only for the sake of old friendship, stop and tell me your fifth question.'

The impatient Simon sank into a chair by the door and said briefly: 'The head and shoulders were cut about in a queer way. It seemed to be done after death.'

'Yes,' said the motionless priest, 'it was done so as to make you assume exactly the one simple falsehood that you did assume. It was done to make you take for granted that the head belonged to the body.'

The borderland of the brain, where all the monsters are made, moved horribly in the Gaelic O'Brien. He felt the chaotic presence of all the horse-men and fish-women that man's unnatural fancy has begotten. A voice older than his first fathers seemed saying in his ear: 'Keep out of the monstrous garden where grows the tree with double fruit. Avoid the evil garden where died the man with two heads.' Yet, while these shameful symbolic shapes passed across the ancient mirror of his Irish soul, his Frenchified intellect was quite alert, and was watching the odd priest[11] as closely and incredulously as all the rest.

Father Brown had turned round at last, and stood against the window with his face in dense shadow; but even in that shadow they could see it was pale as ashes. Nevertheless, he spoke quite sensibly, as if there were no Gaelic souls on earth.

'Gentlemen,' he said, 'you did not find the strange body of Becker in the garden. You did not find any strange body in the

---

example, is either odd or even. But the outside world is fuzzy, and it is difficult to find precise applications of the excluded-middle law. Is it always the case that a basket of apples contains either an odd or an even number of apples? No, because among the whole apples there may be half an apple. Father Brown's cryptic remarks spring from the fuzziness of the concept 'man' as it is being used by the doctor.

11. In the story's magazine printing Chesterton called him the 'old priest'. This could have been a printer's error. If not, G.K. may later have decided that Father Brown was a younger man.

garden. In face of Dr Simon's rationalism, I still affirm that Becker was only partly present. Look here!' (pointing to the black bulk of the mysterious corpse) 'you never saw that man in your lives. Did you ever see this man?'

He rapidly rolled away the bald, yellow head of the unknown, and put in its place the white-maned head beside it. And there, complete, unified, unmistakable, lay Julius K. Brayne.

'The murderer,' went on Brown quietly, 'hacked off his enemy's head and flung the sword far over the wall. But he was too clever to fling the sword only. He flung the *head* over the wall also. Then he had only to clap on another head to the corpse, and (as he insisted on a private inquest) you all imagined a totally new man.'

'Clap on another head!' said O'Brien staring. 'What other head? Heads don't grow on garden bushes, do they?'

'No,' said Father Brown huskily, and looking at his boots; 'there is only one place where they grow. They grow in the basket of the guillotine, beside which the Chief of Police, Aristide Valentin, was standing not an hour before the murder. Oh, my friends, hear me a minute more before you tear me in pieces. Valentin is an honest man, if being mad for an arguable cause is honesty. But did you never see in that cold, grey eye of his that he is mad? He would do anything, *anything*, to break what he calls the superstition of the Cross. He has fought for it and starved for it, and now he has murdered for it. Brayne's crazy millions had hitherto been scattered among so many sects that they did little to alter the balance of things. But Valentin heard a whisper that Brayne, like so many scatterbrained sceptics,[12] was drifting to us; and that was quite a different thing. Brayne would pour supplies into the impoverished and pugnacious Church of France; he would support six Nationalist newspapers like *The Guillotine*. The battle was already balanced on a point, and the fanatic took flame at the risk. He resolved to destroy the millionaire, and he did it as one would expect the greatest of detectives to commit his only crime. He abstracted the severed head of Becker on some criminological excuse, and took it home in his official box. He had that

---

12. It is easy to miss the puns. In the previous sentence we were told how Brayne's 'crazy millions' had been scattered among numerous sects.

last argument with Brayne, that Lord Galloway did not hear the end of; that failing, he led him out into the sealed garden, talked about swordsmanship, used twigs and a sabre for illustration, and——'

Ivan of the Scar sprang up. 'You lunatic,' he yelled; 'you'll go to my master now, if I take you by——'

'Why, I was going there,' said Brown heavily; 'I must ask him to confess, and all that.'

Driving the unhappy Brown before them like a hostage or sacrifice, they rushed together into the sudden stillness of Valentin's study.

The great detective sat at his desk apparently too occupied to hear their turbulent entrance. They paused a moment, and then something in the look of that upright and elegant back made the doctor run forward suddenly. A touch and a glance showed him that there was a small box of pills at Valentin's elbow, and that Valentin was dead in his chair; and on the blind face of the suicide was more than the pride of Cato.[13]

---

**13.** Marcus Porcius Cato (95–46 BC), known as Cato the Younger, was a Roman statesman who supported Pompey against Caesar in a civil war. After a military defeat by Caesar's troops in Africa, Cato stabbed himself. Joseph Addison wrote a tragedy about him. The pride that Chesterton considers greater than Cato's is, of course, the pride of Satan.

### AFTERWORD

Surely this is the most improbable of all Father Brown stories, redeemed only by the crazy ingenuity of the plot. No man as mad as Valentin could have become an admired chief of police. No atheist who hated religion enough to kill a man because he intended to become a Catholic would have taken off his hat, as Valentin did in the previous story, to a priest and called him 'master'. No expert on crime would have dreamed up such a clumsy way to kill a man, especially at a large party, not to mention a party at which his 'master' was a guest. Then there is the miraculous coincidence of a criminal having an identical twin brother, and the impossibility of borrowing a freshly severed head without that fact becoming known. G.K. has here pushed the detective puzzle-story to its outer limits of the absurd.

Christopher Hollis, making the above points in his *The Mind of Chesterton*, thinks the horror of the plot suggests a 'streak of strange morbidity' in Chesterton that later was kept in check by religious faith after G.K.'s conversion to Catholicism. 'The problem that the story really raises is not so much: "What sort of guilty man would have committed so revolting a crime?" as: "What sort of innocent man would have imagined it?" '

Hollis is too hard on Chesterton. Although G.K. was not a Catholic when he wrote this story, he certainly was a devout Christian, and to a Christian a dead body is, or should be, no more a person than is a piece of fingernail. I believe that Chesterton considered the exchange of heads as simply an amusing gimmick for a puzzling murder, and that his story contains nothing comparable to the morbid atmosphere of a horror tale by Poe. Moreover, the story allowed Chesterton to show how a man of the cloth, long accustomed to giving last rites and preaching funeral sermons, can lose all sense of revulsion over the proximity of dead bodies and severed heads.

'Take the most horrible of Grimm's tales in incident and imagery,' wrote G.K. in his essay on 'The Red Angel' (*Tremendous Trifles*), 'the excellent tale of the "Boy Who Could Not Shudder" . . . There are some living shocks in that tale. I remember specially a man's legs which fell down a chimney by themselves and walked about the room, until they were rejoined by the severed head and body which fell down the chimney after them. That is very good.'

Chesterton's essay is a defence of terror in fairy tales, and a marvellous defence it is. Here is a portion:

Fairy tales do not give a child his first idea of bogey. What fairy tales give the child is his first clear idea of the possible defeat of bogey. The baby has known the dragon intimately ever since he had an imagination. What the fairy tale provides for him is a St. George to kill the dragon.

Exactly what the fairy tale does is this: it accustoms him for a series of clear pictures to the idea that these limitless terrors had a limit, that these shapeless enemies have enemies, that these strong enemies of man have enemies in the knights of God, that there is something in the universe more mystical than darkness, and stronger than strong fear.

'I do not think', writes Hollis, 'that the post-war, converted Chesterton of the later Father Brown stories would ever have allowed his imagination even to dwell on things so horrible. But *The Secret Garden* shows the horrors to which he was tempted.' Mr Hollis should have reread 'The Man with Two Beards' in *The Secret of Father Brown*.

# 3

# The Queer Feet*

IF you meet a member of that select club, 'The Twelve True Fishermen,'[1] entering the Vernon Hotel for the annual club dinner, you will observe, as he takes off his overcoat, that his evening coat is green and not black. If (supposing that you have the star-defying audacity to address such a being) you ask him why, he will probably answer that he does it to avoid being mistaken for a waiter. You will then retire crushed. But you will leave behind you a mystery as yet unsolved and a tale worth telling.

If (to pursue the same vein of improbable conjecture) you were to meet a mild, hard-working little priest, named Father Brown, and were to ask him what he thought was the most singular luck of his life, he would probably reply that upon the whole his best stroke was at the Vernon Hotel, where he had averted a crime and, perhaps, saved a soul, merely by listening to a few footsteps in a passage. He is perhaps a little proud of this wild and wonderful guess of his, and it is possible that he might refer to it. But since it is immeasurably unlikely that you will ever rise high enough in the social world to find 'The Twelve True Fishermen,' or that you will ever sink low enough among slums and criminals to find Father Brown, I fear you will never hear the story at all unless you hear it from me.

The Vernon Hotel at which the Twelve True Fishermen held their annual dinners was an institution such as can only exist in

---

* The sound of footsteps that keep abruptly altering their pace is the clue that enables Father Brown to guess how a thief managed to steal a club's valuable silver. The story first appeared in the *Storyteller* (November 1910).

1. London has always been noted for its curious clubs, and Chesterton relished inventing even more curious ones. They figure prominently in his fiction. Members of his most outlandish club provide the mysteries in *The Club of Queer Trades*, G.K.'s first book of short stories.

an oligarchical society which has almost gone mad on good manners. It was that topsy-turvy product—an 'exclusive' commercial enterprise. That is, it was a thing which paid not by attracting people, but actually by turning people away. In the heart of a plutocracy tradesmen become cunning enough to be more fastidious than their customers. They positively create difficulties so that their wealthy and weary clients may spend money and diplomacy in overcoming them. If there were a fashionable hotel in London which no man could enter who was under six foot, society would meekly make up parties of six-foot men to dine in it. If there were an expensive restaurant which by a mere caprice of its proprietor was only open on Thursday afternoon, it would be crowded on Thursday afternoon. The Vernon Hotel stood, as if by accident, in the corner of a square in Belgravia.[2] It was a small hotel; and a very inconvenient one. But its very inconveniences were considered as walls protecting a particular class. One inconvenience, in particular, was held to be of vital importance: the fact that practically only twenty-four people could dine in the place at once. The only big dinner table was the celebrated terrace table, which stood open to the air on a sort of veranda overlooking one of the most exquisite old gardens in London. Thus it happened that even the twenty-four seats at this table could only be enjoyed in warm weather; and this making the enjoyment yet more difficult made it yet more desired. The existing owner of the hotel was a Jew named Lever; and he made nearly a million out of it, by making it difficult to get into. Of course he combined with this limitation in the scope of his enterprise the most careful polish in its performance. The wines and cooking were really as good as any in Europe, and the demeanour of the attendants exactly mirrored the fixed mood of the English upper class. The proprietor knew all his waiters like the fingers on his hand; there were only fifteen of them all told. It was much easier to become a Member of Parliament than to become a waiter in that hotel. Each waiter was trained in terrible silence and smoothness, as if he were a gentleman's servant. And, indeed, there was generally at least one waiter to every gentleman who dined.

---

**2.** Belgravia is a fashionable residential district adjacent to Hyde Park and to the Buckingham Palace gardens.

The club of the Twelve True Fishermen would not have consented to dine anywhere but in such a place, for it insisted on a luxurious privacy; and would have been quite upset by the mere thought that any other club was even dining in the same building. On the occasion of their annual dinner the Fishermen were in the habit of exposing all their treasures, as if they were in a private house, especially the celebrated set of fish knives and forks which were, as it were, the insignia of the society, each being exquisitely wrought in silver in the form of a fish, and each loaded at the hilt with one large pearl. These were always laid out for the fish course, and the fish course was always the most magnificent in that magnificent repast. The society had a vast number of ceremonies and observances, but it had no history and no object; that was where it was so very aristocratic. You did not have to be anything in order to be one of the Twelve Fishers; unless you were already a certain sort of person, you never even heard of them. It had been in existence twelve years. Its president was Mr Audley. Its vice-president was the Duke of Chester.

If I have in any degree conveyed the atmosphere of this appalling hotel, the reader may feel a natural wonder as to how I came to know anything about it, and may even speculate as to how so ordinary a person as my friend Father Brown came to find himself in that golden galley. As far as that is concerned, my story is simple, or even vulgar. There is in the world a very aged rioter and demagogue who breaks into the most refined retreats with the dreadful information that all men are brothers, and wherever this leveller went on his pale horse[3] it was Father Brown's trade to follow. One of the waiters, an Italian, had been struck down with a paralytic stroke that afternoon; and his Jewish employer, marvelling mildly at such superstitions, had consented to send for the nearest Popish priest. With what the waiter confessed to Father Brown we are not concerned, for the excellent reason that the cleric kept it to himself; but apparently it involved him in writing out a note or statement for the conveying of some message or the righting of some wrong. Father Brown, therefore, with a meek impudence which he would have shown equally in Buck-

---

**3.** 'And I looked, and behold, a pale horse: and his name that sat on him was Death, and hell followed with him.' (Revelation 6: 8).

ingham Palace, asked to be provided with a room and writing materials. Mr Lever was torn in two. He was a kind man, and had also that bad imitation of kindness, the dislike of any difficulty or scene. At the same time the presence of one unusual stranger in his hotel that evening was like a speck of dirt on something just cleaned. There was never any borderland or ante-room in the Vernon Hotel, no people waiting in the hall, no customers coming in on chance. There were fifteen waiters. There were twelve guests. It would be as startling to find a new guest in the hotel that night as to find a new brother taking breakfast or tea in one's own family. Moreover, the priest's appearance was second-rate and his clothes muddy; a mere glimpse of him afar off might precipitate a crisis in the club. Mr. Lever at last hit on a plan to cover, since he might not obliterate, the disgrace. When you enter (as you never will) the Vernon Hotel, you pass down a short passage decorated with a few dingy but important pictures, and come to the main vestibule and lounge which opens on your right into passages leading to the public rooms, and on your left to a similar passage pointing to the kitchens and offices of the hotel. Immediately on your left hand is the corner of a glass office, which abuts upon the lounge—a house within a house, so to speak, like the old hotel bar which probably once occupied its place.

In this office sat the representative of the proprietor (nobody in this place ever appeared in person if he could help it), and just beyond the office, on the way to the servants' quarters, was the gentlemen's cloak room, the last boundary of the gentlemen's domain. But between the office and the cloak room was a small private room without other outlet, sometimes used by the proprietor for delicate and important matters, such as lending a duke a thousand pounds or declining to lend him sixpence. It is a mark of the magnificent tolerance of Mr Lever that he permitted this holy place to be for about half an hour profaned by a mere priest, scribbling away on a piece of paper. The story which Father Brown was writing down was very likely a much better story than this one, only it will never be known. I can merely state that it was very nearly as long, and that the last two or three paragraphs of it were the least exciting and absorbing.

For it was by the time he had reached these that the priest began a little to allow his thoughts to wander and his animal senses, which were commonly keen, to awaken. The time of darkness and dinner was drawing on; his own forgotten little room was without a light, and perhaps the gathering gloom, as occasionally happens, sharpened the sense of sound. As Father Brown wrote the last and least essential part of his document, he caught himself writing to the rhythm of a recurrent noise outside, just as one sometimes thinks to the tune of a railway train. When he became conscious of the thing he found what it was: only the ordinary patter of feet passing the door, which in an hotel was no very unlikely matter. Nevertheless, he stared at the darkened ceiling, and listened to the sound. After he had listened for a few seconds dreamily, he got to his feet and listened intently, with his head a little on one side. Then he sat down again and buried his brow in his hands, now not merely listening, but listening and thinking also.

The footsteps outside at any given moment were such as one might hear in any hotel; and yet, taken as a whole, there was something very strange about them. There were no other footsteps. It was always a very silent house, for the few familiar guests went at once to their own apartments, and the well-trained waiters were told to be almost invisible until they were wanted. One could not conceive any place where there was less reason to apprehend anything irregular. But these footsteps were so odd that one could not decide to call them regular or irregular. Father Brown followed them with his finger on the edge of the table, like a man trying to learn a tune on the piano.

First, there came a long rush of rapid little steps, such as a light man might make in winning a walking race. At a certain point they stopped and changed to a sort of slow, swinging stamp, numbering not a quarter of the steps, but occupying about the same time. The moment the last echoing stamp had died away would come again the run or ripple of light, hurrying feet, and then again the thud of the heavier walking. It was certainly the same pair of boots, partly because (as has been said) there were no other boots about, and partly because they had a small but unmistakable creak in them. Father Brown had the kind of head that cannot help asking questions; and on this apparently trivial question his head almost split. He had seen men run in order to jump. He had seen men run in order to slide. But why on earth should a man run in order to walk? Or, again, why should he walk in order to run? Yet no other description would cover the antics of this invisible pair of legs. The man was either walking very fast down one-half of the corridor in order to walk very slow down the other half; or he was walking very slow at one end to have the rapture of walking fast at the other. Neither suggestion seemed to make much sense. His brain was growing darker and darker, like his room.

Yet, as he began to think steadily, the very blackness of his cell seemed to make his thoughts more vivid; he began to see as in a kind of vision the fantastic feet capering along the corridor in unnatural or symbolic attitudes. Was it a heathen religious dance? Or some entirely new kind of scientific exercise? Father Brown began to ask himself with more exactness what the steps suggested. Taking the slow step first: it certainly was not the step of the proprietor. Men of his type walk with a rapid waddle, or they sit still. It could not be any servant or messenger waiting for directions. It did not sound like it. The poorer orders (in an oligarchy) sometimes lurch about when they are slightly drunk, but generally, and especially in such gorgeous scenes, they stand or sit in constrained attitudes. No; that heavy yet springy step, with a kind of careless emphasis, not specially noisy, yet not caring what noise it made, belonged to only one of the animals of this earth. It was a gentleman of western Europe, and probably one who had never worked for his living.

Just as he came to this solid certainty, the step changed to the quicker one, and ran past the door as feverishly as a rat. The listener remarked that though this step was much swifter it was also much more noiseless, almost as if the man were walking on tiptoe. Yet it was not associated in his mind with secrecy, but with something else—something that he could not remember. He was maddened by one of those half-memories that make a man feel half-witted. Surely he had heard that strange, swift walking somewhere. Suddenly he sprang to his feet with a new idea in his head, and walked to the door. His room had no direct outlet on the passage, but let on one side into the glass office, and on the other into the cloak room beyond. He tried the door into the office, and found it locked. Then he looked at the window, now a square pane full of purple cloud cleft by livid sunset, and for an instant he smelt evil as a dog smells rats.

The rational part of him (whether the wiser or not) regained its supremacy. He remembered that the proprietor had told him that he should lock the door, and would come later to release him. He told himself that twenty things he had not thought of might explain the eccentric sounds outside; he reminded himself that there was just enough light left to finish his own proper work. Bringing his paper to the window so as to catch the last stormy evening light, he resolutely plunged once more into the almost completed record. He had written for about twenty minutes, bending closer and closer to his paper in the lessening light; then suddenly he sat upright. He had heard the strange feet once more.

This time they had a third oddity. Previously the unknown man had walked, with levity indeed and lightning quickness, but he had walked. This time he ran. One could hear the swift, soft, bounding steps coming along the corridor, like the pads of a fleeing and leaping panther. Whoever was coming was a very strong, active man, in still yet tearing excitement. Yet, when the sound had swept up to the office like a sort of whispering whirlwind, it suddenly changed again to the old slow, swaggering stamp.

Father Brown flung down his paper, and, knowing the office door to be locked, went at once into the cloak room on the other side. The attendant of this place was temporarily absent, probably because the only guests were at dinner and his office was a sinecure. After groping through a grey forest of overcoats, he found that the dim cloak room opened on the lighted corridor in the form of a sort of counter or half-door, like most of the counters across which we have all handed umbrellas and received tickets. There was a light immediately above the semicircular arch of this opening. It threw little illumination on Father Brown himself, who seemed a mere dark outline against the dim sunset window behind him. But it threw an almost theatrical light on the man who stood outside the cloak room in the corridor.

He was an elegant man in very plain evening dress; tall, but with an air of not taking up much room; one felt that he could have slid along like a shadow where many smaller men would have been obvious and obstructive. His face, now flung back in the lamplight, was swarthy and vivacious, the face of a foreigner. His figure was good, his manners good humoured and confident; a critic could only say that his black coat was a shade below his figure and manners, and even bulged and bagged in an odd way. The moment he caught sight of Brown's black silhouette against the sunset, he tossed down a scrap of paper with a number and called out with amiable authority: 'I want my hat and coat, please; I find I have to go away at once.'

Father Brown took the paper without a word, and obediently went to look for the coat; it was not the first menial work he had done in his life. He brought it and laid it on the counter; meanwhile, the strange gentleman who had been feeling in his waist-coat pocket, said laughing: 'I haven't got any silver; you can keep this.' And he threw down half a sovereign, and caught up his coat.

Father Brown's figure remained quite dark and still; but in that instant he had lost his head. His head was always most valuable when he had lost it. In such moments he put two and two together and made four million. Often the Catholic Church (which is wedded to common sense) did not approve of it. Often he did not approve of it himself. But it was real inspiration—important at rare crises—when whosoever shall lose his head the same shall save it.

'I think, sir', he said civilly, 'that you have some silver in your pocket.'

The tall gentleman stared. 'Hang it,' he cried, 'if I choose to give you gold, why should you complain?'

'Because silver is sometimes more valuable than gold,' said the priest mildly; 'that is, in large quantities.'

The stranger looked at him curiously. Then he looked still more curiously up the passage towards the main entrance. Then he looked back at Brown again, and then he looked very carefully at the window beyond Brown's head, still coloured with the afterglow of the storm. Then he seemed to make up his mind. He put one hand on the counter, vaulted over as easily as an acrobat and towered above the priest, putting one tremendous hand upon his collar.

'Stand still,' he said, in a hacking whisper. 'I don't want to threaten you, but——'

'I do want to threaten you,' said Father Brown, in a voice like a rolling drum, 'I want to threaten you with the worm that dieth not, and the fire that is not quenched.'

'You're a rum sort of cloak-room clerk,' said the other.

'I am a priest, Monsieur Flambeau,'[4] said Brown, 'and I am ready to hear your confession.'

The other stood gasping for a few moments, and then staggered back into a chair.

The first two courses of the dinner of the Twelve True Fishermen had proceeded with placid success. I do not possess a copy of the menu; and if I did it would not convey anything to anybody. It was written in a sort of super-French employed by cooks, but quite unintelligible to Frenchmen. There was a tradition in the club that the *hors d'œuvres* should be various and manifold to the point of madness. They were taken seriously because they were avowedly useless extras, like the whole dinner and the whole club. There was also a tradition that the soup course should be light and unpretending—a sort of simple and austere vigil for the feast of fish that was to come. The talk was that strange, slight talk which governs the British Empire, which governs it in secret, and yet would scarcely enlighten an ordinary Englishman even if he could overhear it. Cabinet ministers on both sides were alluded to by their Christian names with a sort of bored benignity. The Radical Chancellor of the Exchequer, whom the whole Tory party was supposed to be cursing for his extortions, was praised for his minor poetry, or his saddle in the hunting field. The Tory leader, whom all Liberals were supposed to hate as a tyrant, was discussed and, on the whole, praised—as a Liberal. It seemed somehow that politicians were very important. And yet, anything seemed important about them except their politics. Mr Audley, the chairman, was an amiable, elderly man who still wore Gladstone collars;[5] he was a kind of symbol of all that phantasmal and yet fixed society. He had never done anything—not even anything wrong. He was not fast; he was not even particularly rich. He was simply in the thing; and there was an end of it. No party could ignore him, and if he had wished to be in the

---

4. Should you wonder why Flambeau does not recognize Father Brown as the priest who earlier had thwarted his attempt to steal the blue cross, you must remember that the cloakroom is too dark for the priest's features to be seen. What Chesterton leaves unexplained is why Flambeau, arrested in the first story, is still at large. Did he escape before sentencing?

5. Gladstone collars were high, stiff, winged, white collars such as were worn by England's prime minister William Gladstone.

Cabinet he certainly would have been put there. The Duke of Chester, the vice-president, was a young and rising politician. That is to say, he was a pleasant youth, with flat, fair hair and a freckled face, with moderate intelligence and enormous estates. In public his appearances were always successful and his principle was simple enough. When he thought of a joke he made it, and was called brilliant. When he could not think of a joke he said that this was no time for trifling, and was called able. In private, in a club of his own class, he was simply quite pleasantly frank and silly, like a schoolboy. Mr Audley, never having been in politics, treated them a little more seriously. Sometimes he even embarrassed the company by phrases suggesting that there was some difference between a Liberal and a Conservative. He himself was a Conservative, even in private life. He had a roll of grey hair over the back of his collar, like certain old-fashioned statesmen, and seen from behind he looked like the man the empire wants. Seen from the front he looked like a mild, self-indulgent bachelor, with rooms in the Albany[6]—which he was.

As has been remarked, there were twenty-four seats at the terrace table, and only twelve members of the club. Thus they could occupy the terrace in the most luxurious style of all, being ranged along the inner side of the table, with no one opposite, commanding an uninterrupted view of the garden, the colours of which were still vivid, though evening was closing in somewhat luridly for the time of year. The chairman sat in the centre of the line, and the vice-president at the right-hand end of it. When the twelve guests first trooped into their seats it was the custom (for some unknown reason) for all the fifteen waiters to stand lining the wall like troops presenting arms to the king, while the fat proprietor stood and bowed to the club with radiant surprise, as if he had never heard of them before. But before the first chink of knife and fork this army of retainers had vanished, only the one or two required to collect and distribute the plates darting about in deathly silence. Mr Lever, the proprietor, of course

---

**6.** The Albany is a block of residential chambers in London between Burlington Gardens and Piccadilly where many writers, including Lord Byron, once lived. Designed in 1770 by Sir William Chambers, the most famous British architect of his day, it was in Chesterton's day a favourite residence of well-to-do bachelors. It is no longer restricted to men.

had disappeared in convulsions of courtesy long before. It would be exaggerative, indeed irreverent, to say that he ever positively appeared again. But when the important course, the fish course, was being brought on, there was—how shall I put it?—a vivid shadow, a projection of his personality, which told that he was hovering near. The sacred fish course consisted (to the eyes of the vulgar) in a sort of monstrous pudding, about the size and shape of a wedding cake, in which some considerable number of interesting fishes had finally lost the shapes which God had given to them. The Twelve True Fishermen took up their celebrated fish knives and fish forks, and approached it as gravely as if every inch of the pudding cost as much as the silver fork it was eaten with. So it did, for all I know. This course was dealt with in eager and devouring silence; and it was only when his plate was nearly empty that the young duke made the ritual remark: 'They can't do this anywhere but here.'

'Nowhere,' said Mr Audley, in a deep bass voice, turning to the speaker and nodding his venerable head a number of times. 'Nowhere, assuredly, except here. It was represented to me that at the Café Anglais——'

Here he was interrupted and even agitated for a moment by the removal of his plate, but he recaptured the valuable thread of his thoughts. 'It was represented to me that the same could be done at the Café Anglais. Nothing like it, sir,' he said, shaking his head ruthlessly, like a hanging judge. 'Nothing like it.'

'Overrated place,' said a certain Colonel Pound, speaking (by the look of him) for the first time for some months.

'Oh, I don't know,' said the Duke of Chester, who was an optimist, 'it's jolly good for some things. You can't beat it at——'

A waiter came swiftly along the room, and then stopped dead. His stoppage was as silent as his tread; but all those vague and kindly gentlemen were so used to the utter smoothness of the unseen machinery which surrounded and supported their lives, that a waiter doing anything unexpected was a start and a jar. They felt as you and I would feel if the inanimate world disobeyed—if a chair ran away from us.

The waiter stood staring a few seconds, while there deepened on every face at table a strange shame which is wholly the product of our time. It is the combination of modern humanitarianism with the horrible modern abyss between the souls of the rich and poor. A genuine historic aristocrat would have thrown things at the waiter, beginning with empty bottles, and very probably ending with money. A genuine democrat would have asked him, with a comrade-like clearness of speech, what the devil he was doing. But these modern plutocrats could not bear a poor man near to them, either as a slave or as a friend. That something had gone wrong with the servants was merely a dull, hot embarrassment. They did not want to be brutal, and they dreaded the need to be benevolent. They wanted the thing, whatever it was, to be over. It was over. The waiter, after standing for some seconds rigid, like a cataleptic, turned round and ran madly out of the room.

When he reappeared in the room, or rather in the doorway, it was in company with another waiter, with whom he whispered and gesticulated with southern fierceness. Then the first waiter went away, leaving the second waiter, and reappeared with a third waiter. By the time a fourth waiter had joined this hurried synod, Mr Audley felt it necessary to break the silence in the interests of Tact. He used a very loud cough, instead of a presidential hammer, and said: 'Splendid work young Moocher's doing in Burmah. Now, no other nation in the world could have——'

A fifth waiter had sped towards him like an arrow, and was whispering in his ear: 'So sorry. Important! Might the proprietor speak to you?'

The chairman turned in disorder, and with a dazed stare saw Mr Lever coming towards them with his lumbering quickness. The gait of the good proprietor was indeed his usual gait, but his face was by no means usual. Generally it was a genial copper-brown; now it was a sickly yellow.

'You will pardon me, Mr Audley,' he said, with asthmatic breathlessness. 'I have great apprehensions. Your fish-plates, they are cleared away with the knife and fork on them!'

'Well, I hope so,' said the chairman, with some warmth.

'You see him?' panted the excited hotel keeper; 'you see the waiter who took them away? You know him?'

'Know the waiter?' answered Mr Audley indignantly. 'Certainly not!'

Mr Lever opened his hands with a gesture of agony. 'I never send him,' he said. 'I know not when or why he come. I send my waiter to take away the plates, and he find them already away.'

Mr Audley still looked rather too bewildered to be really the man the empire wants; none of the company could say anything except the man of wood—Colonel Pound—who seemed galvanised into an unnatural life. He rose rigidly from his chair, leaving all the rest sitting, screwed his eyeglass into his eye, and spoke in a raucous undertone as if he had half-forgotten how to speak. 'Do you mean,' he said 'that somebody has stolen our silver fish service?'

The proprietor repeated the open-handed gesture with even greater helplessness; and in a flash all the men at the table were on their feet.

'Are all your waiters here?' demanded the colonel, in his low, harsh accent.

'Yes; they're all here. I noticed it myself,' cried the young duke, pushing his boyish face into the inmost ring. 'Always count 'em as I come in; they look so queer standing up against the wall.

'But surely one cannot exactly remember,' began Mr Audley, with heavy hesitation.

'I remember exactly, I tell you,' cried the duke excitedly. 'There never have been more than fifteen waiters at this place, and there were no more than fifteen to-night, I'll swear; no more and no less.'

The proprietor turned upon him, quaking in a kind of palsy of surprise. 'You say—you say,' he stammered, 'that you see all my fifteen waiters?'

'As usual,' assented the duke. 'What is the matter with that?'

'Nothing,' said Lever, with a deepening accent, 'only you did not. For one of zem is dead upstairs.'

There was a shocking stillness for an instant in that room. It may be (so supernatural is the word death) that each of those idle men looked for a second at his soul, and saw it as a small dried pea.[7] One of them—the duke, I think—even said with the idiotic kindness of wealth: 'Is there anything we can do?'

---

7. In *The Club of Queer Trades* the prime minister of England appears in court to give evidence against his valet. After details of the stateman's household have been aired, the judge asks the prime minister to step forward. 'Get a new soul,' he advises. 'That thing's not fit for a dog. Get a new soul.' Watson tell us that Holmes 'loathed society with his whole Bohemian soul'. The same can be said for Father Brown and his creator.

'He has had a priest,' said the Jew, not untouched.

Then, as to the clang of doom, they awoke to their own position. For a few weird seconds they had really felt as if the fifteenth waiter might be the ghost of the dead man upstairs. They had been dumb under that oppression, for ghosts were to them an embarrassment, like beggars. But the remembrance of the silver broke the spell of the miraculous; broke it abruptly and with a brutal reaction. The colonel flung over his chair and strode to the door. 'If there was a fifteenth man here, friends,' he said, 'that fifteenth fellow was a thief. Down at once to the front and back doors and secure everything; then we'll talk. The twenty-four pearls of the club are worth recovering.'

Mr Audley seemed at first to hesitate about whether it was gentlemanly to be in such a hurry about anything; but, seeing the duke dash down the stairs with youthful energy, he followed with a more mature motion.

At the same instant a sixth waiter ran into the room, and declared that he had found the pile of fish plates on a sideboard, with no trace of the silver.

The crowd of diners and attendants that tumbled helter-skelter down the passages divided into two groups. Most of the Fishermen followed the proprietor to the front room to demand news of any exit. Colonel Pound, with the chairman, the vice-president, and one or two others darted down the corridor leading to the servants' quarters, as the more likely line of escape. As they did so they passed the dim alcove or cavern of the cloak room, and saw a short, black-coated figure, presumably an attendant, standing a little way back in the shadow of it.

'Hallo, there!' called out the duke. 'Have you seen anyone pass?'

The short figure did not answer the question directly, but merely said: 'Perhaps I have got what you are looking for, gentlemen.'

They paused, wavering and wondering, while he quietly went to the back of the cloak room, and came back with both hands full of shining silver, which he laid out on the counter as calmly as a salesman. It took the form of a dozen quaintly shaped forks and knives.

'You—you——' began the colonel, quite thrown off his balance at last. Then he peered into the dim little room and saw two things: first, that the short, black-clad man was dressed like a clergyman; and, second, that the window of the room behind him was burst, as if someone had passed violently through.

'Valuable things to deposit in a cloak room, aren't they?' remarked the clergyman, with cheerful composure.

'Did—did you steal those things?' stammered Mr Audley, with staring eyes.

'If I did,' said the cleric pleasantly, 'at least I am bringing them back again.'

'But you didn't,' said Colonel Pound, still staring at the broken window.

'To make a clean breast of it, I didn't,' said the other, with some humour. And he seated himself quite gravely on a stool.

'But you know who did,' said the colonel.

'I don't know his real name,' said the priest placidly, 'but I know something of his fighting weight, and a great deal about his spiritual difficulties. I formed the physical estimate when he was trying to throttle me, and the moral estimate when he repented.'

'Oh, I say—repented!' cried young Chester, with a sort of crow of laughter.

Father Brown got to his feet, putting his hands behind him. 'Odd, isn't it,' he said, 'that a thief and a vagabond should repent, when so many who are rich and secure remain hard and frivolous, and without fruit for God or man? But there, if you will excuse me, you trespass a little upon my province. If you doubt the penitence as a practical fact, there are your knives and forks. You are the Twelve True Fishers, and there are all your silver fish. But He has made me a fisher of men.'[8]

'Did you catch this man?' asked the colonel, frowning.

Father Brown looked him full in his frowning face. 'Yes,' he said, 'I caught him, with an unseen hook and an invisible line which is long enough to let him wander to the ends of the world,

---

8. Father Brown is recalling the remark by Jesus (Mark 1: 17) when he saw the brothers Simon and Andrew casting their net into the Sea of Galilee. 'Come after me, and I will make you to become fishers of men.' The Twelve True Fishermen are fishers only in a trivial sense—they like to dine on expensive sea food. Father Brown is the One True Fisherman of the story.

and still to bring him back with a twitch upon the thread.'[9]

There was a long silence. All the other men present drifted away to carry the recovered silver to their comrades, or to consult the proprietor about the queer condition of affairs. But the grim-faced colonel still sat sideways on the counter, swinging his long, lank legs and biting his dark moustache.

At last he said quietly to the priest: 'He must have been a clever fellow, but I think I know a cleverer.'

'He was a clever fellow,' answered the other, 'but I am not quite sure of what other you mean.'

'I mean you,' said the colonel, with a short laugh. 'I don't want to get the fellow jailed; make yourself easy about that. But I'd give a good many silver forks to know exactly how you fell into this affair, and how you got the stuff out of him. I reckon you're the most up-to-date devil of the present company.'

Father Brown seemed rather to like the saturnine candour of the soldier. 'Well,' he said, smiling, 'I mustn't tell you anything of the man's identity, or his own story, of course; but there's no particular reason why I shouldn't tell you of the mere outside facts which I found out for myself.'

He hopped over the barrier with unexpected activity, and sat beside Colonel Pound, kicking his short legs like a little boy on a gate. He began to tell the story as easily as if he were telling it to an old friend by a Christmas fire.

'You see, colonel,' he said, 'I was shut up in that small room there doing some writing, when I heard a pair of feet in this passage doing a dance that was as queer as the dance of death. First came quick, funny little steps, like a man walking on tiptoe for a wager; then came slow, careless, creaking steps, as of a big man

---

**9.** Evelyn Waugh chose 'a twitch upon the thread' as the title of the second book of his novel *Brideshead Revisited*. Here is how Cordelia, a character in the story, explains the title:

'D'you know what Papa said when he became a Catholic? Mummy told me once. He said to her: "You have brought back my family to the faith of their ancestors." Pompous, you know. It takes people different ways. Anyhow, the family haven't been very constant, have they? There's him and Sebastian gone and Julia gone. But God won't let them go for long, you know. I wonder if you remember the story Mummy read us the evening Sebastian first got drunk—I mean the *bad* evening. Father Brown said something like "I caught him" [the thief] "with an unseen hook and an invisible line which is long enough to let him wander to the ends of the world and still to bring him back with a twitch upon the thread." '

walking about with a cigar. But they were both made by the same feet, I swear, and they came in rotation; first the run and then the walk, and then the run again. I wondered at first idly and then wildly why a man should act these two parts at once. One walk I knew; it was just like yours, colonel. It was the walk of a well-fed gentleman waiting for something, who strolls about rather because he is physically alert than because he is mentally impatient. I knew that I knew the other walk, too, but I could not remember what it was. What wild creature had I met on my travels that tore along on tiptoe in that extraordinary style? Then I heard a clink of plates somewhere; and the answer stood up as plain as St. Peter's. It was the walk of a waiter—that walk with the body slanted forward, the eyes looking down, the ball of the toe spurning away the ground, the coat tails and napkin flying. Then I thought for a minute and a half more. And I believe I saw the manner of the crime, as clearly as if I were going to commit it.'

Colonel Pound looked at him keenly, but the speaker's mild grey eyes were fixed upon the ceiling with almost empty wistfulness.[10]

'A crime,' he said slowly, 'is like any other work of art. Don't look surprised; crimes are by no means the only works of art that come from an infernal workshop. But every work of art, divine or diabolic, has one indispensable mark—I mean, that the centre of it is simple, however much the fulfilment may be complicated. Thus, in *Hamlet,* let us say, the grotesqueness of the grave-digger, the flowers of the mad girl, the fantastic finery of Osric, the pallor of the ghost and the grin of the skull are all oddities in a sort of tangled wreath round one plain tragic figure of a man in black. Well, this also,' he said, getting slowly down from his seat with a smile, 'this also is the plain tragedy of a man in black. Yes,' he went on, seeing the colonel look up in some wonder, 'the whole of this tale turns on a black coat. In this, as in *Hamlet,* there are the rococo excrescences—yourselves, let us say. There is the dead

---

**10.** We learn for the first time that Father Brown's eyes are grey. Sherlock Holmes also had grey eyes, although Watson delayed disclosing this until Chapter 12 of *The Hound of the Baskervilles,* the fifth book in the canon. Flambeau's eyes, by the way, are 'dark', we are told in the sixth story, and a 'fierce black', as we learn in 'The Duel of Dr Hirsch' (*The Wisdom of Father Brown*).

waiter, who was there when he could not be there. There is the
invisible hand that swept your table clear of silver and melted
into air. But every clever crime is founded ultimately on some
one quite simple fact—some fact that is not itself mysterious. The
mystification comes in covering it up, in leading men's thoughts
away from it. This large and subtle and (in the ordinary course)
most profitable crime, was built on the plain fact that a gentleman's evening dress is the same as a waiter's. All the rest was
acting, and thundering good acting, too.'

'Still,' said the colonel, getting up and frowning at his boots, 'I
am not sure that I understand.'

'Colonel,' said Father Brown, 'I tell you that this archangel of
impudence who stole your forks walked up and down this passage twenty times in the blaze of all the lamps, in the glare of all
the eyes. He did not go and hide in dim corners where suspicion
might have searched for him. He kept constantly on the move in
the lighted corridors, and everywhere that he went he seemed to
be there by right. Don't ask me what he was like; you have seen
him yourself six or seven times to-night. You were waiting with
all the other grand people in the reception room at the end of the
passage there, with the terrace just beyond. Whenever he came
among you gentlemen, he came in the lightning style of a waiter,
with bent head, flapping napkin and flying feet. He shot out on to
the terrace, did something to the table cloth, and shot back again
towards the office and the waiters' quarters. By the time he had
come under the eye of the office clerk and the waiters he had
become another man in every inch of his body, in every instinctive gesture. He strolled among the servants with the absent-
minded insolence which they have all seen in their patrons. It
was no new thing to them that a swell from the dinner party
should pace all parts of the house like an animal at the Zoo; they
know that nothing marks the Smart Set more than a habit of
walking where one chooses. When he was magnificently weary of
walking down that particular passage he would wheel round and
pace back past the office; in the shadow of the arch just beyond
he was altered as by a blast of magic, and went hurrying forward
again among the Twelve Fishermen, an obsequious attendant.
Why should the gentlemen look at a chance waiter? Why should
the waiters suspect a first-rate walking gentleman? Once or twice
he played the coolest tricks. In the proprietor's private quarters

he called out breezily for a syphon of soda water, saying he was thirsty. He said genially that he would carry it himself, and he did; he carried it quickly and correctly through the thick of you, a waiter with an obvious errand. Of course, it could not have been kept up long, but it only had to be kept up till the end of the fish course.

'His worst moment was when the waiters stood in a row; but even then he contrived to lean against the wall just round the corner in such a way that for that important instant the waiters thought him a gentleman, while the gentlemen thought him a waiter. The rest went like winking. If any waiter caught him away from the table, that waiter caught a languid aristocrat. He had only to time himself two minutes before the fish was cleared, become a swift servant, and clear it himself. He put the plates down on a sideboard, stuffed the silver in his breast pocket, giving it a bulgy look, and ran like a hare (I heard him coming) till he came to the cloak room. There he had only to be a plutocrat again—a plutocrat called away suddenly on business. He had only to give his ticket to the cloak-room attendant, and go out again elegantly as he had come in. Only—only I happened to be the cloak-room attendant.'

'What did you do to him?' cried the colonel, with unusual intensity. 'What did he tell you?'

'I beg your pardon,' said the priest immovably, 'that is where the story ends.'

'And the interesting story begins,' muttered Pound. 'I think I understand his professional trick. But I don't seem to have got hold of yours.'

'I must be going,' said Father Brown.

They walked together along the passage to the entrance hall, where they saw the fresh, freckled face of the Duke of Chester, who was bounding buoyantly along towards them.

'Come along, Pound,' he cried breathlessly. 'I've been looking for you everywhere. The dinner's going again in spanking style, and old Audley has got to make a speech in honour of the forks being saved. We want to start some new ceremony, don't you know, to commemorate the occasion. I say, you really got the goods back, what do you suggest?'

'Why,' said the colonel, eyeing him with a certain sardonic approval, 'I should suggest that henceforward we wear green coats, instead of black. One never knows what mistakes may arise when one looks so like a waiter.'

'Oh, hang it all!' said the young man, 'a gentleman never looks like a waiter.'

'Nor a waiter like a gentleman, I suppose,' said Colonel Pound, with the same lowering laughter on his face. 'Reverend sir, your friend must have been very smart to act the gentleman.'

Father Brown buttoned up his commonplace overcoat to the neck, for the night was stormy, and took his commonplace umbrella from the stand.

'Yes,' he said, 'it must be very hard work to be a gentleman; but, do you know, I have sometimes thought that it may be almost as laborious to be a waiter.'

And saying 'Good evening,' he pushed open the heavy doors of that palace of pleasures. The golden gates closed behind him, and he went at a brisk walk through the damp, dark streets in search of a penny omnibus.

## AFTERWORD

A key element in the success of Flambeau's remarkable plan was the inability of any of the aristocratic club members to recall the face of the waiter who took away the silver. 'Know the waiter?' says Mr Audley. 'Certainly not!' The waiters in this much-anthologized story were almost as invisible as the invisible man in Chapter 5.

# 4

●■●■●■●■●■●■●■●■●■●■●■●■●■●■●■●■●■●■●■●■●■●

# The Flying Stars*

'THE most beautiful crime I ever committed,' Flambeau would say in his highly moral old age, 'was also, by a singular coincidence, my last. It was committed at Christmas. As an artist I had always attempted to provide crimes suitable to the special season or landscapes in which I found myself, choosing this or that terrace or garden for a catastrophe, as if for a statuary group. Thus squires should be swindled in long rooms panelled with oak; while Jews, on the other hand, should rather find themselves unexpectedly penniless among the lights and screens of the Café Riche.[1] Thus, in England, if I wished to relieve a dean of his riches (which is not so easy as you might suppose), I wished to frame him, if I make myself clear, in the green lawns and grey

---

\* Flambeau devises a characteristically outlandish way to steal three large diamonds in the course of a Christmas harlequinade. It is the last and most colourful of his many crimes. The story was first published in *Cassell's Magazine* (June 1911), with illustrations by Sidney Lucas.

1. Although many of Chesterton's lifelong friends were Jews—forgive the hackneyed apology—there is no denying the fact that, like his brother Cecil and his friend Hilaire Belloc, and like many another Christian writer in Edwardian England, Chesterton allowed numerous antisemitic remarks to mar his writing. Among mystery writers Agatha Christie and Dorothy Sayers were often guilty of the same practice. We encountered some evidence of G.K.'s bias in the previous chapter. We shall encounter more later on.

There is a sense in which no conservative Christian, for whom the Old Testament is a divine revelation, can avoid holding opinions that many Jews consider antisemitic. He must believe, to go at once to the heart of the matter, that Jehovah carefully selected the Jews to prepare the way for His First Coming. Eventually God did arrive on earth, born of a Jewish mother. He selected a band of disciples, all Jews, including Peter whom Catholics consider their first Pope. Then after all this elaborate preparation, over thousands of years, God's own chosen people refused to believe that Jesus was their promised messiah.

towers of some cathedral town. Similarly, in France, when I had got money out of a rich and wicked peasant (which is almost impossible), it gratified me to get his indignant head relieved against a grey line of clipped poplars, and those solemn plains of Gaul over which broods the mighty spirit of Millet.[2]

'Well, my last crime was a Christmas crime, a cheery, cosy, English middle-class crime; a crime of Charles Dickens. I did it in a good old middle-class house near Putney,[3] a house with a crescent of carriage drive, a house with a stable by the side of it, a house with the name on the two outer gates, a house with a

---

There are two ways to view this refusal. Either God made a gross error of judgement, or the Jews of Jesus's time were guilty of a wilful, inexplicable rebellion against their own God. Since the first is unthinkable to a conservative Christian, the second view became the accepted one. Can anyone doubt that it fanned the flames of the great Jewish persecutions in Europe? It continues to be the view that underlies even such twentieth-century Catholic books as Belloc's *The Jews* and Jacques Maritain's *A Christian Looks at the Jewish Question*. Jews are assumed to be a peculiar people, under a mysterious curse that will not be lifted until the time of the Second Coming. That Chesterton took this for granted there can be no doubt. See in particular his final chapter of *The New Jerusalem* and the unfortunate thirteenth chapter of *The End of the Armistice*.

Maisie Ward, discussing G.K.'s antisemitism in *Return to Chesterton* (Chapter 8) quotes the following mock epitaph by Humbert Wolfe:

> Here lies Mr Chesterton
> who to Heaven might have gone,
> but didn't when he heard the news
> that the place was run by Jews

The lines provoke a smile. Yet they touch on one of the saddest of all the dilemmas that torment, or should torment, today's conservative Christians.

Antisemitism is now so muted in the rhetoric of Christian thinkers and leaders that it is hard to comprehend how passionate it was in earlier centuries before it reached its monstrous climax in Hitler's Germany. And who was the Fatherland's leading pre-Hitler antisemite? It was none other than the founder of Protestantism, Martin Luther. In an early work, *That Jesus Christ Was Born a Jew* (1523) he urged tolerance and kindness toward Jews, expecting them to become converts to his new version of Christian doctrine. Twenty years later, when it became clear this would not happen, he wrote his most infamous pamphlet, *Concerning the Jews and Their Lies* (1543). It was a small step from Luther's violent sentiments to Hitler's 'final solution'.

**2.** Jean-François Millet (1814–1875), the French painter best known for his *Angelus* and *The Gleaners*.

**3.** Putney is a London suburb on the south side of the Thames. The poet Algernon Charles Swinburne was one of its famous literary residents.

monkey tree.[4] Enough, you know the species. I really think my imitation of Dickens's style was dexterous and literary. It seems almost a pity I repented the same evening.'

Flambeau would then proceed to tell the story from the inside; and even from the inside it was odd. Seen from the outside it was perfectly incomprehensible, and it is from the outside that the stranger must study it. From this standpoint the drama may be said to have begun when the front doors of the house with the stable opened on the garden with the monkey tree, and a young girl came out with bread to feed the birds on the afternoon of Boxing Day.[5] She had a pretty face, with brave brown eyes; but her figure was beyond conjecture, for she was so wrapped up in brown furs that it was hard to say which was hair and which was fur. But for the attractive face she might have been a small toddling bear.

The winter afternoon was reddening towards evening, and already a ruby light was rolled over the bloomless beds, filling them, as it were, with the ghosts of the dead roses. On one side of the house stood the stable, on the other an alley or cloister of laurels led to the larger garden behind. The young lady, having scattered bread for the birds (for the fourth or fifth time that day, because the dog ate it), passed unobtrusively down the lane of laurels and into a glimmering plantation of evergreens behind. Here she gave an exclamation of wonder, real or ritual, and looking up at the high garden wall above her, beheld it fantastically bestridden by a somewhat fantastic figure.

'Oh, don't jump, Mr Crook,' she called out in some alarm; 'it's much too high.'

---

4. This odd-looking pine tree (*Araucaria araucana*) from Chile was introduced into England in 1776, and is now widespread throughout Europe. In the US it flourishes in California and along the Gulf coast. It is a tall tree, with a strangely wrinkled trunk that resembles the leg of a huge elephant. The small leaves have points as sharp as needles. It is usually called a 'monkey-puzzle tree', I assume because a monkey would be puzzled over how to climb it.

5. Boxing Day is the first weekday after Christmas. A legal holiday in England, it is the day on which boxes with gifts used to be given to servants, the postman, and others who performed services during the year for a family. The boxes were prepared during the previous evening. Boxing Day is also called St. Stephen's Day after the Feast of St. Stephen.

The individual riding the party wall like an aerial horse was a tall, angular young man,[6] with dark hair sticking up like a hair brush, intelligent and even distinguished lineaments, but a sallow and almost alien complexion. This showed the more plainly because he wore an aggressive red tie, the only part of his costume of which he seemed to take any care. Perhaps it was a symbol. He took no notice of the girl's alarmed adjuration, but leapt like a grasshopper to the ground beside her, where he might very well have broken his legs.

'I think I was meant to be a burglar,' he said placidly, 'and I have no doubt I should have been if I hadn't happened to be born in that nice house next door. I can't see any harm in it, anyhow.'

'How can you say such things?' she remonstrated.

'Well,' said the young man, 'if you're born on the wrong side of the wall, I can't see that it's wrong to climb over it.'

'I never know what you will say or do next,' she said.

'I don't often know myself,' replied Mr Crook; 'but then I am on the right side of the wall now.'

'And which is the right side of wall?' asked the young lady, smiling.

'Whichever side you are on,' said the young man named Crook.

As they went together through the laurels towards the front garden a motor horn sounded thrice, coming nearer and nearer, and a car of splendid speed, great elegance, and a pale green colour swept up to the front doors like a bird and stood throbbing.

'Hullo, hullo!' said the young man with the red tie, 'here's somebody born on the right side, anyhow. I didn't know, Miss Adams, that your Santa Claus was so modern as this.'

'Oh, that's my godfather, Sir Leopold Fischer. He always comes on Boxing Day.'

Then, after an innocent pause, which unconsciously betrayed some lack of enthusiasm, Ruby Adams added:

'He is very kind.'

John Crook, journalist, had heard of that eminent City magnate; and it was not his fault if the City magnate had not heard of

---

**6.** See Note 30 of Chapter 1.

him; for in certain articles in *The Clarion* or *The New Age* Sir Leopold had been dealt with austerely. But he said nothing and grimly watched the unloading of the motor-car, which was rather a long process. A large, neat chauffeur in green got out from the front, and a small, neat manservant in grey got out from the back, and between them they deposited Sir Leopold on the doorstep and began to unpack him, like some very carefully protected parcel. Rugs enough to stock a bazaar, furs of all the beasts of the forest, and scarves of all the colours of the rainbow were unwrapped one by one, till they revealed something resembling the human form; the form of a friendly, but foreign-looking old gentleman, with a grey goat-like beard and a beaming smile, who rubbed his big fur gloves together.

Long before this revelation was complete the two big doors of the porch had opened in the middle, and Colonel Adams (father of the furry young lady) had come out himself to invite his eminent guest inside. He was a tall, sunburnt, and very silent man, who wore a red smoking-cap like a fez, making him look like one of the English Sirdars or Pashas in Egypt.[7] With him was his brother-in-law, lately come from Canada, a big and rather boisterous young gentleman-farmer, with a yellow beard, by name James Blount. With him also was the more insignificant figure of the priest from the neighbouring Roman Church; for the colonel's late wife had been a Catholic, and the children, as is common in such cases, had been trained to follow her. Everything seemed undistinguished about the priest, even down to his name, which was Brown; yet the colonel had always found something companionable about him, and frequently asked him to such family gatherings.

In the large entrance hall of the house there was ample room even for Sir Leopold and the removal of his wraps. Porch and vestibule, indeed, were unduly large in proportion to the house, and formed, as it were, a big room with the front door at one end, and the bottom of the staircase at the other. In front of the large hall fire, over which hung the colonel's sword, the process was

---

7. Sirdars and Pashas are persons of high rank rank in India and Egypt respectively. Chesterton is here referring to British military and political leaders in the two countries.

completed and the company, including the saturnine Crook, presented to Sir Leopold Fischer. That venerable financier, however, still seemed struggling with portions of his well-lined attire, and at length produced from a very interior tail-coat pocket, a black oval case which he radiantly explained to be his Christmas present for his god-daughter. With an unaffected vainglory that had something disarming about it he held out the case before them all; it flew open at a touch and half-blinded them. It was just as if a crystal fountain had spurted in their eyes. In a nest of orange velvet lay like three eggs, three white and vivid diamonds that seemed to set the very air on fire all round them. Fischer stood beaming benevolently and drinking deep of the astonishment and ecstasy of the girl, the grim admiration and gruff thanks of the colonel, the wonder of the whole group.

'I'll put 'em back now, my dear,' said Fischer, returning the case to the tails of his coat. 'I had to be careful of 'em coming down. They're the three great African diamonds called "The Flying Stars," because they've been stolen so often. All the big criminals are on the track; but even the rough men about in the streets and hotels could hardly have kept their hands off them. I might have lost them on the road here. It was quite possible.'

'Quite natural, I should say,' growled the man in the red tie. 'I shouldn't blame 'em if they had taken 'em. When they ask for bread, and you don't even give them a stone, I think they might take the stone for themselves.'

'I won't have you talking like that,' cried the girl, who was in a curious glow. 'You've only talked like that since you became a horrid what's-his-name. You know what I mean. What do you call a man who wants to embrace the chimney-sweep?'

'A saint,' said Father Brown.

'I think,' said Sir Leopold, with a supercilious smile, 'that Ruby means a Socialist.'

'A Radical does not mean a man who lives on radishes,' remarked Crook, with some impatience; 'and a Conservative does not mean a man who preserves jam. Neither, I assure you, does a Socialist mean a man who desires a social evening with the chimney-sweep. A Socialist means a man who wants all the chimneys swept and all the chimney-sweeps paid for it.'

'But who won't allow you,' put in the priest in a low voice, 'to own your own soot.'

Crook looked at him with an eye of interest and even respect. 'Does one want to own soot?' he asked.

'One might,' answered Brown, with speculation in his eye. 'I've heard that gardeners use it. And I once made six children happy at Christmas when the conjuror didn't come, entirely with soot—applied externally.'[8]

'Oh, splendid,' cried Ruby. 'Oh, I wish you'd do it to this company.'

The boisterous Canadian, Mr Blount, was lifting his loud voice in applause, and the astonished financier his (in some considerable deprecation), when a knock sounded at the double front doors. The priest opened them, and they showed again the front garden of evergreens, monkey tree and all, now gathering gloom against a gorgeous violet sunset. The scene thus framed was so coloured and quaint, like a back scene in a play, that they forgot for a moment the insignificant figure standing in the door. He was dusty-looking and in a frayed coat, evidently a common messenger. 'Any of you gentlemen Mr Blount?' he asked, and held forward a letter doubtfully. Mr Blount started, and stopped in his shout of assent. Ripping up the envelope with evident astonishment he read it; his face clouded a little, and then cleared, and he turned to his brother-in-law and host.

'I'm sick at being such a nuisance, colonel,' he said, with the cheery colonial convention; 'but would it upset you if an old acquaintance called on me here to-night on business? In point of fact it's Florian, that famous French acrobat and comic actor; I knew him years ago out West (he was a French-Canadian by birth), and he seems to have business for me, though I hardly guess what.'

'Of course, of course,' replied the colonel carelessly. 'My dear chap, any friend of yours. No doubt he will prove an acquisition.'

'He'll black his face, if that's what you mean,' cried Blount,

---

8. Father Brown could be recalling an old parlour prank involving two plates. One has secretly been covered on the bottom with soot. It is given to the victim. The entertainer holds a clean plate. The victim is told to keep his eyes fixed on the eyes of the entertainer who will attempt to hypnotize him. The victim must imitate all the entertainer's actions. The actions consist of rubbing fingers on the bottom of the plate, then rubbing the same fingers on the forehead, chin, each cheek, and the nose. The poor victim cannot understand why the audience keeps laughing.

laughing. 'I don't doubt he'd black everyone else's eyes. I don't care; I'm not refined. I like the jolly old pantomime where a man sits on his top hat.'

'Not on mine, please,' said Sir Leopold Fischer, with dignity.

'Well, well,' observed Crook, airily, 'don't let's quarrel. There are lower jokes than sitting on a top hat.'

Dislike of the red-tied youth, both of his predatory opinions and evident intimacy with the pretty godchild, led Fischer to say, in his most sarcastic, magisterial manner: 'No doubt you have found something much lower than sitting on a top hat. What is it, pray?'

'Letting a top hat sit on you, for instance,' said the Socialist.

'Now, now, now,' cried the Canadian farmer with his barbarian benevolence, 'don't let's spoil a jolly evening. What I say is, let's do something for the company to-night. Not blacking faces or sitting on hats, if you don't like those—but something of the sort. Why couldn't we have a proper old English pantomime—clown, columbine, and so on.[9] I saw one when I left England at

---

**9.** The British harlequinade is a traditional pantomime comedy borrowed from Italy, and featuring four main characters. Harlequin is an acrobatic young man who wears a black cat-face mask, variegated tights spangled with stage diamonds, and carries a wooden lath that serves as both magic wand and bat. (It is no accident that the initial letters of Vladimir Nabokov's novel *Look at the Harlequins* spell LATH.)

Harlequin is in love with Columbine, a saucy young woman in ballet dress, with roses in her hair. She elopes with Harlequin. Pantaloon, her foolish, tottering father, bespectacled and in slippers, pursues the couple. The Clown is Pantaloon's comic servant who constantly plays jokes on his master. Minor characters frequently include a policeman.

In Shakespeare's *As You Like It* (II, vii. 139–66), the seven ages of man are described in a famous passage that begins with 'All the world's a stage, and all the men and women merely players . . . ' The pantaloon stage is the sixth:

> The sixth age shifts
> Into the lean and slipper'd pantaloon,
> With spectacles on nose and pouch on side,
> His youthful hose, well saved, a world too wide
> For his shrunk shank; and his big manly voice,
> Turning again toward childish treble, pipes
> And whistles in his sound.

William J. Scheick, in a splendid essay on 'The Twilight Harlequinade of Chesterton's Father Brown Stories' (*The Chesterton Review*, Fall–Winter,

twelve years old, and it's blazed in my brain like a bonfire ever since. I came back to the old country only last year, and I find the thing's extinct. Nothing but a lot of snivelling fairy plays. I want a hot poker and a policeman made into sausages, and they give me princesses moralising by moonlight, Blue Birds, or something. Blue Beard's more in my line, and him I liked best when he turned into the pantaloon.'

'I'm all for making a policeman into sausages,' said John Crook. 'It's a better definition of Socialism than some recently given. But surely the get-up would be too big a business.'

'Not a scrap,' cried Blount, quite carried away. 'A harlequinade's the quickest thing we can do, for two reasons. First, one can gag to any degree; and, second, all the objects are household things—tables and towel-horses and washing baskets,[10] and things like that.'

'That's true,' admitted Crook, nodding eagerly and walking about. 'But I'm afraid I can't have my policeman's uniform. Haven't killed a policeman lately.'

Blount frowned thoughtfully a space, and then smote his thigh. 'Yes, we can!' he cried. 'I've got Florian's address here, and he knows every *costumier* in London. I'll 'phone him to bring a police dress when he comes.' And he went bounding away to the telephone.

'Oh, it's glorious, godfather,' cried Ruby, almost dancing. 'I'll be columbine and you shall be pantaloon.'

---

1977–78), persuasively maintains that G.K., like Shakespeare and Dickens, liked to think of life as a fantastic, dreamlike harlequinade taking place in a perpetual gloaming—a mix of light and darkness that symbolizes our ignorance of the play's meaning and the fact that the actors too are souls in a twilight realm midway between beast and angel.

The Father Brown stories, Scheick points out, swarm with references to stage acting, and an extraordinary number of them—not just the Father Brown tales but G.K.'s other stories as well—have twilight settings. Moreover, Chesterton's characters are masked in the sense that we learn little about their inner lives. This is true of Father Brown. When we finish the canon's fifty-two acts we know a great deal about his opinions, almost nothing about his early history or his life as a parish priest. The ordinary pudding face, with its empty eyes, is Father Brown's mask as he acts out his curious roles in the canon's harlequinade.

**10.** Towel horses are wooden frames on which to hang towels, and washing baskets are for storing laundry.

The millionaire held himself stiff with a sort of heathen solemnity. 'I think, my dear,' he said, 'you must get someone else for pantaloon.'

'I will be pantaloon, if you like,' said Colonel Adams, taking his cigar out of his mouth, and speaking for the first and last time.

'You ought to have a statue,' cried the Canadian, as he came back, radiant, from the telephone. 'There, we are all fitted. Mr Crook shall be clown; he's a journalist and knows all the oldest jokes. I can be harlequin, that only wants long legs and jumping about. My friend Florian 'phones he's bringing the police costume; he's changing on the way. We can act it in this very hall, the audience sitting on those broad stairs opposite, one row above another. These front doors can be the back scene, either open or shut. Shut, you see an English interior. Open, a moonlit garden. It all goes by magic.' And snatching a chance piece of billiard chalk[11] from his pocket, he ran it across the hall floor, half-way between the front door and the staircase, to mark the line of the footlights.

How even such a banquet of bosh was got ready in the time remained a riddle. But they went at it with that mixture of recklessness and industry that lives when youth is in a house; and youth was in that house that night, though not all may have isolated the two faces and hearts from which it flamed. As always happens, the invention grew wilder and wilder through the very tameness of the *bourgeois* conventions from which it had to create. The columbine looked charming in an outstanding skirt that strangely resembled the large lamp-shade in the drawing-room. The clown and pantaloon made themselves white with flour from the cook, and red with rouge from some other domestic, who remained (like all true Christian benefactors) anonymous. The harlequin, already clad in silver paper out of cigar boxes, was, with difficulty, prevented from smashing the old Victorian lustre chandeliers, that he might cover himself with resplendent crystals. In fact he would certainly have done so, had not Ruby unearthed some old pantomime paste jewels she had worn at a fancy dress party as the Queen of Diamonds. Indeed, her uncle,

---

11. Billiard chalk is the chalk that players apply to the tips of their cues.

James Blount, was getting almost out of hand in his excitement; he was like a schoolboy. He put a paper donkey's head unexpectedly on Father Brown, who bore it patiently, and even found some private manner of moving his ears. He even essayed to pin the paper donkey's tail to the coat-tails of Sir Leopold Fischer. This, however, was frowned down. 'Uncle is too absurd,' cried Ruby to Crook, round whose shoulders she had seriously placed a string of sausages. 'Why is he so wild?'

'He is harlequin to your columbine,' said Crook. 'I am only the clown who makes the old jokes.'

'I wish you were the harlequin,' she said, and left the string of sausages swinging.

Father Brown, though he knew every detail done behind the scenes, and had even evoked applause by his transformation of a pillow into a pantomime baby, went round to the front and sat among the audience with all the solemn expectation of a child at his first matinée. The spectators were few, relations, one or two local friends, and the servants; Sir Leopold sat in the front seat, his full and still fur-collared figure largely obscuring the view of the little cleric behind him; but it has never been settled by artistic authorities whether the cleric lost much. The pantomime was utterly chaotic, yet not contemptible; there ran through it a rage of improvisation which came chiefly from Crook the clown. Commonly he was a clever man, and he was inspired to-night with a wild omniscience, a folly wiser than the world, that which comes to a young man who has seen for an instant a particular expression on a particular face. He was supposed to be the clown, but he was really almost everything else, the author (so far as there was an author), the prompter, the scene-painter, the scene-shifter, and, above all, the orchestra. At abrupt intervals in the outrageous performance he would hurl himself in full costume at the piano and bang out some popular music equally absurd and appropriate.

The climax of this, as of all else, was the moment when the two front doors at the back of the scene flew open, showing the lovely moonlit garden, but showing more prominently the famous professional guest; the great Florian, dressed up as a policeman. The clown at the piano played the constabulary chorus in the 'Pirates of Penzance,' but it was drowned in the deafening applause, for every gesture of the great comic actor was an admirable though restrained version of the carriage and manner of the police. The harlequin leapt upon him and hit him over the helmet; the pianist playing 'Where did you get that hat?' he faced about in admirably simulated astonishment, and then the leaping harlequin hit him again (the pianist suggesting a few bars of 'Then we had another one'). Then the harlequin rushed right into the arms of the policeman and fell on top of him, amid a roar of applause. Then it was that the strange actor gave that celebrated imitation of a dead man, of which the fame still lingers round Putney. It was almost impossible to believe that a living person could appear so limp.

The athletic harlequin swung him about like a sack or twisted or tossed him like an Indian club; all the time to the most maddeningly ludicrous tunes from the piano. When the harlequin heaved the comic constable heavily off the floor the clown played 'I arise from dreams of thee.' When he shuffled him across his back, 'With my bundle on my shoulder,' and when the harlequin finally let fall the policeman with a most convincing thud, the lunatic at the instrument struck into a jingling measure with some words which are still believed to have been, 'I sent a letter to my love and on the way I dropped it.'[12]

At about this limit of mental anarchy Father Brown's view was obscured altogether; for the City magnate in front of him rose to his full height and thrust his hands savagely into all his pockets. Then he sat down nervously, still fumbling, and then stood up again. For an instant it seemed seriously likely that he would stride across the footlights; then he turned a glare at the clown playing the piano; and then he burst in silence out of the room.

The priest had only watched for a few more minutes the absurd but not inelegant dance of the amateur harlequin over his splendidly unconscious foe. With real though rude art, the harlequin danced slowly backwards out of the door into the garden, which was full of moonlight and stillness. The vamped dress of silver paper and paste, which had been too glaring in the footlights, looked more and more magical and silvery as it danced away under a brillant moon. The audience was closing in with a

---

12. These are all songs then popular in England. In the story's magazine text, this last line continues: 'and some of you have picked it up and put it in your pocket'.

cataract of applause, when Brown felt his arm abruptly touched, and he was asked in a whisper to come into the colonel's study.

He followed his summoner with increasing doubt, which was not dispelled by a solemn comicality in the scene of the study. There sat Colonel Adams, still unaffectedly dressed as a pantaloon, with the knobbed whalebone nodding above his brow, but with his poor old eyes sad enough to have sobered a Saturnalia. Sir Leopold Fischer was leaning against the mantelpiece and heaving with all the importance of panic.

'This is a very painful matter, Father Brown,' said Adams. 'The truth is, those diamonds we all saw this afternoon seem to have vanished from my friend's tail-coat pocket. And as you——'

'As I,' supplemented Father Brown, with a broad grin, 'was sitting just behind him——'

'Nothing of the sort shall be suggested,' said Colonel Adams, with a firm look at Fischer, which rather implied that some such thing *had* been suggested. 'I only ask you to give me the assistance that any gentleman might give.'

'Which is turning out his pockets,' said Father Brown, and proceeded to do so, displaying seven and sixpence, a return ticket, a small silver crucifix, a small breviary, and a stick of chocolate.

The colonel looked at him long, and then said, 'Do you know, I should like to see the inside of your head more than the inside of your pockets. My daughter is one of your people, I know; well, she has lately——' and he stopped.

'She has lately,' cried out old Fischer, 'opened her father's house to a cut-throat Socialist, who says openly he would steal anything from a richer man. This is the end of it. Here is the richer man—and none the richer.'

'If you want the inside of my head you can have it,' said Brown rather wearily. 'What it's worth you can say afterwards. But the first thing I find in that disused pocket is this; that men who mean to steal diamonds don't talk Socialism. They are more likely,' he added demurely, 'to denounce it.'

Both the others shifted sharply and the priest went on:

'You see, we know these people, more or less. That Socialist would no more steal a diamond than a Pyramid. We ought to look at once to the one man we don't know. The fellow acting the policeman—Florian. Where is he exactly at this minute, I wonder.'

The pantaloon sprang erect and strode out of the room. An interlude ensued, during which the millionaire stared at the priest, and the priest at his breviary; then the pantaloon returned and said, with *staccato* gravity, 'The policeman is still lying on the stage. The curtain has gone up and down six times; he is still lying there.'

Father Brown dropped his book and stood staring with a look of blank mental ruin. Very slowly a light began to creep back in his grey eyes, and then he made the scarcely obvious answer.

'Please forgive me, colonel, but when did your wife die?'

'My wife!' replied the staring soldier, 'she died this year two months. Her brother James arrived just a week too late to see her.'

The little priest bounded like a rabbit shot. 'Come on!' he cried in quite unusual excitement. 'Come on! We've got to go and look at that policeman!'

They rushed on to the now curtained stage, breaking rudely past the columbine and clown (who seemed whispering quite contentedly), and Father Brown bent over the prostrate comic policeman.

'Chloroform,' he said as he rose; 'I only guessed it just now.'

There was a startled stillness, and then the colonel said slowly, 'Please say seriously what all this means.'

Father Brown suddenly shouted with laughter,[13] then stopped, and only struggled with it for instants during the rest of his speech. 'Gentlemen,' he gasped, 'there's not much time to talk. I must run after the criminal. But this great French actor who played the policeman—this clever corpse the harlequin waltzed with and dandled and threw about—he was——' His voice again failed him, and he turned his back to run.

'He was?' called Fischer inquiringly.

'A real policeman,' said Father Brown, and ran away into the dark.

There were hollows and bowers at the extreme end of that

---

13. Father Brown is unable to check his surprise and admiration for the ingenuity and humour of Flambeau's method of stealing the jewels. The priest stops suddenly when he realizes it is not a laughing matter.

leafy garden, in which the laurels and other immortal shrubs showed against sapphire sky and silver moon, even in that mid-winter, warm colours as of the south. The green gaiety of the waving laurels, the rich purple indigo of the night, the moon like a monstrous crystal, make an almost irresponsibly romantic picture; and among the top branches of the garden trees a strange figure is climbing, who looks not so much romantic as impossible. He sparkles from head to heel, as if clad in ten million moons; the real moon catches him at every movement and sets a new inch of him on fire. But he swings, flashing and successful, from the short tree in this garden to the tall, rambling tree in the other, and only stops there because a shade has slid under the smaller tree and has unmistakably called up to him.

'Well, Flambeau,' says the voice, 'you really look like a Flying Star; but that always means a Falling Star at last.'

The silver, sparkling figure above seems to lean forward in the laurels and, confident of escape, listens to the little figure below.

'You never did anything better, Flambeau. It was clever to come from Canada (with a Paris ticket, I suppose) just a week after Mrs Adams died, when no one was in a mood to ask questions. It was cleverer to have marked down the Flying Stars and the very day of Fischer's coming. But there's no cleverness, but mere genius, in what followed. Stealing the stones, I suppose, was nothing to you. You could have done it by sleight of hand in a hundred other ways besides that pretence of putting a paper donkey's tail to Fischer's coat. But in the rest you eclipsed yourself.'

The silvery figure among the green leaves seems to linger as if hypnotised, though his escape is easy behind him; he is staring at the man below.

'Oh, yes,' says the man below, 'I know all about it. I know you not only forced the pantomime, but put it to a double use. You were going to steal the stones quietly; news came by an accomplice that you were already suspected, and a capable police officer was coming to rout you up that very night. A common thief would have been thankful for the warning and fled; but you are a poet. You already had the clever notion of hiding the jewels in a blaze of false stage jewellery. Now, you saw that if the dress were a harlequin's the appearance of a policeman would be quite in keeping. The worthy officer started from Putney police station to find you, and walked into the queerest trap ever set in this world. When the front door opened he walked straight on to the stage of a Christmas pantomime, where he could be kicked, clubbed, stunned and drugged by the dancing harlequin, amid roars of laughter from all the most respectable people in Putney. Oh, you will never do anything better. And now, by the way, you might give me back those diamonds.'

The green branch on which the glittering figure swung, rustled as if in astonishment; but the voice went on:

'I want you to give them back, Flambeau, and I want you to give up this life. There is still youth and honour and humour in you; don't fancy they will last in that trade. Men may keep a sort of level of good, but no man has ever been able to keep on one level of evil. That road goes down and down. The kind man drinks and turns cruel; the frank man kills and lies about it. Many a man I've known started like you to be an honest outlaw, a merry robber of the rich, and ended stamped into slime. Maurice Blum started out as an anarchist of principle, a father of the poor; he ended a greasy spy and tale-bearer that both sides used and despised. Harry Burke started his free money movement sincerely enough; now he's sponging on a half-starved sister for endless brandies and sodas. Lord Amber went into wild society in a sort of chivalry; now he's paying blackmail to the lowest vultures in London. Captain Barillon[14] was the great gentleman-apache before your time; he died in a madhouse, screaming with fear of the 'narks'[15] and receivers that had betrayed him and hunted him down. I know the woods look very free behind you, Flambeau; I know that in a flash you could melt into them like a monkey.[16] But some day you will be an old grey monkey,

---

14. Blum, Burke, Amber, Barillon. I assume these are all invented names.

15. Today, mainly in the US, the term 'nark' refers to a narcotic agent, but in Edwardian England a nark was a police informer—sometimes called a 'nose'—(from the Romany *nak*, meaning 'nose'). 'Had Johnson been a "nark" of the police he would soon have been exposed,' writes Watson in 'The Adventure of the Illustrious Client' (*The Case Book of Sherlock Holmes*).

16. Flambeau's athletic prowess enables him to climb a tree as easily as a monkey, though it surely is not the monkey tree mentioned earlier, with its needle-sharp leaves.

Flambeau. You will sit up in your free forest cold at heart and close to death, and the tree-tops will be very bare.'

Everything continued still, as if the small man below held the other in the tree in some long invisible leash; and he went on:

'Your downward steps have begun. You used to boast of doing nothing mean, but you are doing something mean to-night. You are leaving suspicion on an honest boy with a good deal against him already; you are separating him from the woman he loves and who loves him. But you will do meaner things than that before you die.'

Three flashing diamonds fell from the tree to the turf. The small man stooped to pick them up, and when he looked up again the green cage of the tree was emptied of its silver bird.

The restoration of the gems (accidentally picked up by Father Brown, of all people) ended the evening in uproarious triumph; and Sir Leopold, in his height of good humour, even told the priest that though he himself had broader views, he could respect those whose creed required them to be cloistered and ignorant of this world.

### AFTERWORD

There was good reason in the previous chapter why Flambeau did not recognize Father Brown in a dark cloakroom, but here we have a problem. Why did Flambeau and the priest fail to recognize each other when they arrived together at the party? Let us speculate. Flambeau may have known at once that his former Nemesis was a guest, and maybe this heightened the challenge of his plans. It is more difficult to believe that Flambeau's yellow beard was sufficient to hide his identity from Father Brown. Perhaps Flambeau used clever makeup to further disguise his features, and adopted a different way of speaking that aroused no suspicions in Father Brown's mind until he realized that only Flambeau could have orchestrated such a brilliant scenario.

In 'The Secret of Flambeau' (*The Secret of Father Brown*), Flambeau recalls the occasion in this story when he decided to abandon his life of crime:

'There is nothing mystical or metaphorical, or vicarious about my confession,' said Flambeau. 'I stole for twenty years with these two hands; I fled from the police on these two feet. I hope you will admit that my activities were practical. I hope you will admit that my judges and pursuers really had to deal with crime. Do you think I do not know all about their way of reprehending it? Have I not heard the sermons of the righteous and seen the cold stare of the respectable; have I not been lectured in the lofty and distant style, asked how it was possible for anyone to fall so low, told that no decent person could ever have dreamed of such depravity? Do you think all that ever did anything but make me laugh? Only my friend told me that he knew exactly why I stole; and I have never stolen since.'

# 5

# The Invisible Man*

IN the cool blue twilight of two steep streets in Camden Town, the shop at the corner, a confectioner's, glowed like the butt of a cigar. One should rather say, perhaps, like the butt of a firework, for the light was of many colours and some complexity, broken up by many mirrors and dancing on many gilt and gaily-coloured cakes and sweetmeats. Against this one fiery glass were glued the noses of many gutter-snipes, for the chocolates were all wrapped in those red and gold and green metallic colours which are almost better than chocolate itself; and the huge white wedding-cake in the window was somehow at once remote and satisfying, just as if the whole North Pole were good to eat. Such rainbow provocations could naturally collect the youth of the neighbourhood up to the ages of ten or twelve. But this corner was also attractive to youth at a later stage; and a young man, not less than twenty-four, was staring into the same shop window. To him, also, the shop was of fiery charm, but this attraction was not wholly to be explained by chocolates; which, however, he was far from despising.

He was a tall, burly, red-haired young man, with a resolute face but a listless manner. He carried under his arm a flat, grey portfolio of black-and-white sketches, which he had sold with more or less success to publishers ever since his uncle (who was an admiral) had disinherited him for Socialism, because of a lecture which he had delivered against that economic theory. His name was John Turnbull Angus.[1]

---

* How could a murderer enter the victim's apartment in daylight and remove his body without being seen? This is perhaps the best known, most anthologized of all Father Brown stories. It first appeared, with pictures by Sidney Lucas, in *Cassell's Magazine* (February 1911).

1. This young red-haired Scotsman may be a relative of James Turnbull, the Scottish atheist in Chesterton's fantasy *The Ball and the Cross*.

Entering at last, he walked through the confectioner's shop into the back room, which was a sort of pastry-cook restaurant, merely raising his hat to the young lady who was serving there. She was a dark, elegant, alert girl in black, with a high colour and very quick, dark eyes; and after the ordinary interval she followed him into the inner room to take his order.

His order was evidently a usual one. 'I want, please,' he said with precision, 'one halfpenny bun and a small cup of black coffee.' An instant before the girl could turn away he added, 'Also, I want you to marry me.'

The young lady of the shop stiffened suddenly, and said, 'Those are jokes I don't allow.'[2]

The red-haired young man lifted grey eyes of an unexpected gravity.

'Really and truly,' he said, 'it's as serious—as serious as the halfpenny bun. It is expensive, like the bun; one pays for it. It is indigestible, like the bun. It hurts.'

The dark young lady had never taken her dark eyes off him, but seemed to be studying him with almost tragic exactitude. At the end of her scrutiny she had something like the shadow of a smile, and she sat down in a chair.

'Don't you think,' observed Angus, absently, 'that it's rather cruel to eat these halfpenny buns? They might grow up into penny buns. I shall give up these brutal sports when we are married.'

The dark young lady rose from her chair and walked to the window, evidently in a state of strong but not unsympathetic cogitation. When at last she swung round again with an air of resolution she was bewildered to observe that the young man was carefully laying out on the table various objects from the shop window. They included a pyramid of highly coloured sweets, several plates of sandwiches, and the two decanters containing that mysterious port and sherry which are peculiar to pastrycooks. In the middle of this neat arrangement he had carefully let down the enormous load of white sugared cake which had been the huge ornament of the window.

---

2. In the magazine text Chesterton adds that the woman made her remark 'with a snap of her black eyes'.

'What on earth are you doing?' she asked.

'Duty, my dear Laura,' he began.

'Oh, for the Lord's sake, stop a minute,' she cried, 'and don't talk to me in that way. I mean, what is all that?'

'A ceremonial meal, Miss Hope.'

'And what is *that?*' she asked impatiently, pointing to the mountain of sugar.

'The wedding-cake, Mrs Angus,' he said.

The girl marched to that article, removed it with some clatter, and put it back in the shop window; she then returned, and, putting her elegant elbows on the table, regarded the young man not unfavourably but with considerable exasperation.

'You don't give me any time to think,' she said.

'I'm not such a fool,' he answered; 'that's my Christian humility.'

She was still looking at him; but she had grown considerably graver behind the smile.

'Mr Angus,' she said steadily, 'before there is a minute more of this nonsense I must tell you something about myself as shortly as I can.'

'Delighted,' replied Angus gravely. 'You might tell me something about myself, too, while you are about it.'

'Oh, do hold your tongue and listen,' she said. 'It's nothing that I'm ashamed of, and it isn't even anything that I'm specially sorry about. But what would you say if there were something that is no business of mine and yet is my nightmare?'

'In that case,' said the man seriously, 'I should suggest that you bring back the cake.'

'Well, you must listen to the story first,' said Laura, persistently. 'To begin with, I must tell you that my father owned the inn called the "Red Fish" at Ludbury,[3] and I used to serve people in the bar.'

---

3. Chesterton invented the name of Ludbury, but in the story's magazine form it is Sudbury, an actual town on the River Stour in Suffolk. The famous English painter John Gainsborough was born in Sudbury and for a time lived there. Chesterton may have disguised the name because he described some unpleasant characters who frequented one of the town's inns. I assume that the inn's name, The Red Fish, was also invented by G.K.

'I have often wondered,' he said, 'why there was a kind of a Christian air about this one confectioner's shop.'

'Ludbury is a sleepy, grassy little hole in the Eastern Counties, and the only kind of people who ever came to the "Red Fish" were occasional commercial travellers, and for the rest, the most awful people you can see, only you've never seen them. I mean little, loungy men, who had just enough to live on and had nothing to do but lean about in bar-rooms and bet on horses, in bad clothes that were just too good for them. Even these wretched young rotters were not very common at our house; but there were two of them that were a lot too common—common in every sort of way. They both lived on money of their own, and were wearisomely idle and over-dressed. But yet I was a bit sorry for them, because I half believe they slunk into our little empty bar because each of them had a slight deformity; the sort of thing that some yokels laugh at. It wasn't exactly a deformity either; it was more an oddity. One of them was a surprisingly small man, something like a dwarf, or at least like a jockey. He was not at all jockeyish to look at, though; he had a round black head and a well-trimmed black beard, bright eyes like a bird's; he jingled money in his pockets; he jangled a great gold watch chain; and he never turned up except dressed just too much like a gentleman to be one. He was no fool though, though a futile idler; he was curiously clever at all kinds of things that couldn't be the slightest use; a sort of impromptu conjuring; making fifteen matches set fire to each other like a regular firework; or cutting a banana or some such thing into a dancing doll. His name was Isidore Smythe; and I can see him still, with his little dark face, just coming up to the counter, making a jumping kangaroo out of five cigars.

'The other fellow was more silent and more ordinary; but somehow he alarmed me much more than poor little Smythe. He was very tall and slight, and light-haired; his nose had a high bridge, and he might almost have been handsome in a spectral sort of way; but he had one of the most appalling squints I have ever seen or heard of. When he looked straight at you, you didn't know where you were yourself, let alone what he was looking at. I fancy this sort of disfigurement embittered the poor chap a little; for while Smythe was ready to show off his monkey tricks anywhere, James Welkin (that was the squinting man's name) never did anything except soak in our bar parlour, and go for great walks by himself in the flat, grey country all round. All the same, I think Smythe, too, was a little sensitive about being so small, though he carried it off more smartly. And so it was that I was really puzzled, as well as startled, and very sorry, when they both offered to marry me in the same week.

'Well, I did what I've since thought was perhaps a silly thing. But, after all, these freaks were my friends in a way; and I had a horror of their thinking I refused them for the real reason, which was that they were so impossibly ugly. So I made up some gas of another sort, about never meaning to marry anyone who hadn't carved his way in the world. I said it was a point of principle with me not to live on money that was just inherited like theirs. Two days after I had talked in this well-meaning sort of way, the whole trouble began. The first thing I heard was that both of them had gone off to seek their fortunes, as if they were in some silly fairy tale.

'Well, I've never seen either of them from that day to this. But I've had two letters from the little man called Smythe, and really they were rather exciting.'

'Ever heard of the other man?' asked Angus.

'No, he never wrote,' said the girl, after an instant's hesitation. 'Smythe's first letter was simply to say that he had started out walking with Welkin to London; but Welkin was such a good walker that the little man dropped out of it, and took a rest by the roadside. He happened to be picked up by some travelling show, and, partly because he was nearly a dwarf, and partly because he was really a clever little wretch, he got on quite well in the show business, and was soon sent up to the Aquarium, to do some tricks that I forget. That was his first letter. His second was much more of a startler, and I only got it last week.'

The man called Angus emptied his coffee-cup and regarded her with mild and patient eyes. Her own mouth took a slight twist of laughter as she resumed, 'I suppose you've seen on the hoardings[4] all about this "Smythe's Silent Service"? Or you must be the only person that hasn't. Oh, I don't know much

---

4. 'Hoardings' is a British term for a board fence on which bills and advertisements are posted.

about it, it's some clockwork invention[5] for doing all the house-work by machinery. You know the sort of thing: "Press a but-ton—A Butler who Never Drinks." "Turn a Handle—Ten Housemaids who Never Flirt." You must have seen the adver-tisements. Well, whatever these machines are, they are making pots of money; and they are making it all for that little imp whom I knew down in Ludbury. I can't help feeling pleased the poor little chap has fallen on his feet; but the plain fact is, I'm in terror of his turning up any minute and telling me he's carved his way in the world—as he certainly has.'

'And the other man?' repeated Angus with a sort of obstinate quietude.

Laura Hope got to her feet suddenly. 'My friend,' she said, 'I think you are a witch. Yes, you are quite right. I have not seen a line of the other man's writing; and I have no more notion than the dead of what or where he is. But it is of him that I am fright-ened. It is he who is all about my path. It is he who has half driven me mad. Indeed, I think he has driven me mad; for I have felt him where he could not have been, and I have heard his voice when he could not have spoken.'

'Well, my dear,' said the young man, cheerfully, 'if he were Satan himself, he is done for now you have told somebody. One goes mad all alone, old girl. But when was it you fancied you felt and heard our squinting friend?'

'I heard James Welkin laugh as plainly as I hear you speak,'

---

**5.** In Chesterton's time no one anticipated electronic, computer-controlled machines; the best G.K. could imagine was an elaborate clockwork robot similar to L. Frank Baum's Tik-Tok of Oz except it was headless. Had anyone suggested that before the century was over robots would be con-structing cars, Chesterton would have been incredulous. Today the 'butler who never drinks' and the 'housemaid who never flirts' are no more imposs-ible than the automated factory workers who never tire or go on strike.

The headless robots of G.K.'s story are, of course, symbols of how some members of the upper classes look upon their servants, seeing them as little more than useful machines, faceless robots with no individuality. This heartless tendency not to comprehend the complexity of simple, ordinary people returns as a theme in one of the best of the later Father Brown stor-ies, 'The Blast of the Book' (*The Scandal of Father Brown*). The tale is about an erudite professor who is easily hoodwinked by his clerk Berridge. The pro-fessor liked to call him Babbage (after Charles Babbage, inventor of a pio-neering mechanical computer) because he considered Berridge no more than an inhuman 'calculating machine'.

said the girl, steadily. 'There was nobody there, for I stood just outside the shop at the corner, and could see down both streets at once. I had forgotten how he laughed, though his laugh was as odd as his squint. I had not thought of him for nearly a year. But it's a solemn truth that a few seconds later the first letter came from his rival.'

'Did you ever make the spectre speak or squeak, or anything?' asked Angus, with some interest.

Laura suddenly shuddered, and then said, with an unshaken voice, 'Yes. Just when I had finished reading the second letter from Isidore Smythe announcing his success, just then, I heard Welkin say, "He shan't have you, though." It was quite plain, as if he were in the room. It is awful; I think I must be mad.'

'If you really were mad,' said the young man, 'you would think you must be sane. But certainly there seems to me to be something a little rum about this unseen gentleman. Two heads are better than one—I spare you allusions to any other organs—and really, if you would allow me, as a sturdy, practical man, to bring back the wedding-cake out of the window——'

Even as he spoke, there was a sort of steely shriek in the street outside, and a small motor, driven at devilish speed, shot up to the door of the shop and stuck there. In the same flash of time a small man in a shiny top hat stood stamping in the outer room.

Angus, who had hitherto maintained hilarious ease from motives of mental hygiene, revealed the strain of his soul by striding abruptly out of the inner room and confronting the newcomer. A glance at him was quite sufficient to confirm the savage guesswork of a man in love. This very dapper but dwarfish figure, with the spike of black beard carried insolently forward, the clever unrestful eyes, the neat but very nervous fingers, could be none other than the man just described to him: Isidore Smythe, who made dolls out of banana skins and match-boxes; Isidore Smythe, who made millions out of undrinking butlers and unflirting housemaids of metal. For a moment the two men, instinctively understanding each other's air of possession, looked at each other with that curious cold generosity which is the soul of rivalry.[6]

6. In *Cassell's Magazine* Chesterton added to this sentence: 'and goes down to the roots of the soul'.

Mr Smythe, however, made no allusion to the ultimate ground of their antagonism, but said simply and explosively, 'Has Miss Hope seen that thing on the window?'

'On the window?' repeated the staring Angus.

'There's no time to explain other things,' said the small million-aire shortly. 'There's some tomfoolery going on here that has to be investigated.'

He pointed his polished walking-stick at the window, recently depleted by the bridal preparations of Mr Angus; and that gentle-man was astonished to see along the front of the glass a long strip of paper pasted, which had certainly not been on the window when he had looked through it some time before. Following the energetic Smythe outside into the street, he found that some yard and a half of stamp paper[7] had been carefully gummed along the glass outside, and on this was written in straggly characters, 'If you marry Smythe, he will die.'

'Laura,' said Angus, putting his big red head into the shop, 'you're not mad.'

'It's the writing of that fellow Welkin,' said Smythe gruffly. 'I haven't seen him for years, but he's always bothering me. Five times in the last fortnight he's had threatening letters left at my flat, and I can't even find out who leaves them, let alone if it is Welkin himself. The porter of the flats swears that no suspicious characters have been seen, and here he has pasted up a sort of dado[8] on a public shop window, while the people in the shop——'

'Quite so,' said Angus modestly, 'while the people in the shop were having tea. Well, sir, I can assure you I appreciate your common sense in dealing so directly with the matter. We can talk about other things afterwards. The fellow cannot be very far off yet, for I swear there was no paper there when I went last to the window, ten or fifteen minutes ago. On the other hand, he's too far off to be chased, as we don't even know the direction. If you'll take my advice, Mr Smythe, you'll put this at once in the hands of some energetic inquiry man, private rather than public. I know an extremely clever fellow, who has set up in business five

---

7. Stamp paper is the blank marginal paper on sheets of postage stamps, often used at the time as paper sticking tape.

8. Dado: 'Any lining, painting, or papering of the lower part of an interior wall, of a different material or colour from that of the upper part' (*OED*).

minutes from here in your car. His name's Flambeau, and
though his youth was a bit stormy, he's a strictly honest man
now, and his brains are worth money.[9] He lives in Lucknow
Mansions, Hampstead.'

'That is odd,' said the little man, arching his black eyebrows.
'I live, myself, in Himalaya Mansions, round the corner. Perhaps
you might care to come with me; I can go to my rooms and sort
out these queer Welkin documents, while you run round and get
your friend the detective.'

'You are very good,' said Angus politely. 'Well, the sooner we
act the better.'

Both men, with a queer kind of impromptu fairness, took the
same sort of formal farewell of the lady, and both jumped into the
brisk little car. As Smythe took the handles and they turned the
great corner of the street, Angus was amused to see a gigantesque
poster of 'Smythe's Silent Service,' with a picture of a huge headless iron doll, carrying a saucepan with legend, 'A Cook Who is
Never Cross.'

'I use them in my own flat,' said the little black-bearded man,
laughing, 'partly for advertisement, and partly for real convenience. Honestly, and all above board, those big clockwork
dolls of mine do bring you coals or claret or a time-table quicker
than any live servants I've ever known, if you know which knob
to press. But I'll never deny, between ourselves, that such servants have their disadvantages, too.'

'Indeed?' said Angus; 'is there something they can't do?'

'Yes,' replied Smythe coolly; 'they can't tell me who left those
threatening letters at my flat.'

The man's motor was small and swift like himself; in fact, like
his domestic service, it was of his own invention. If he was an

---

**9.** Flambeau's business is that of private detective, and his office (we
learn in later stories) is in Westminster across from the Abbey. His speciality is catching jewel thieves. On one occasion ('The Insoluble Problem', the
last story in the last Father Brown book) 'he had torn the tiara of the Duchess of Dulwich out of the very hand of the bandit as he bolted through the
garden'. Indeed, his exploits as a crime investigator soon rival in flam-
boyance some of his youthful crimes. 'He laid so ingenious a trap for the
criminal who planned to carry off the celebrated Sapphire Necklace,' to continue the above quote, 'that the artist in question actually carried off the
copy which he had himself planned to leave as a substitute.'

advertising quack, he was one who believed in his own wares. The sense of something tiny and flying was accentuated as they swept up long white curves of road in the dead but open daylight of evening. Soon the white curves came sharper and dizzier; they were upon ascending spirals, as they say in the modern religions. For, indeed, they were cresting a corner of London which is almost as precipitous as Edinburgh, if not quite so picturesque. Terrace rose above terrace, and the special tower of flats they sought rose above them all to almost Egyptian height, gilt by the level sunset. The change, as they turned the corner and entered the crescent known as Himalaya Mansions, was as abrupt as the opening of a window; for they found that pile of flats sitting above London as above a green sea of slate. Opposite to the mansions, on the other side of the gravel crescent, was a bushy enclosure more like a steep hedge or dyke than a garden, and some way below that ran a strip of artificial water, a sort of canal, like the moat of that embowered fortress. As the car swept round the crescent it passed, at one corner, the stray stall of a man selling chestnuts; and right away at the other end of the curve, Angus could see a dim blue policeman walking slowly. These were the only human shapes in that high suburban solitude; but he had an irrational sense that they expressed the speechless poetry of London. He felt as if they were figures in a story.

The little car shot up to the right house like a bullet, and shot out its owner like a bomb shell. He was immediately inquiring of a tall commissionaire in shining braid, and a short porter in shirt sleeves, whether anybody or anything had been seeking his apartments. He was assured that nobody and nothing had passed these officials since his last inquiries; whereupon he and the slightly bewildered Angus were shot up in the lift like a rocket, till they reached the top floor.

'Just come in for a minute,' said the breathless Smythe. 'I want to show you those Welkin letters. Then you might run round the corner and fetch your friend.' He pressed a button concealed in the wall, and the door opened of itself.

It opened on a long, commodious ante-room, of which the only arresting features, ordinarily speaking, were the rows of tall half-human mechanical figures that stood up on both sides like tailors' dummies. Like tailors' dummies they were headless; and like tailors' dummies they had a handsome unnecessary humpiness in the shoulders, and a pigeon-breasted protuberance of chest; but barring this, they were not much more like a human figure than any automatic machine at a station that is about the human height. They had two great hooks like arms, for carrying trays; and they were painted pea-green, or vermilion, or black for convenience of distinction; in every other way they were only automatic machines and nobody would have looked twice at them. On this occasion, at least, nobody did. For between the two rows of these domestic dummies lay something more interesting than most of the mechanics of the world. It was a white, tattered scrap of paper scrawled with red ink; and the agile inventor had snatched it up almost as soon as the door flew open. He handed it to Angus without a word. The red ink on it actually was not dry, and the message ran, 'If you have been to see her to-day, I shall kill you.'

There was a short silence, and then Isidore Smythe said quietly, 'Would you like a little whisky? I rather feel as if I should.'

'Thank you; I should like a little Flambeau,'[10] said Angus, gloomily. 'This business seems to me to be getting rather grave. I'm going round at once to fetch him.'

'Right you are,' said the other, with admirable cheerfulness. 'Bring him round here as quick as you can.'

But as Angus closed the front door behind him he saw Smythe push back a button, and one of the clockwork images glided from its place and slid along a groove in the floor carrying a tray with syphon and decanter. There did seem something a trifle weird about leaving the little man alone among those dead servants, who were coming to life as the door closed.

Six steps down from Smythe's landing the man in shirt sleeves was doing something with a pail. Angus stopped to extract a promise, fortified with a prospective bribe, that he would remain in that place until the return with the detective, and would keep count of any kind of stranger coming up those stairs. Dashing down to the front hall he then laid similar charges of vigilance on the commissionaire at the front door, from whom he learned the simplifying circumstance that there was no back door. Not content with this, he captured the floating policeman and induced

10. I take it that Angus means he wants some light shed on the situation.

him to stand opposite the entrance and watch it; and finally paused an instant for a pennyworth of chestnuts, and an inquiry as to the probable length of the merchant's stay in the neighbourhood.

The chestnut seller, turning up the collar of his coat, told him he should probably be moving shortly, as he thought it was going to snow. Indeed, the evening was growing grey and bitter, but Angus, with all his eloquence, proceeded to nail the chestnut man to his post.

'Keep yourself warm on your own chestnuts,' he said earnestly. 'Eat up your whole stock; I'll make it worth your while. I'll give you a sovereign if you'll wait here till I come back, and then tell me whether any man, woman, or child has gone into that house where the commissionaire is standing.'

He then walked away smartly, with a last look at the besieged tower.

'I've made a ring round that room, anyhow,' he said. 'They can't all four of them be Mr Welkin's accomplices.'

Lucknow Mansions were, so to speak, on a lower platform of that hill of houses, of which Himalaya Mansions might be called the peak. Mr Flambeau's semi-official flat was on the ground floor, and presented in every way a marked contrast to the American machinery and cold hotel-like luxury of the flat of the Silent Service. Flambeau, who was a friend of Angus, received him in a rococo artistic den behind his office, of which the ornaments were sabres, harquebuses,[11] Eastern curiosities, flasks of Italian wine, savage cooking-pots, a plumy Persian cat, and a small dusty-looking Roman Catholic priest, who looked particularly out of place.

'This is my friend Father Brown,' said Flambeau. 'I've often wanted you to meet him. Splendid weather, this; a little cold for Southerners like me.'

'Yes, I think it will keep clear,' said Angus, sitting down on a violet-striped Eastern ottoman.

'No,' said the priest quietly, 'it has begun to snow.'

---

11. 'Harquebuses' comes from the German 'hook-gun', a sixteenth-century military gun. Too heavy to be held, it was supported on a tripod or some similar device. A hook on the barrel allowed it to be attached to its support.

And, indeed, as he spoke, the first few flakes, foreseen by the man of chestnuts, began to drift across the darkening window-pane.

'Well,' said Angus heavily. 'I'm afraid I've come on business, and rather jumpy business at that. The fact is, Flambeau, within a stone's throw of your house is a fellow who badly wants your help; he's perpetually being haunted and threatened by an invisible enemy—a scoundrel whom nobody has even seen.' As Angus proceeded to tell the whole tale of Smythe and Welkin, beginning with Laura's story, and going on with his own, the supernatural laugh at the corner of two empty streets, the strange distinct words spoken in an empty room, Flambeau grew more and more vividly concerned, and the little priest seemed to be left out of it, like a piece of furniture. When it came to the scribbled stamp paper pasted on the window, Flambeau rose, seeming to fill the room with his huge shoulders.

'If you don't mind,' he said, 'I think you had better tell me the rest on the nearest road to this man's house. It strikes me, somehow, that there is no time to be lost.'

'Delighted,' said Angus, rising also, 'though he's safe enough for the present, for I've set four men to watch the only hole to his burrow.'

They turned out into the street, the small priest trundling after them with the docility of a small dog. He merely said, in a cheerful way, like one making conversation, 'How quick the snow gets thick on the ground.'

As they threaded the steep side streets already powdered with silver, Angus finished his story; and by the time they reached the crescent with the towering flats, he had leisure to turn his attention to the four sentinels. The chestnut seller, both before and after receiving a sovereign, swore stubbornly that he had watched the door and seen no visitor enter. The policeman was even more emphatic. He said he had had experience of crooks of all kinds, in top hats and in rags; he wasn't so green as to expect suspicious characters to look suspicious; he looked out for anybody, and, so help him, there had been nobody. And when all three men gathered round the gilded commissionaire, who still stood smiling astride of the porch, the verdict was more final still.

'I've got a right to ask any man, duke or dustman, what he wants in these flats,' said the genial and gold-laced giant, 'and

I'll swear there's been nobody to ask since this gentleman went away.'

The unimportant Father Brown, who stood back, looking modestly at the pavement, here ventured to say meekly, 'Has nobody been up and down stairs, then, since the snow began to fall? It began while we were all round at Flambeau's.'

'Nobody's been in here, sir, you can take it from me,' said the official, with beaming authority.

'Then I wonder what that is?' said the priest, and stared at the ground blankly like a fish.

The others all looked down also; and Flambeau used a fierce exclamation and a French gesture. For it was unquestionably true that down the middle of the entrance guarded by the man in gold lace, actually between the arrogant, stretched legs of that colossus, ran a stringy pattern of grey footprints stamped upon the white snow.

'God!' cried Angus involuntarily, 'the Invisible Man!'[12]

Without another word he turned and dashed up the stairs, with Flambeau following; but Father Brown still stood looking about him in the snowclad street as if he had lost interest in his query.

Flambeau was plainly in a mood to break down the door with

---

12. When Chesterton entitled this story he may have had in mind the popular short novel (1897) of the same title by his friend and antagonist H. G. Wells. Ralph Ellison's 1925 novel, *Invisible Man*, has a theme essentially the same as G.K.'s story. Ellison's black protagonist is a man who loses his identity, becoming as invisible to blacks as he is to whites.

Chesterton's story is often likened to Poe's 'The Purloined Letter', in which an important document is concealed by putting it in a spot too obvious to be noticed by the police.

I must add an anecdote about the renowned physicist Eugene Wigner that involves a brown sack like the postman's—though one of paper, not cloth. When Enrico Fermi obtained the first nuclear chain reaction in a laboratory under the University of Chicago's football stadium, Wigner suddenly produced a bottle of wine to celebrate. Because no one had seen him carry in a bottle, the wine seemed to appear by magic. Some of those present thought he had concealed the bottle for hours under his jacket. I once had the pleasure of asking Wigner how he had performed this miracle. He laughed, reminded me of Poe's story, and said he had brought the bottle in an ordinary brown paper sack which he simply placed unobtrusively aside until he needed it.

his big shoulder; but the Scotsman, with more reason, if less intuition, fumbled about on the frame of the door till he found the invisible button; and the door swung slowly open.

It showed substantially the same serried interior;[13] the hall had grown darker, though it was still struck here and there with the last crimson shafts of sunset, and one or two of the headless machines had been moved from their places for this or that purpose, and stood here and there about the twilit place. The green and red of their coats were all darkened in the dusk; and their likeness to human shapes slightly increased by their very shapelessness. But in the middle of them all, exactly where the paper with the red ink had lain, there lay something that looked very like red ink spilt out of its bottle. But it was not red ink.

With a French combination of reason and violence Flambeau simply said 'Murder!' and, plunging into the flat, had explored every corner and cupboard of it in five minutes. But if he expected to find a corpse he found none. Isidore Smythe simply was not in the place, either dead or alive. After the most tearing search the two men met each other in the outer hall, with streaming faces and staring eyes. 'My friend,' said Flambeau, talking French in his excitement, 'not only is your murderer invisible, but he makes invisible also the murdered man.'

Angus looked round at the dim room full of dummies, and in some Celtic corner of his Scotch soul a shudder started. One of the life-size dolls stood immediately overshadowing the blood stain, summoned, perhaps, by the slain man an instant before he fell. One of the high-shouldered hooks that served the thing for arms, was a little lifted, and Angus had suddenly the horrid fancy that poor Smythe's own iron child had struck him down. Matter had rebelled, and these machines had killed their master.[14] But even so, what had they done with him?

'Eaten him?' said the nightmare at his ear; and he sickened for an instant at the idea of rent, human remains absorbed and crushed into all that acephalous clockwork.

---

13. 'Serried' is commonly used to describe ranks of soldiers who stand shoulder to shoulder.

14. Chesterton probably had in mind the famous story by Ambrose Bierce, 'Moxon's Master', in which an angry clockwork chess machine kills its inventor after losing a game.

He recovered his mental health by an emphatic effort, and said to Flambeau, 'Well, there it is. The poor fellow has evaporated like a cloud and left a red streak on the floor. The tale does not belong to this world.'

'There is only one thing to be done,' said Flambeau, 'whether it belongs to this world or the other, I must go down and talk to my friend.'

They descended, passing the man with the pail, who again asseverated that he had let no intruder pass, down to the commissionaire and the hovering chestnut man, who rigidly reasserted their own watchfulness. But when Angus looked round for his fourth confirmation he could not see it, and called out with some nervousness, 'Where is the policeman?'

'I beg your pardon,' said Father Brown; 'that is my fault. I just sent him down the road to investigate something—that I just thought worth investigating.'

'Well, we want him back pretty soon,' said Angus abruptly, 'for the wretched man upstairs has not only been murdered, but wiped out.'

'How?' asked the priest.

'Father,' said Flambeau, after a pause, 'upon my soul I believe it is more in your department than mine. No friend or foe has entered the house, but Smythe is gone, as if stolen by the fairies. If that is not supernatural, I——'

As he spoke they were all checked by an unusual sight; the big blue policeman came round the corner of the crescent, running. He came straight up to Brown.

'You're right, sir,' he panted, 'they've just found poor Mr Smythe's body in the canal down below.'

Angus put his hand wildly to his head. 'Did he run down and drown himself?' he asked.

'He never came down, I'll swear,' said the constable, 'and he wasn't drowned either, for he died of a great stab over the heart.'

'And yet you saw no one enter?' said Flambeau in a grave voice.

'Let us walk down the road a little,' said the priest.

As they reached the other end of the crescent he observed abruptly, 'Stupid of me! I forgot to ask the policeman something. I wonder if they found a light brown sack.'

'Why a light brown sack?' asked Angus, astonished.

'Because if it was any other coloured sack, the case must begin over again,' said Father Brown; 'but if it was a light brown sack, why, the case is finished.'

'I am pleased to hear it', said Angus with hearty irony. 'It hasn't begun, so far as I am concerned.'

'You must tell us all about it,' said Flambeau with a strange heavy simplicity, like a child.

Unconsciously they were walking with quickening steps down the long sweep of road on the other side of the high crescent, Father Brown leading briskly, though in silence. At last he said with an almost touching vagueness, 'Well, I'm afraid you'll think it so prosy. We always begin at the abstract end of things, and you can't begin this story anywhere else.

'Have you ever noticed this—that people never answer what you say? They answer what you mean—or what they think you mean. Suppose one lady says to another in a country house, "Is anybody staying with you?" the lady doesn't answer "Yes; the butler, the three footmen, the parlourmaid, and so on," though the parlourmaid may be in the room, or the butler behind her chair. She says "There is *nobody* staying with us," meaning nobody of the sort you mean. But suppose a doctor inquiring into an epidemic asks, "Who is staying in the house?" then the lady will remember the butler, parlourmaid, and the rest. All language is used like that; you never get a question answered literally, even when you get it answered truly. When those four quite honest men said that no man had gone into the Mansions, they did not really mean that *no man* had gone into them. They meant no man whom they could suspect of being your man. A man did go into the house, and did come out of it, but they never noticed him.'

'An invisible man?' inquired Angus, raising his red eyebrows.

'A mentally invisible man,' said Father Brown.

A minute or two after he resumed in the same unassuming voice, like a man thinking his way. 'Of course you can't think of such a man, until you do think of him. That's where his clever-ness comes in. But I came to think of him through two or three little things in the tale Mr Angus told us. First, there was the fact that this Welkin went for long walks. And then there was the vast lot of stamp paper on the window. And then, most of all, there were the two things the young lady said—things that couldn't be true. Don't get annoyed,' he added hastily, noting a sudden movement of the Scotsman's head; 'she thought they were true all right, but they couldn't be true. A person *can't* be quite alone in a street a second before she receives a letter. She can't be quite alone in a street when she starts reading a letter just received. There must be somebody pretty near her; he must be mentally invisible.'

'Why must there be somebody near her?' asked Angus.

'Because,' said Father Brown, 'barring carrier-pigeons, somebody must have brought her the letter.'

'Do you really mean to say,' asked Flambeau, with energy, 'that Welkin carried his rival's letters to his lady?'

'Yes,' said the priest. 'Welkin carried his rival's letters to his lady. You see, he had to.'

'Oh, I can't stand much more of this,' exploded Flambeau. 'Who is this fellow? What does he look like? What is the usual get-up of a mentally invisible man?'

'He is dressed rather handsomely in red, blue and gold,' replied the priest promptly with precision, 'and in this striking, and even showy, costume he entered Himalaya Mansions under eight human eyes; he killed Smythe in cold blood, and came down into the street again carrying the dead body in his arms——'

'Reverend sir,' cried Angus, standing still, 'are you raving mad, or am I?'

'You are not mad,' said Brown, 'only a little unobservant. You have not noticed such a man as this, for example.'

He took three quick strides forward, and put his hand on the shoulder of an ordinary passing postman who had bustled by them unnoticed under the shade of the trees.

'Nobody ever notices postmen somehow,' he said thoughtfully; 'yet they have passions like other men, and even carry large bags where a small corpse can be stowed quite easily.'

The postman, instead of turning naturally, had ducked and tumbled against the garden fence. He was a lean fair-bearded man of very ordinary appearance, but as he turned an alarmed face over his shoulder, all three men were fixed with an almost fiendish squint.

Flambeau went back to his sabres, purple rugs and Persian cat, having many things to attend to. John Turnbull Angus went back to the lady at the shop, with whom that imprudent young man contrives to be extremely comfortable. But Father Brown walked those snow-covered hills under the stars for many hours with a murderer, and what they said to each other will never be known.

### AFTERWORD

Perhaps a tiny midget could be stowed in a postman's bag, but a small man? This has often been cited as an example of unbelievable aspects of Father Brown plots. 'Surely no postman ever at any time carried a bag large enough to conceal even a small man's body,' writes Gertrude M. White in *The Chesterton Review* (May 1984).

In a later issue of the same magazine (May 1985) Bernard Bell disagreed. 'In those far-off days, the postman delivered both letters and parcels in a large mail bag, and he became the model for drawings of Santa Claus and his bag of goodies. Even I dimly remember that, when I was young, I used a surplus mail bag as a sleeping bag on weekend hikes.'

Not knowing anything about the size of bags carried by postmen in Edwardian London, I must leave this question open. In any case, the tale is clearly a semi-fantasy with an eternal moral. Servants and tradespeople with whom we come in frequent contact should never be invisible.

# 6

# The Honour of Israel Gow*

A STORMY evening of olive and silver was closing in, as Father Brown, wrapped in a grey Scotch plaid, came to the end of a grey Scotch valley and beheld the strange castle of Glengyle. It stopped one end of the glen or hollow like a blind alley; and it looked like the end of the world. Rising in steep roofs and spires of seagreen slate in the manner of the old French-Scottish châteaux, it reminded an Englishman of the sinister steeple-hats of witches in fairy tales; and the pine woods that rocked round the green turrets looked, by comparison, as black as numberless flocks of ravens. This note of a dreamy, almost a sleepy devilry, was no mere fancy from the landscape. For there did rest on the place one of those clouds of pride and madness and mysterious sorrow which lie more heavily on the noble houses of Scotland than on any other of the children of men. For Scotland has a double dose of the poison called heredity; the sense of blood in the aristocrat, and the sense of doom in the Calvinist.

The priest had snatched a day from his business at Glasgow to meet his friend Flambeau, the amateur detective, who was at Glengyle Castle with another more formal officer investigating the life and death of the late Earl of Glengyle. That mysterious person was the last representative of a race whose valour, insanity, and violent cunning had made them terrible even among the sinister nobility of their nation in the sixteenth century. None were deeper in that labyrinthine ambition, in chamber within chamber of that palace of lies that was built up around Mary Queen of Scots.

---

* Why were diamonds, candles, snuff, and loose clockwork scattered about the castle of a dead Scottish earl, and why were golden halos and ornamental letters removed from the castle's religious pictures? Originally titled 'The Strange Justice', the story appeared in *Cassell's Magazine* (April 1911), with illustrations by Sidney Lucas.

The rhyme in the country-side attested the motive and the result of their machinations candidly:

'As green sap to the simmer trees
Is red gold to the Ogilvies.'

For many centuries there had never been a decent lord in Glengyle Castle; and with the Victorian era one would have thought that all eccentricities were exhausted. The last Glengyle, however, satisfied his tribal tradition by doing the only thing that was left for him to do; he disappeared. I do not mean that he went abroad; by all accounts he was still in the castle, if he was anywhere. But though his name was in the church register and the big red Peerage, nobody ever saw him under the sun.

If anyone saw him it was a solitary man-servant, something between a groom and a gardener. He was so deaf that the more business-like assumed him to be dumb; while the more penetrating declared him to be half-witted. A gaunt, red-haired labourer, with a dogged jaw and chin, but quite blank blue eyes, he went by the name of Israel Gow, and was the one silent servant on that deserted estate. But the energy with which he dug potatoes, and the regularity with which he disappeared into the kitchen gave people an impression that he was providing for the meals of a superior, and that the strange earl was still concealed in the castle. If society needed any further proof that he was there, the servant persistently asserted that he was not at home. One morning the provost and the minister (for the Glengyles were Presbyterian) were summoned to the castle. There they found that the gardener, groom and cook had added to his many professions that of an undertaker, and had nailed up his noble master in a coffin. With how much or how little further inquiry this odd fact was passed, did not as yet very plainly appear; for the thing had never been legally investigated till Flambeau had gone north two or three days before. By then the body of Lord Glengyle (if it was the body) had lain for some time in the little churchyard on the hill.

As Father Brown passed through the dim garden and came under the shadow of the château, the clouds were thick and the whole air damp and thundery. Against the last stripe of the green-gold sunset he saw a black human silhouette; a man in a chimney-pot hat,[1] with a big spade over his shoulder. The combination was queerly suggestive of a sexton; but when Brown remembered the deaf servant who dug potatoes, he thought it natural enough. He knew something of the Scotch peasant; he knew the respectability which might well feel it necessary to wear 'blacks' for an official inquiry; he knew also the economy that would not lose an hour's digging for that. Even the man's start and suspicious stare as the priest went by were consonant enough with the vigilance and jealousy of such a type.

The great door was opened by Flambeau himself, who had with him a lean man with iron-grey hair and papers in his hand: Inspector Craven from Scotland Yard. The entrance hall was mostly stripped and empty; but the pale, sneering faces of one or two of the wicked Ogilvies looked down out of black periwigs and blackening canvas.

Following them into an inner room, Father Brown found that the allies had been seated at a long oak table, of which their end was covered with scribbled papers, flanked with whisky and cigars. Through the whole of its remaining length it was occupied by detached objects arranged at intervals; objects about as inexplicable as any objects could be. One looked like a small heap of glittering broken glass. Another looked like a high heap of brown dust. A third appeared to be a plain stick of wood.

'You seem to have a sort of geological museum here,' he said, as he sat down, jerking his head briefly in the direction of the brown dust and the crystalline fragments.

'Not a geological museum,' replied Flambeau; 'say a psychological museum.'

'Oh, for the Lord's sake,' cried the police detective laughing, 'don't let's begin with such long words.'

'Don't you know what psychology means?' asked Flambeau with friendly surprise. 'Psychology means being off your chump.'[2]

'Still I hardly follow,' replied the official.

'Well,' said Flambeau, with decision, 'I mean that we've only found out one thing about Lord Glengyle. He was a maniac.'

---

1. A chimney-pot hat is a cylindrical black silk hat, or top hat.
2. 'Off your chump' means off your head, out of your senses.

The black silhouette of Gow with his top hat and spade passed the window, dimly outlined against the darkening sky. Father Brown stared passively at it and answered:

'I can understand there must have been something odd about the man, or he wouldn't have buried himself alive—nor been in such a hurry to bury himself dead. But what makes you think it was lunacy?'

'Well,' said Flambeau, 'you just listen to the list of things Mr Craven has found in the house.'

'We must get a candle,' said Craven, suddenly, 'A storm is getting up, and it's too dark to read.'

'Have you found any candles,' asked Brown smiling, 'among your oddities?'

Flambeau raised a grave face, and fixed his dark eyes on his friend.

'That is curious, too,' he said. 'Twenty-five candles, and not a trace of a candlestick.'

In the rapidly darkening room and rapidly rising wind, Brown went along the table to where a bundle of wax candles lay among the other scrappy exhibits. As he did so he bent accidentally over the heap of red-brown dust; and a sharp sneeze cracked the silence.

'Hullo!' he said, 'snuff!'

He took one of the candles, lit it carefully, came back and stuck it in the neck of the whisky bottle. The unrestful night air, blowing through the crazy window, waved the long flame like a banner. And on every side of the castle they could hear the miles and miles of black pine wood seething like a black sea around a rock.

'I will read the inventory,' began Craven gravely, picking up one of the papers, 'the inventory of what we found loose and unexplained in the castle. You are to understand that the place generally was dismantled and neglected; but one or two rooms had plainly been inhabited in a simple but not squalid style by somebody; somebody who was not the servant Gow. The list is as follows:

'First item. A very considerable hoard of precious stones, nearly all diamonds, and all of them loose, without any setting whatever. Of course, it is natural that the Ogilvies should have family jewels; but those are exactly the jewels that are almost always set in particular articles of ornament. The Ogilvies would seem to have kept theirs loose in their pockets, like coppers.

'Second item. Heaps and heaps of loose snuff, not kept in a horn, or even a pouch, but lying in heaps on the mantelpieces, on the sideboard, on the piano, anywhere. It looks as if the old gentleman would not take the trouble to look in a pocket or lift a lid.

'Third item. Here and there about the house curious little heaps of minute pieces of metal, some like steel springs and some in the form of microscopic wheels. As if they had gutted some mechanical toy.

'Fourth item. The wax candles, which have to be stuck in bottle necks because there is nothing else to stick them in. Now I wish you to note how very much queerer all this is than anything we anticipated. For the central riddle we are prepared; we have all seen at a glance that there was something wrong about the last earl. We have come here to find out whether he really lived here, whether he really died here, whether that red-haired scarecrow who did his burying had anything to do with his dying. But suppose the worst in all this, the most lurid or melodramatic solution you like. Suppose the servant really killed the master, or suppose the master isn't really dead, or suppose the master is dressed up as the servant, or suppose the servant is buried for the master; invent what Wilkie Collins' tragedy you like,[3] and you still have not explained a candle without a candlestick, or why an elderly gentleman of good family should habitually spill snuff on the piano. The core of the tale we could imagine; it is the fringes that are mysterious. By no stretch of fancy can the human mind connect together snuff and diamonds and wax and loose clockwork.'

'I think I see the connection,' said the priest. 'This Glengyle was mad against the French Revolution. He was an enthusiast for the *ancien régime*, and was trying to re-enact literally the family life of the last Bourbons. He had snuff because it was the eighteenth-century luxury; wax candles, because they were the eighteenth-

---

**3.** Wilkie Collins was the author of that classic murder mystery *The Moonstone*. Incidentally, Chesterton once drew a set of illustrations for *The Moonstone*, but they were never published. The original sketches are in the John B. Shaw collection of Chesterton, at the University of Notre Dame, in Notre Dame, Indiana.

century lighting; the mechanical bits of iron represent the lock-smith hobby of Louis XVI;[4] the diamonds are for the Diamond Necklace of Marie Antoinette.'

Both the other men were staring at him with round eyes. 'What a perfectly extraordinary notion!' cried Flambeau. 'Do you really think that is the truth?'

'I am perfectly sure it isn't,' answered Father Brown, 'only you said that nobody could connect snuff and diamonds and clock-work and candles. I give you that connection off-hand. The real truth, I am very sure, lies deeper.'

He paused a moment and listened to the wailing of the wind in the turrets. Then he said, 'The late Earl of Glengyle was a thief. He lived a second and darker life as a desperate house-breaker. He did not have any candlesticks because he only used these candles cut short in the little lantern he carried. The snuff he employed as the fiercest French criminals have used pepper: to fling it suddenly in dense masses in the face of a captor or pur-suer. But the final proof is in the curious coincidence of the dia-monds and the small steel wheels. Surely that makes everything plain to you? Diamonds and small steel wheels are the only two instruments with which you can cut out a pane of glass.'

The bough of a broken pine tree lashed heavily in the blast against the windowpane behind them, as if in parody of a burg-lar, but they did not turn round. Their eyes were fastened on Father Brown.

'Diamonds and small wheels,' repeated Craven ruminating. 'Is that all that makes you think it the true explanation?'

'I don't think it the true explanation,' replied the priest pla-cidly; 'but you said that nobody could connect the four things. The true tale, of course, is something much more humdrum. Glengyle had found, or thought he had found, precious stones on his estate. Somebody had bamboozled him with those loose bril-liants, saying they were found in the castle caverns. The little wheels are some diamond-cutting affair. He had to do the thing very roughly and in a small way, with the help of a few shepherds

---

4. Louis XVI was the dull-witted king of France from 1765 to 1793, and husband of Marie Antoinette. He was guillotined in 1793 for treason. Next to hunting, his principal pastime was making locks.

or rude fellows on these hills. Snuff is the one great luxury of such Scotch shepherds; it's the one thing with which you can bribe them. They didn't have candlesticks because they didn't want them; they held the candles in their hands when they explored the caves.'

'Is that all?' asked Flambeau after a long pause. 'Have we got to the dull truth at last?'

'Oh, no,' said Father Brown.

As the wind died in the most distant pine woods with a long hoot as of mockery Father Brown, with an utterly impassive face, went on:

'I only suggested that because you said one could not plausibly connect snuff with clockwork or candles with bright stones. Ten false philosophies will fit the universe; ten false theories will fit Glengyle Castle. But we want the real explanation of the castle and the universe.[5] But are there no other exhibits?'

Craven laughed, and Flambeau rose smiling to his feet and strolled down the long table.

'Items five, six, seven, etc.,' he said, 'are certainly more varied than instructive. A curious collection, not of lead pencils, but of the lead out of lead pencils. A senseless stick of bamboo, with the top rather splintered. It might be the instrument of the crime. Only, there isn't any crime. The only other things are a few old missals and little Catholic pictures, which the Ogilvies kept, I suppose, from the Middle Ages—their family pride being stronger than their Puritanism. We only put them in the museum because they seem curiously cut about and defaced.'

The heady tempest without drove a dreadful wrack of clouds across Glengyle and threw the long room into darkness as Father Brown picked up the little illuminated pages to examine them.

---

**5.** The history of science is filled with theories that fitted the universe extremely well until later evidence proved them false. As Father Brown says, science seeks the 'real explanation' about how the universe works. It is fashionable now to insist that 'real truth' or 'final truth' is a meaningless concept. Philosophers of science divide over whether the changing conjectures of science keep moving closer to ultimate truth (as I believe) or whether they are more like changing fashions in art that bear no relation to anything beyond human cultures.

He spoke before the drift of darkness had passed; but it was the voice of an utterly new man.

'Mr Craven,' said he, talking like a man ten years younger, 'you have got a legal warrant, haven't you, to go up and examine that grave? The sooner we do it the better, and get to the bottom of this horrible affair. If I were you I should start now.'

'Now,' repeated the astonished detective, 'and why now?'

'Because this is serious,' answered Brown; 'this is not spilt snuff or loose pebbles, that might be there for a hundred reasons. There is only one reason I know of for *this* being done; and the reason goes down to the roots of the world. These religious pictures are not just dirtied or torn or scrawled over, which might be done in idleness or bigotry, by children or by Protestants. These have been treated very carefully—and very queerly. In every place where the great ornamented name of God comes in the old illuminations it has been elaborately taken out. The only other thing that has been removed is the halo round the head of the Child Jesus. Therefore, I say, let us get our warrant and our spade and our hatchet, and go up and break open that coffin.'

'What *do* you mean?' demanded the London officer.

'I mean,' answered the little priest, and his voice seemed to rise slightly in the roar of the gale. 'I mean that the great devil of the universe may be sitting on the top tower of this castle at this moment, as big as a hundred elephants, and roaring like the Apocalypse. There is black magic somewhere at the bottom of this.'

'Black magic,'[6] repeated Flambeau in a low voice, for he was too enlightened a man not to know of such things; 'but what can these other things mean?'

'Oh, something damnable, I suppose,' replied Brown impatiently. 'How should I know? How can I guess all their mazes down below? Perhaps you can make a torture out of snuff and

---

**6.** Black magic. Flambeau and Father Brown, like all conservative Catholics, believe in the reality of black magic; that is, in paranormal phenomena of Satanic origin. In his autobiography (Chapter 4) Chesterton writes about his youthful experiences with a Ouija board that convinced him of such things. He acknowledges that the movements of the planchette may have been caused by some 'subconscious but still human force', but he does not rule out a paranormal force of evil origin.

bamboo. Perhaps lunatics lust after wax and steel filings. Perhaps there is a maddening drug made of lead pencils! Our shortest cut to the mystery is up the hill to the grave.'

His comrades hardly knew that they had obeyed and followed him till a blast of the night wind nearly flung them on their faces in the garden.[7] Nevertheless they had obeyed him like automata; for Craven found a hatchet in his hand, and the warrant in his pocket; Flambeau was carrying the heavy spade of the strange gardener; Father Brown was carrying the little gilt book from which had been torn the name of God.

The path up the hill to the churchyard was crooked but short; only under that stress of wind it seemed laborious and long. Far as the eye could see, farther and farther as they mounted the slope, were seas beyond seas of pines, now all aslope one way under the wind. And that universal gesture seemed as vain as it was vast, as vain as if that wind were whistling about some unpeopled and purposeless planet. Through all that infinite growth of grey-blue forests sang, shrill and high, that ancient sorrow that is in the heart of all heathen things.[8] One could fancy

---

7. Strong winds blow through much of Chesterton's fiction, like the great wind that opens and closes his novel *Manalive*, and like the winds that blow through so many of Ray Bradbury's fantasies. 'I happen to be so constituted', Chesterton once said (*The Resurrection of Rome*, Section V), 'that I can enjoy almost any weather, except what is called glorious weather.'

8. Chesterton frequently wrote about the sorrow at the heart of pagan mythologies, but nowhere more eloquently than in the last chapter of *Orthodoxy*:

The really interesting thing is this, that the pagan was (in the main) happier and happier as he approached the earth, but sadder and sadder as he approached the heavens. The gaiety of the best Paganism . . . is, indeed, an eternal gaiety never to be forgotten . . . But it is all a gaiety about the facts of life, not about its origin. To the pagan the small things are as sweet as the small brooks breaking out of the mountain; but the broad things are as bitter as the sea. When the pagan looks at the very core of the cosmos he is struck cold. Behind the gods, who are merely despotic, sit the fates, who are deadly . . . Giotto lived in a gloomier town than Euripides, but he lived in a gayer universe . . .

The vault above us is not deaf because the universe is an idiot; the silence is not the heartless silence of an endless and aimless world. Rather the silence around us is a small and pitiful stillness like the prompt stillness in a sick-room. We are perhaps permitted tragedy as a sort of merciful comedy: because the frantic energy of divine things would knock us down like a drunken farce. We can take our own tears more lightly than we could take the tremendous levities of the angels. So we sit perhaps in a starry chamber of silence, while the laughter of the heavens is too loud for us to hear.

that the voices from the under world of unfathomable foliage were cries of the lost and wandering pagan gods: gods who had gone roaming in that irrational forest, and who will never find their way back to heaven.

'You see,' said Father Brown in low but easy tone, 'Scotch people before Scotland existed were a curious lot. In fact, they're a curious lot still. But in the prehistoric times I fancy they really worshipped demons. That,' he added genially, 'is why they jumped at the Puritan theology.'[9]

'My friend,' said Flambeau, turning in a kind of fury, 'what does all that snuff mean?'

'My friend,' replied Brown, with equal seriousness, 'there is one mark of all genuine religions: materialism. Now, devil-worship is a perfectly genuine religion.'

They had come up on the grassy scalp of the hill, one of the few bald spots that stood clear of the crashing and roaring pine forest. A mean enclosure, partly timber and partly wire, rattled in the tempest to tell them the border of the graveyard. But by the time Inspector Craven had come to the corner of the grave, and Flambeau had planted his spade point downwards and leaned on it, they were both almost as shaken as the shaky wood and wire. At the foot of the grave grew great tall thistles, grey and silver in their decay. Once or twice, when a ball of thistledown broke under the breeze and flew past him, Craven jumped slightly as if it had been an arrow.

Flambeau drove the blade of his spade through the whistling grass into the wet clay below. Then he seemed to stop and lean on it as on a staff.

'Go on,' said the priest very gently. 'We are only trying to find the truth. What are you afraid of?'

'I am afraid of finding it,' said Flambeau.

The London detective spoke suddenly in a high crowing voice that was meant to be conversational and cheery. 'I wonder why he really did hide himself like that. Something nasty, I suppose; was he a leper?'

---

9. The Puritan theological movement in England was dominated by Calvinism, which Chesterton, like Father Brown, considered evil. See Chapter 9, Note 11.

'Something worse than that,' said Flambeau.

'And what do you imagine,' asked the other, 'would be worse than a leper?'

'I don't imagine it,' said Flambeau.

He dug for some dreadful minutes in silence, and then said in a choked voice, 'I'm afraid of his not being the right shape.'

'Nor was that piece of paper, you know,' said Father Brown quietly, 'and we survived even that piece of paper.'[10]

Flambeau dug on with a blind energy. But the tempest had shouldered away the choking grey clouds that clung to the hills like smoke and revealed grey fields of faint starlight before he cleared the shape of a rude timber coffin, and somehow tipped it up upon the turf. Craven stepped forward with his axe; a thistle-top touched him, and he flinched. Then he took a firmer stride, and hacked and wrenched with an energy like Flambeau's till the lid was torn off, and all that was there lay glimmering in the grey starlight.

'Bones,' said Craven; and then he added, 'but it is a man,' as if that were something unexpected.

'Is he,' asked Flambeau in a voice that went oddly up and down, 'is he all right?'

'Seems so,' said the officer huskily, bending over the obscure and decaying skeleton in the box. 'Wait a minute.'

A vast heave went over Flambeau's huge figure. 'And now I come to think of it,' he cried, 'why in the name of madness shouldn't he be all right? What is it gets hold of a man on these cursed cold mountains? I think it's the black, brainless repetition; all these forests, and over all an ancient horror of unconsciousness. It's like the dream of an atheist. Pine-trees and more pine-trees and millions more pine-trees——'

'God!' cried the man by the coffin, 'but he hasn't got a head.'

While the others stood rigid the priest, for the first time, showed a leap of startled concern.

'No head!' he repeated. *'No head?'* as if he had almost expected some other deficiency.

Half-witted visions of a headless baby born to Glengyle, of a headless youth hiding himself in the castle, of a headless man

10. Father Brown is referring here to an earlier case that is recounted in the next chapter. See the opening note to Chapter 7.

pacing those ancient halls or that gorgeous garden, passed in panorama through their minds. But even in that stiffened instant the tale took no root in them and seemed to have no reason in it. They stood listening to the loud woods and the shrieking sky quite foolishly, like exhausted animals. Thought seemed to be something enormous that had suddenly slipped out of their grasp.

'There are three headless men,' said Father Brown, 'standing round this open grave.'

The pale detective from London opened his mouth to speak, and left it open like a yokel, while a long scream of wind tore the sky; then he looked at the axe in his hands as if it did not belong to him, and dropped it.

'Father,' said Flambeau in that infantile and heavy voice he used very seldom, 'what are we to do?'

His friend's reply came with the pent promptitude of a gun going off.

'Sleep!' cried Father Brown. 'Sleep. We have come to the end of the ways. Do you know what sleep is? Do you know that every man who sleeps believes in God?[11] It is a sacrament; for it is an act of faith and it is a food. And we need a sacrament, if only a natural one. Something has fallen on us that falls very seldom on men; perhaps the worst thing that can fall on them.'

Craven's parted lips came together to say, 'What do you mean?'

The priest had turned his face to the castle as he answered:

'We have found the truth; and the truth makes no sense.'[12]

---

11. Father Brown's dubious point is that everyone who goes to sleep believes he will wake up in the morning. The priest sees this as an act of faith in the uniformity of nature, hence in a deity responsible for that uniformity.

12. Father Brown's remark is quoted by Felix Browder in his stimulating essay 'Does Pure Mathematics Have a Relation to the Sciences?' (*American Scientist*, Volume 64, 1976, pages 542–9). Although pure mathematics always makes sense, Browder writes, its applications to the real world sometimes do not. This is especially true of quantum mechanics, the structure of which is more purely mathematical than that of any other theory. Yet its paradoxes are much more counterintuitive than the milder paradoxes of relativity theory. It was for just such a reason that Einstein, Schrödinger, and other architects of quantum mechanics were repelled by the very theory they helped establish. [*cont. opposite*]

He went down the path in front of them with a plunging and reckless step very rare with him, and when they reached the castle again he threw himself upon sleep with the simplicity of a dog.

Despite his mystic praise of slumber, Father Brown was up earlier than anyone else except the silent gardener; and was found smoking a big pipe and watching that expert at his speechless labours in the kitchen garden. Towards daybreak the rocking storm had ended in roaring rains, and the day came with a curious freshness. The gardener seemed even to have been conversing, but at sight of the detectives he planted his spade sullenly in a bed and, saying something about his breakfast, shifted along the lines of cabbages and shut himself in the kitchen. 'He's a valuable man, that,' said Father Brown. 'He does the potatoes amazingly. Still,' he added, with a dispassionate charity, 'he has his faults; which of us hasn't? He doesn't dig this bank quite regularly. There, for instance,' and he stamped suddenly on one spot. 'I'm really very doubtful about that potato.'

'And why?' asked Craven, amused with the little man's new hobby.

'I'm doubtful about it,' said the other 'because old Gow was doubtful about it himself. He put his spade in methodically in every place but just this. There must be a mighty fine potato just here.'

Flambeau pulled up the spade and impetuously drove it into the place. He turned up, under a load of soil, something that did not look like a potato, but rather like a monstrous, over-domed mushroom. But it struck the spade with a cold click; it rolled over like a ball, and grinned up at them.

'The Earl of Glengyle,' said Brown sadly, and looked down heavily at the skull.

Then, after a momentary meditation, he plucked the spade from Flambeau, and, saying 'We must hide it again,' clamped the skull down in the earth. Then he leaned his little body and

---

Einstein and two of his younger friends, Boris Podolsky and Nathan Rosen, devised a famous paradox (known as the EPR paradox after the alphabetized initials of their last names) which Einstein believed proved that quantum mechanics is seriously flawed. Were he alive today to study recent laboratory confirmations of his paradox, he might well exclaim with Father Brown, 'We have found the truth; and the truth makes no sense.'

huge head on the great handle of the spade, that stood up stiffly in the earth, and his eyes were empty and his forehead full of wrinkles. 'If one could only conceive,' he muttered, 'the meaning of this last monstrosity.' And leaning on the large spade handle, he buried his brows in his hands, as men do in church.

All the corners of the sky were brightening into blue and silver; the birds were chattering in the tiny garden trees; so loud it seemed as if the trees themselves were talking. But the three men were silent enough.

'Well, I give it all up,' said Flambeau at last boisterously. 'My brain and this world don't fit each other; and there's an end of it. Snuff, spoilt Prayer Books, and the insides of musical boxes—what——'

Brown threw up his bothered brow and rapped on the spade handle with an intolerance quite unusual with him. 'Oh, tut, tut, tut, tut!' he cried. 'All that is as plain as a pikestaff. I understood the snuff and clockwork, and so on, when I first opened my eyes this morning. And since then I've had it out with old Gow, the gardener, who is neither so deaf nor so stupid as he pretends. There's nothing amiss about the loose items. I was wrong about the torn mass-book, too; there's no harm in that. But it's this last business. Desecrating graves and stealing dead men's heads—surely there's harm in that? Surely there's black magic still in that? That doesn't fit in to the quite simple story of the snuff and the candles.' And, striding about again, he smoked moodily.

'My friend,' said Flambeau, with a grim humour, 'you must be careful with me and remember I was once a criminal. The great advantage of that estate was that I always made up the story myself, and acted it as quick as I chose. This detective business of waiting about is too much for my French impatience. All my life, for good or evil, I have done things at the instant; I always fought duels the next morning; I always paid bills on the nail;[13] I never even put off a visit to the dentist——'

Father Brown's pipe fell out of his mouth and broke into three pieces on the gravel path. He stood rolling his eyes, the exact picture of an idiot. 'Lord, what a turnip I am!' he kept saying.

---

**13.** 'On the nail' is an old British expression, used most often with reference to the prompt payment of a debt. It means, as the *OED* has it, 'on the spot, at once, without the least delay'. The origin of the phrase is obscure.

'Lord, what a turnip!' Then, in a somewhat groggy kind of way, he began to laugh.

'The dentist!' he repeated. 'Six hours in the spiritual abyss, and all because I never thought of the dentist! Such a simple, such a beautiful and peaceful thought! Friends, we have passed a night in hell; but now the sun is risen, the birds are singing, and the radiant form of the dentist consoles the world.'

'I will get some sense out of this,' cried Flambeau, striding forward, 'if I use the tortures of the Inquisition.'

Father Brown repressed what appeared to be a momentary disposition to dance on the now sunlit lawn and cried quite piteously, like a child, 'Oh, let me be silly a little. You don't know how unhappy I have been. And now I know that there has been no deep sin in this business at all. Only a little lunacy, perhaps—and who minds that?'

He spun round once, then faced them with gravity.

'This is not a story of crime,' he said; 'rather it is the story of a strange and crooked honesty. We are dealing with the one man on earth, perhaps, who has taken no more than his due. It is a study in the savage living logic that has been the religion of this race.

'That old local rhyme about the house of Glengyle—

> "As green sap to the simmer trees
> Is red gold to the Ogilvies"—

was literal as well as metaphorical. It did not merely mean that the Glengyles sought for wealth; it was also true that they literally gathered gold; they had a huge collection of ornaments and utensils in that metal. They were, in fact, misers whose mania took that turn. In the light of that fact, run through all the things we found in the castle. Diamonds without their gold rings; candles without their gold candlesticks; snuff without the gold snuff-boxes; pencil-leads without the gold pencil-cases; a walking stick without its gold top; clockwork without the gold clocks—or rather watches. And, mad as it sounds, because the halos and the name of God in the old missals were of real gold; these also were taken away.'

The garden seemed to brighten, the grass to grow gayer in the strengthening sun, as the crazy truth was told. Flambeau lit a cigarette as his friend went on.

'Were taken away,' continued Father Brown; 'were taken away—but not stolen. Thieves would never have left this mystery. Thieves would have taken the gold snuff-boxes, snuff and all; the gold pencil-cases, lead and all. We have to deal with a man with a peculiar conscience, but certainly a conscience. I found that mad moralist this morning in the kitchen garden yonder, and I heard the whole story.

'The late Archibald Ogilvie was the nearest approach to a good man ever born at Glengyle. But his bitter virtue took the turn of the misanthrope; he moped over the dishonesty of his ancestors, from which, somehow, he generalised a dishonesty of all men. More especially he distrusted philanthropy or free-giving;[14] and he swore if he could find one man who took his exact rights he should have all the gold of Glengyle. Having delivered this defiance to humanity he shut himself up, without the smallest expectation of its being answered. One day, however, a deaf and seemingly senseless lad from a distant village brought him a belated telegram; and Glengyle, in his acrid pleasantry, gave him a new farthing. At least he thought he had done so, but when he turned over his change he found the new farthing still there and a sovereign gone. The accident offered him vistas of sneering speculation. Either way, the boy would show the greasy greed of the species. Either he would vanish, a thief stealing a coin; or he would sneak back with it virtuously, a snob seeking a reward. In the middle of that night Lord Glengyle was knocked up[15] out of his bed—for he lived alone—and forced to open the door to the deaf idiot. The idiot brought with him, not the sovereign, but exactly nineteen shillings and elevenpence three-farthings in change.

'Then the wild exactitude of this action took hold on the mad lord's brain like fire. He swore he was Diogenes, that had long sought an honest man, and at last had found one. He made a new

---

**14.** After the words 'free-giving', in the story's magazine version, Chesterton added 'regarding it as a cover for free-taking'.

**15.** 'Knocked up' is a common British expression for being awakened, as if someone had knocked loudly on a bedroom door. 'Very sorry to knock you up, Watson,' says Holmes when he awakens Watson in 'The Adventures of the Speckled Band', 'but it's the common lot this morning. Mrs Hudson has been knocked up, she retorted upon me, and I on you.'

will, which I have seen.[16] He took the literal youth into his huge, neglected house, and trained him up as his solitary servant and—after an odd manner—his heir. And whatever that queer creature understands, he understood absolutely his lord's two fixed ideas: first, that the letter of right is everything; and second, that he himself was to have the gold of Glengyle. So far, that is all; and that is simple. He has stripped the house of gold, and taken not a grain that was not gold; not so much as a grain of snuff. He lifted the gold leaf off an old illumination, fully satisfied that he left the rest unspoilt. All that I understood; but I could not understand this skull business. I was really uneasy about that human head buried among the potatoes. It distressed me—till Flambeau said the word.

'It will be all right. He will put the skull back in the grave, when he has taken the gold out of the tooth.'

And, indeed, when Flambeau crossed the hill that morning, he saw that strange being, the just miser, digging at the desecrated grave, the plaid round his throat thrashing out in the mountain wind; the sober top hat on his head.

---

**16.** The fact that Father Brown saw the Earl's will, but the reader did not, is one of those annoying flaws so common in detective stories. Sherlock Holmes had a similar habit of occasionally withholding information from Watson, and therefore from the reader, which would make guessing the solution of a mystery much easier.

# 7

# The Wrong Shape*

CERTAIN of the great roads going north out of London continue far into the country a sort of attenuated and interrupted spectre of a street, with great gaps in the building, but preserving the line. Here will be a group of shops, followed by a fenced field or paddock, and then a famous public-house, and then perhaps a market garden or a nursery garden, and then one large private house, and then another field and another inn, and so on. If anyone walks along one of these roads he will pass a house which will probably catch his eye, though he may not be able to explain its attraction. It is a long, low house, running parallel with the road, painted mostly white and pale green, with a veranda and sun-blinds, and porches capped with those quaint sort of cupolas like wooden umbrellas that one sees in some old-fashioned houses. In fact, it is an old-fashioned house, very English and very suburban in the good old wealthy Clapham sense.[1] And yet

---

* A poet's suicide note strikes Father Brown as having a wrong shape, like the dagger that killed him. It is a clue that helps the priest solve the mystery of the man's death. The story was first published in the *Storyteller* ( January 1911).

'The Wrong Shape' was the fifth Father Brown story to see print, but in all editions of *The Innocence of Father Brown* it is the seventh chapter. This explains why Flambeau is mentioned only as a friend of the priest, not a detective. It also explains Father Brown's reference in the previous story to 'that piece of paper' with the wrong shape. (See Chapter 6, Note 10.)

1. In the sixth chapter of his autobiography Chesterton recalls a youthful occasion on which he had written an article for the *Daily News* that contained the sentence, 'Clapham, like every other city, is built on a volcano.' An editor, who lived in Clapham (a residential suburb in south-west London), took this to be a taunt, and changed the town to Kensington, where G.K. then lived.

'But I was glorifying Clapham!' Chesterton said the next day to the editor. 'I was showing it as epical and elemental and founded in the holy flame.' The editor's 'horrid secret', G.K. continues, was not that he was proud of Clapham, but that he was ashamed of Clapham. 'There was

the house has a look of having been built chiefly for the hot weather. Looking at its white paint and sun-blinds one thinks vaguely of pugarees[2] and even of palm trees. I cannot trace the feeling to its root; perhaps the place was built by an Anglo-Indian.

Anyone passing this house, I say, would be namelessly fascinated by it; would feel that it was a place about which some story was to be told. And he would have been right, as you shall shortly hear. For this is the story—the story of the strange things that did really happen in it in the Whitsuntide[3] of the year 18—:

Anyone passing the house on the Thursday before Whit-Sunday at about half-past four p.m. would have seen the front door open, and Father Brown, of the small church of St. Mungo,[4] come out smoking a large pipe in company with a very tall French friend of his called Flambeau, who was smoking a very small cigarette. These persons may or may not be of interest to the reader, but the truth is that they were not the only interesting

---

utterly veiled from his sight the visionary Clapham, the volcanic Clapham, what I may be allowed to put upon the cosmic map as Thunderclapham.'

For several pages Chesterton enlarges on what he considers the central motive of his writing—to arouse in people a sense of the 'wonder and splendour of being alive' in cities as mean as Clapham. The suburbs of London were all mean cities, in Chesterton's eyes, but he wanted their inhabitants to see their home towns in a mystical light.

What was called my medievalism was simply that I was very much interested in the historic meaning of Clapham Common. What was called my dislike of Imperialism was a dislike of making England an Empire, in the sense of something more like Clapham Junction. For my own visionary Clapham consisted of houses standing still; and not of trucks and trains rattling by . . .

**2.** Pugarees are the light scarves of silk or muslin that East Indians wrap around their sun helmets or hats, allowing the cloth to hang down in the back to shade their necks.

**3.** Whitsuntide is the week (especially its first three days) that begins with Whit Sunday, or White Sunday, the seventh Sunday after Easter. It commemorates the New Testament's day of Pentecost on which the Holy Spirit descended on leaders of the first church. The name derives from the white clothing traditionally worn by candidates for baptism during this period.

**4.** St. Mungo is presumably Father Brown's church in Cobhole. St. Mungo, also known as St. Kentigern, was a sixth-century bishop who founded the See Glasgow. In Scotland his festival is celebrated on 13 January, and his remains are said to be in the crypt of the St. Mungo Cathedral in Glasgow. Mungo, the name given to him, means 'amiable' in Gaelic.

things that were displayed when the front door of the white-and-green house was opened. There are further peculiarities about this house, which must be described to start with, not only that the reader may understand this tragic tale, but also that he may realise what it was that the opening of the door revealed.

The whole house was built upon the plan of a T, but a T with a very long cross piece and a very short tail piece. The long cross piece was the frontage that ran along in face of the street, with the front door in the middle; it was two stories high, and contained nearly all the important rooms. The short tail piece, which ran out at the back immediately opposite the front door, was one story high, and consisted only of two long rooms, the one leading into the other. The first of these two rooms was the study in which the celebrated Mr Quinton wrote his wild Oriental poems and romances. The farther room was a glass conservatory full of tropical blossoms of quite unique and almost monstrous beauty, and on such afternoons as these glowing with gorgeous sunlight. Thus when the hall door was open, many a passer-by literally stopped to stare and gasp; for he looked down a perspective of rich apartments to something really like a transformation scene in a fairy play: purple clouds and golden suns and crimson stars that were at once scorchingly vivid and yet transparent and far away.

Leonard Quinton, the poet, had himself most carefully arranged this effect; and it is doubtful whether he so perfectly expressed his personality in any of his poems. For he was a man who drank and bathed in colours, who indulged his lust for colour somewhat to the neglect of form—even of good form. This it was that had turned his genius so wholly to Eastern art and imagery; to those bewildering carpets or blinding embroideries in which all the colours seem fallen into a fortunate chaos, having nothing to typify or to teach. He had attempted, not perhaps with complete artistic success, but with acknowledged imagination and invention, to compose epics and love stories reflecting the riot of violent and even cruel colour; tales of tropical heavens of burning gold or blood-red copper; of Eastern heroes who rode with twelve-turbaned mitres upon elephants painted purple or peacock green; of gigantic jewels that a hundred negroes could not carry, but which burned with ancient and strange-hued fires.

In short (to put the matter from the more common point of

view), he dealt much in Eastern heavens, rather worse than most Western hells; in Eastern monarchs, whom we might possibly call maniacs; and in Eastern jewels which a Bond Street[5] jeweller (if the hundred staggering negroes brought them into his shop) might possibly not regard as genuine. Quinton was a genius, if a morbid one; and even his morbidity appeared more in his life than in his work. In temperament he was weak and waspish, and his health had suffered heavily from Oriental experiments with opium. His wife—a handsome, hard-working, and, indeed, over-worked woman—objected to the opium, but objected much more to a live Indian hermit in white and yellow robes, whom her husband insisted on entertaining for months together, a Virgil to guide his spirit through the heavens and the hells of the East.

It was out of this artistic household that Father Brown and his friend stepped on to the doorstep; and to judge from their faces, they stepped out of it with much relief. Flambeau had known Quinton in wild student days in Paris, and they had renewed the acquaintance for a week-end; but apart from Flambeau's more responsible developments of late, he did not get on well with the poet now. Choking oneself with opium and writing little erotic verses on vellum was not his notion of how a gentleman should go to the devil. As the two paused on the doorstep, before taking a turn in the garden, the front garden gate was thrown open with violence, and a young man with a billycock[6] hat on the back of his head tumbled up the steps in his eagerness. He was a dissipated-looking youth with a gorgeous red necktie all awry, as if he had slept in it, and he kept fidgeting and lashing about with one of those little jointed canes.

'I say,' he said breathlessly, 'I want to see old Quinton. I must see him. Has he gone?'

'Mr Quinton is in, I believe,' said Father Brown, cleaning his pipe, 'but I do not know if you can see him. The doctor is with him at present.'

---

5. London's Bond Street is noted for its elegant shops and fine art galleries, and for such famous residents as James Boswell and Laurence Sterne.

6. A billycock hat was a round, stiff, low-crowned felt hat worn mainly by men, but sometimes by women. It is an old 'battered billycock' that Sherlock Holmes analyses in a famous scene that opens 'The Adventures of the Blue Carbuncle'.

The young man, who seemed not to be perfectly sober, stumbled into the hall; and at the same moment the doctor came out of Quinton's study, shutting the door and beginning to put on his gloves.

'See Mr Quinton?' said the doctor coolly. 'No, I'm afraid you can't. In fact, you mustn't on any account. Nobody must see him; I've just given him his sleeping draught.'

'No, but look here, old chap,' said the youth in the red tie, trying affectionately to capture the doctor by the lapels of his coat. 'Look here. I'm simply sewn up,[7] I tell you. I——'

'It's no good, Mr Atkinson,' said the doctor, forcing him to fall back; 'when you can alter the effects of a drug I'll alter my decision,' and, settling on his hat, he stepped out into the sunlight with the other two. He was a bull-necked, good-tempered little man with a small moustache, inexpressibly ordinary, yet giving an impression of capability.

The young man in the billycock, who did not seem to be gifted with any tact in dealing with people beyond the general idea of clutching hold of their coats, stood outside the door, as dazed as if he had been thrown out bodily, and silently watched the other three walk away together through the garden.

'That was a sound, spanking lie I told just now,' remarked the medical man, laughing. 'In point of fact, poor Quinton doesn't have his sleeping draught for nearly half an hour. But I'm not going to have him bothered with that little beast, who only wants to borrow money that he wouldn't pay back if he could. He's a dirty little scamp, though he is Mrs Quinton's brother, and she's as fine a woman as ever walked.'

'Yes,' said Father Brown. 'She's a good woman.'

'So I propose to hang about the garden till the creature has cleared off,' went on the doctor, 'and then I'll go in to Quinton with the medicine. Atkinson can't get in, because I locked the door.'

'In that case, Dr Harris,' said Flambeau, 'we might as well walk round at the back by the end of the conservatory. There's no entrance to it that way, but it's worth seeing, even from the outside.'

---

7. 'Sewn up' is a slang expression meaning worn out.

'Yes, and I might get a squint at my patient,' laughed the doctor, 'for he prefers to lie on an ottoman right at the end of the conservatory amid all those blood-red poinsettias; it would give me the creeps. But what are you doing?'

Father Brown had stopped for a moment, and picked up out of the long grass, where it had almost been wholly hidden, a queer, crooked Oriental knife, inlaid exquisitely in coloured stones and metals.

'What is this?' asked Father Brown, regarding it with some disfavour.

'Oh, Quinton's, I suppose,' said Dr Harris carelessly; 'he has all sorts of Chinese knick-knacks about the place. Or perhaps it belongs to that mild Hindoo of his whom he keeps on a string.'

'What Hindoo?' asked Father Brown, still staring at the dagger in his hand.

'Oh, some Indian conjurer,' said the doctor lightly; 'a fraud, of course.'

'You don't believe in magic?' asked Father Brown, without looking up.

'O crikey! magic!' said the doctor.

'It's very beautiful,' said the priest in a low, dreaming voice; 'the colours are very beautiful. But it's the wrong shape.'

'What for?' asked Flambeau, staring.

'For anything. It's the wrong shape in the abstract. Don't you ever feel that about Eastern art? The colours are intoxicatingly lovely; but the shapes are mean and bad—deliberately mean and bad. I have seen wicked things in a Turkey carpet.'[8]

'*Mon Dieu!*' cried Flambeau, laughing.

---

8. Quinton is one of Chesterton's many caricatures of the aesthete for whom beauty is the ultimate value. As a good Aristotelian and Thomist, Father Brown knows that beauty is not equivalent to truth or goodness. A work of art—be it a novel, painting, poem, or decorated instrument—can be beautiful in a formal way, and at the same time be false and wicked.

Chesterton, incidentally, was as fond of large knives as he was of swords. Father John O'Connor, in his book on Chesterton, reports that for almost a quarter of a century G.K. carried with him a knife that was $7\frac{1}{2}$ inches long when shut, 14 inches when open. Mrs Chesterton 'often retrieved it from under his pillow in foreign hotels, for fear of complications . . . He cut new books with it, but once, during a public debate in Dublin, he absent-mindedly drew it to sharpen a pencil, and the opposition speech was drowned in delighted laughter by the audience.'

'They are letters and symbols in a language I don't know; but I know they stand for evil words,' went on the priest, his voice growing lower and lower. 'The lines go wrong on purpose—like serpents doubling to escape.'

'What the devil are you talking about?' said the doctor with a loud laugh.

Flambeau spoke quietly to him in answer. 'The Father sometimes gets this mystic's cloud on him,' he said,: 'but I give you fair warning that I have never known him have it except when there was some evil quite near.'

'Oh, rats!' said the doctor.

'Why, look at it,' cried Father Brown, holding out the crooked knife at arms' length, as if it were some glittering snake. 'Don't you see it is the wrong shape? Don't you see that it has no hearty and plain purpose. It does not point like a spear. It does not sweep like a scythe. It does not *look* like a weapon. It looks like an instrument of torture.'

'Well, as you don't seem to like it,' said the jolly Harris, 'it had better be taken back to its owner. Haven't we come to the end of this confounded conservatory yet? This house is the wrong shape, if you like.'

'You don't understand,' said Father Brown, shaking his head. 'The shape of this house is quaint—it is even laughable. But there is nothing *wrong* about it.'

As they spoke they came round the curve of glass that ended the conservatory, an uninterrupted curve, for there was neither door nor window by which to enter at that end. The glass, however, was clear, and the sun still bright, though beginning to set; and they could see not only the flamboyant blossoms inside, but the frail figure of the poet in a brown velvet coat lying languidly on the sofa, having, apparently, fallen half asleep over a book. He was a pale, slight man, with loose, chestnut hair and a fringe of beard that was the paradox of his face, for the beard made him look less manly. These traits were well known to all three of them; but even had it not been so, it may be doubted whether they would have looked at Quinton just then. Their eyes were riveted on another object.

Exactly in their path, immediately outside the round end of the glass building, was standing a tall man, whose drapery fell to his feet in faultless white, and whose bare, brown skull, face, and neck gleamed in the setting sun like splendid bronze. He was looking through the glass at the sleeper, and he was more motionless than a moutain.

'Who is that?' cried Father Brown, stepping back with a hissing intake of his breath.

'Oh, it is only that Hindoo humbug,' growled Harris; 'but I don't know what the deuce he's doing here.'

'It looks like hypnotism,' said Flambeau, biting his black moustache.

'Why are you unmedical fellows always talking bosh about hypnotism?' cried the doctor. 'It looks a deal more like burglary.'

'Well, we will speak to it, at any rate,' said Flambeau, who was always for action. One long stride took him to the place where the Indian stood. Bowing from his great height, which overtopped even the Oriental's, he said with placid impudence:

'Good evening, sir. Do you want anything?'

Quite slowly, like a great ship turning into a harbour, the great yellow face turned, and looked at last over its white shoulder. They were startled to see that its yellow eyelids were quite sealed, as in sleep. 'Thank you,' said the face in excellent English. 'I want nothing.' Then, half opening the lids, so as to show a slit of opalescent eyeball, he repeated, 'I want nothing.' Then he opened his eyes wide with a startling stare, said, 'I want nothing,' and went rustling away into the rapidly darkening garden.

'The Christian is more modest,' muttered Father Brown; 'he wants something.'

'What on earth was he doing?' asked Flambeau, knitting his black brows and lowering his voice.

'I should like to talk to you later,' said Father Brown.

The sunlight was still a reality, but it was the red light of evening, and the bulk of the garden trees and bushes grew blacker and blacker against it. They turned round the end of the conservatory, and walked in silence down the other side to get round to the front door. As they went they seemed to wake something, as one startles a bird, in the deeper corner between the study and the main building; and again they saw the white-robed fakir slide out of the shadow, and slip round towards the front door. To their surprise, however, he had not been alone. They found themselves abruptly pulled up and forced to banish their bewilderment by the appearance of Mrs Quinton, with her heavy golden hair and square pale face, advancing on them out of the twilight. She looked a little stern, but was entirely courteous.

'Good evening, Dr Harris,' was all she said.

'Good evening, Mrs Quinton,' said the little doctor heartily. 'I am just going to give your husband his sleeping draught.'

'Yes,' she said in a clear voice. 'I think it is quite time.' And she smiled at them, and went sweeping into the house.

'That woman's over-driven,' said Father Brown; 'that's the kind of woman that does her duty for twenty years, and then does something dreadful.'

The little doctor looked at him for the first time with an eye of interest. 'Did you ever study medicine?' he asked.

'You have to know something of the mind as well as the body,' answered the priest; 'we have to know something of the body as well as the mind.'

'Well,' said the doctor, 'I think I'll go and give Quinton his stuff.'

They had turned the corner of the front façade, and were approaching the front doorway. As they turned into it they saw the man in the white robe for the third time. He came so straight towards the front door that it seemed quite incredible that he had not just come out of the study opposite to it. Yet they knew that the study door was locked.

Father Brown and Flambeau, however, kept this weird contradiction to themselves, and Dr Harris was not a man to waste his thoughts on the impossible. He permitted the omnipresent Asiatic to make his exit, and then stepped briskly into the hall. There he found a figure which he had already forgotten. The inane Atkinson was still hanging about, humming and poking things with his knobby cane. The doctor's face had a spasm of disgust and decision, and he whispered rapidly to his companion: 'I must lock the door again, or this rat will get in. But I shall be out again in two minutes.'

He rapidly unlocked the door and locked it again behind him, just balking a blundering charge from the young man in the billy-cock. The young man threw himself impatiently on a hall chair. Flambeau looked at a Persian illumination on the wall; Father Brown, who seemed in a sort of daze, dully eyed the door. In about four minutes the door was opened again. Atkinson was quicker this time. He sprang forward, held the door open for an instant, and called out: 'Oh, I say, Quinton, I want——'

From the other end of the study came the clear voice of Quinton, in something between a yawn and a yell of weary laughter.

'Oh, I know what you want. Take it, and leave me in peace. I'm writing a song about peacocks.'

Before the door closed half a sovereign came flying through the aperture; and Atkinson, stumbling forward, caught it with singular dexterity.

'So that's settled,' said the doctor, and, locking the door savagely, he led the way out into the garden.

'Poor Leonard can get a little peace now,' he added to Father Brown; 'he's locked in all by himself for an hour or two.'

'Yes,' answered the priest; 'and his voice sounded jolly enough when we left him.' Then he looked gravely round the garden, and saw the loose figure of Atkinson standing and jingling the half-sovereign in his pocket, and beyond, in the purple twilight, the figure of the Indian sitting bolt upright upon a bank of grass with his face turned towards the setting sun. Then he said abruptly: 'Where is Mrs Quinton?'

'She has gone up to her room,' said the doctor. 'That is her shadow on the blind.'

Father Brown looked up, and frowningly scrutinised a dark outline at the gas-lit window.

'Yes,' he said, 'that is her shadow,' and he walked a yard or two and threw himself upon a garden seat.

Flambeau sat down beside him; but the doctor was one of those energetic people who live naturally on their legs. He walked away, smoking, into the twilight, and the two friends were left together.

'My father,' said Flambeau in French, 'what is the matter with you?'

Father Brown was silent and motionless for half a minute, then he said: 'Superstition is irreligious, but there is something in the air of this place. I think it's that Indian—at least, partly.'

He sank into silence, and watched the distant outline of the Indian, who still sat rigid as if in prayer. At first sight he seemed motionless, but as Father Brown watched him he saw that the man swayed ever so slightly with a rhythmic movement, just as the dark tree-tops swayed ever so slightly in the little wind that was creeping up the dim garden paths and shuffling the fallen leaves a little.

The landscape was growing rapidly dark, as if for a storm, but they could still see all the figures in their various places. Atkinson was leaning against a tree with a listless face; Quinton's wife was still at her window; the doctor had gone strolling round the end of the conservatory; they could see his cigar like a will-o'-the-wisp; and the fakir still sat rigid and yet rocking, while the trees above him began to rock and almost to roar. Storm was certainly coming.

'When that Indian spoke to us,' went on Brown in a conversational undertone, 'I had a sort of vision, a vision of him and all his universe. Yet he only said the same thing three times. When first he said, "I want nothing," it meant only that he was impenetrable, that Asia does not give itself away. Then he said again, "I want nothing," and I knew that he meant that he was sufficient to himself, like a cosmos, that he needed no God, neither admitted any sins. And when he said the third time, "I want nothing," he said it with blazing eyes. And I knew that he meant literally what he said; that nothing was his desire and his home; that he was weary for nothing as for wine; that annihilation, the mere destruction of everything or anything——'

Two drops of rain fell; and for some reason Flambeau started and looked up, as if they had stung him. And the same instant the doctor down by the end of the conservatory began running towards them, calling out something as he ran.

As he came among them like a bombshell the restless Atkinson happened to be taking a turn nearer to the house front; and the doctor clutched him by the collar in a convulsive grip. 'Foul play!' he cried; 'what have you been doing to him, you dog?'

The priest had sprung erect, and had the voice of steel of a soldier in command.

'No fighting,' he cried coolly; 'we are enough to hold anyone we want to. What is the matter, doctor?'

'Things are not right with Quinton,' said the doctor, quite white. 'I could just see him through the glass, and I don't like the way he's lying. It's not as I left him, anyhow.'

'Let us go in to him,' said Father Brown shortly. 'You can leave Mr Atkinson alone. I have had him in sight since we heard Quinton's voice.'

'I will stop here and watch him,' said Flambeau hurriedly. 'You go in and see.'

The doctor and the priest flew to the study door, unlocked it, and fell into the room. In doing so they nearly fell over the large mahogany table in the centre at which the poet usually wrote; for the place was lit only by a small fire kept for the invalid. In the middle of this table lay a single sheet of paper, evidently left there on purpose. The doctor snatched it up, glanced at it, handed it to Father Brown, and crying, 'Good God, look at that!' plunged towards the glass room beyond, where the terrible tropic flowers still seemed to keep a crimson memory of the sunset.

Father Brown read the words three times before he put down the paper. The words were: 'I die by my own hand; yet I die murdered!' They were in the quite inimitable, not to say illegible, handwriting of Leonard Quinton.

Then Father Brown, still keeping the paper in his hand, strode towards the conservatory, only to meet his medical friend coming back with a face of assurance and collapse. 'He's done it,' said Harris.

They went together through the gorgeous unnatural beauty of cactus and azalea and found Leonard Quinton, poet and romancer, with his head hanging downward off his ottoman and his red curls sweeping the ground. Into his left side was thrust the queer dagger that they had picked up in the garden, and his limp hand still rested on the hilt.

Outside the storm had come at one stride, like the night in Coleridge,[9] and garden and glass roof were darkened with driving rain. Father Brown seemed to be studying the paper more than the corpse; he held it close to his eyes;[10] and seemed trying to

----

9. Chesterton had in mind those lines in *The Ancient Mariner* that speak of how abruptly night falls in the tropics:

> The sun's rim dips; the stars rush out;
> At one stride comes the dark.

10. Here and in later stories Father Brown is unable to read without holding the writing close to his face. There is no mention in the first four Father Brown books of the priest wearing glasses, although he obviously is extremely near-sighted. Chesterton may have supposed for a time that frequent blinking is a sign of near-sightedness, although it is much more characteristic (as he later realized) of near-sighted persons to squint when

read it in the twilight. Then he held it up against the faint light, and, as he did so, lightning stared at them for an instant so white that the paper looked black against it.

Darkness full of thunder followed, and after the thunder Father Brown's voice said out of the dark: 'Doctor, this paper is the wrong shape.'

'What do you mean?' asked Doctor Harris, with a frowning stare.

'It isn't square,' answered Brown. 'It has a sort of edge snipped off at the corner. What does it mean?'

'How the deuce should I know?' growled the doctor. 'Shall we move this poor chap, do you think? He's quite dead.'

'No,' answered the priest; 'we must leave him as he lies and send for the police.' But he was still scrutinising the paper.

As they went back through the study he stopped by the table and picked up a small pair of nail scissors. 'Ah,' he said, with a sort of relief, 'this is what he did it with. But yet——' And he knitted his brows.

'Oh, stop fooling with that scrap of paper,' said the doctor emphatically. 'It was a fad of his. He had hundreds of them. He cut all his paper like that,' as he pointed to a stack of sermon paper[11] still unused on another and smaller table. Father Brown

---

looking at distant scenes. In 'The Worst Crime in the World' (*The Secret of Father Brown*), the priest's eyes are called 'screwed, shortsighted', and there is a reference to his observing a woman through 'half-closed eyes'.

The Father Brown stories in the *Storyteller* were not illustrated, but those in *Cassell's Magazine* had fourteen pictures by Sidney Lucas, eight of which were reprinted in the first British edition. For some reason Lucas put glasses on the priest, and most of the dust jackets of Father Brown books, both in England and the US, gave the priest glasses. (The illustrations by Will F. Foster, in the first US edition, show the priest without glasses.) This is surprising because it is not until the fifth and last Father Brown book, in the story 'The Quick One', that Chesterton speaks of the priest's 'moonlike spectacles'. The glasses are mentioned in later stories in the same volume— 'owlish spectacles' they are called in 'The Point of a Pin'. Either Father Brown did not acquire spectacles until late in life, or Chesterton did not think to mention them until artists reminded him.

**11.** Sermon paper would have been writing paper of foolscap size; that is, 17 by $13\frac{1}{2}$ inches.

went up to it and held up a sheet. It was the same irregular shape.

'Quite so,' he said. 'And here I see the corners that were snipped off.' And to the indignation of his colleague he began to count them.

'That's all right,' he said, with an apologetic smile. 'Twenty-three sheets cut and twenty-two corners cut off them. And as I see you are impatient we will rejoin the others.'

'Who is to tell his wife?' asked Dr Harris. 'Will you go and tell her now, while I send a servant for the police?'

'As you will,' said Father Brown indifferently. And he went out to the hall door.

Here also he found a drama, though of a more grotesque sort. It showed nothing less than his big friend Flambeau in an attitude to which he had long been unaccustomed, while upon the pathway at the bottom of the steps was sprawling with his boots in the air the amiable Atkinson, his billycock hat and walking cane sent flying in opposite directions along the path. Atkinson had at length wearied of Flambeau's almost paternal custody, and had endeavoured to knock him down, which was by no means a smooth game to play with the Roi des Apaches,[12] even after that monarch's abdication.

Flambeau was about to leap upon his enemy and secure him once more, when the priest patted him easily on the shoulder.

'Make it up with Mr Atkinson, my friend,' he said. 'Beg a mutual pardon and say "Good night." We need not detain him any longer.' Then, as Atkinson rose somewhat doubtfully and gathered his hat and stick and went towards the garden gate, Father Brown said in a more serious voice: 'Where is that Indian?'

They all three (for the doctor had joined them) turned involuntarily towards the dim grassy bank amid the tossing trees purple with twilight, where they had last seen the brown man swaying in his strange prayers. The Indian was gone.

---

12. King of the Apaches. The title testifies to Flambeau's eminence in French crime before he 'abdicated'. The Apaches was a name given to Parisian ruffians on the assumption that American Apache Indians were unusually fierce and warlike.

'Confound him,' cried the doctor, stamping furiously. 'Now I know that it was that nigger that did it.'

'I thought you didn't believe in magic,' said Father Brown quietly.

'No more I did,' said the doctor, rolling his eyes. 'I only know that I loathed that yellow devil when I thought he was a sham wizard. And I shall loathe him more if I come to think he was a real one.'

'Well, his having escaped is nothing,' said Flambeau. 'For we could have proved nothing and done nothing against him. One hardly goes to the parish constable with a story of suicide imposed by witchcraft or auto-suggestion.'

Meanwhile Father Brown had made his way into the house, and now went to break the news to the wife of the dead man.

When he came out again he looked a little pale and tragic, but what passed between them in that interview was never known, even when all was known.

Flambeau, who was talking quietly with the doctor, was surprised to see his friend reappear so soon at his elbow; but Brown took no notice, and merely drew the doctor apart. 'You have sent for the police, haven't you?' he asked.

'Yes,' answered Harris. 'They ought to be here in ten minutes.'

'Will you do me a favour?' said the priest quietly. 'The truth is, I make a collection of these curious stories, which often contain, as in the case of our Hindoo friend, elements which can hardly be put into a police report. Now, I want you to write out a report of this case for my private use. Yours is a clever trade,' he said, looking the doctor gravely and steadily in the face. 'I sometimes think that you know some details of this matter which you have not thought fit to mention. Mine is a confidential trade like yours, and I will treat anything you write for me in strict confidence. But write the whole.'

The doctor, who had been listening thoughtfully with his head a little on one side, looked the priest in the face for an instant, and said: 'All right,' and went into the study, closing the door behind him.

'Flambeau,' said Father Brown, 'there is a long seat there under the veranda, where we can smoke out of the rain. You are my only friend in the world, and I want to talk to you.[13] Or, perhaps, be silent with you.'

They established themselves comfortably in the veranda seat; Father Brown, against his common habit, accepted a good cigar and smoked it steadily in silence, while the rain shrieked and rattled on the roof of the veranda.

'My friend,' he said at length, 'this is a very queer case. A very queer case.'

'I should think it was,' said Flambeau, with something like a shudder.

'You call it queer, and I call it queer,' said the other, 'and yet we mean quite opposite things. The modern mind always mixes up two different ideas: mystery in the sense of what is marvellous, and mystery in the sense of what is complicated. That is half its difficulty about miracles. A miracle is startling; but it is simple. It is simple because it *is* a miracle. It is power coming directly from God (or the devil) instead of indirectly through nature or human wills. Now, you mean that this business is marvellous because it is miraculous, because it is witchcraft worked by a wicked Indian. Understand, I do not say that it was not spiritual or diabolic. Heaven and hell only know by what surrounding influences strange sins come into the lives of men. But for the present my point is this: If it was pure magic, as you think, then it is marvellous; but it is not mysterious—that is, it is not complicated. The quality of a miracle is mysterious, but its manner is simple. Now, the manner of this business has been the reverse of simple.'

The storm that had slackened for a little seemed to be swelling again, and there came heavy movements as of faint thunder. Father Brown let fall the ash of his cigar and went on:

'There has been in this incident,' he said, 'a twisted, ugly, complex quality that does not belong to the straight bolts either

---

13. Note the priest's resemblance to Sherlock Holmes, whose only good friend was John Watson. Father Brown speaks of wanting to be silent with his friend. 'For two hours we rambled about together in silence for the most part, as befits two men who know each other intimately,' writes Watson, describing a walk with Holmes through Hyde Park at the beginning of 'The Yellow Face'.

of heaven or hell. As one knows the crooked track of a snail, I know the crooked track of a man.'

The white lightning opened its enormous eye in one wink, the sky shut up again, and the priest went on:

'Of all these crooked things, the crookedest was the shape of that piece of paper. It was crookeder than the dagger that killed him.'

'You mean the paper on which Quinton confessed his suicide,' said Flambeau.

'I mean the paper on which Quinton wrote, "I die by my own hand," ' answered Father Brown. 'The shape of that paper, my friend, was the wrong shape; the wrong shape, if ever I have seen it in this wicked world.'

'It only had a corner snipped off,' said Flambeau, 'and I understand that all Quinton's paper was cut that way.'

'It was a very odd way,' said the other, 'and a very bad way, to my taste and fancy. Look here, Flambeau, this Quinton—God receive his soul!—was perhaps a bit of a cur in some ways, but he really was an artist, with the pencil as well as the pen. His handwriting, though hard to read, was bold and beautiful. I can't prove what I say; I can't prove anything. But I tell you with the full force of conviction that he could never have cut that mean little piece off a sheet of paper. If he had wanted to cut down paper for some purpose of fitting in, or binding up, or what not, he would have made quite a different slash with the scissors. Do you remember the shape? It was a mean shape. It was a wrong shape. Like this. Don't you remember?'

And he waved his burning cigar before him in the darkness,[14] making irregular squares so rapidly that Flambeau really seemed to see them as fiery hieroglyphics upon the darkness—hieroglyphics such as his friend had spoken of, which are undecipherable, yet can have no good meaning.

'But,' said Flambeau, as the priest put his cigar in his mouth again and leaned back, staring at the roof. 'Suppose somebody else did use the scissors. Why should somebody else, cutting pieces off his sermon paper, make Quinton commit suicide?'

---

14. Chesterton liked to wave the burning end of his cigar in night air to trace a fiery symbol of the cross.

Father Brown was still leaning back and staring at the roof, but he took his cigar out of his mouth and said: 'Quinton never did commit suicide.'

Flambeau stared at him. 'Why, confound it all,' he cried, 'then why did he confess to suicide?'

The priest leaned forward again, settled his elbows on his knees, looked at the ground, and said, in a low, distinct voice: 'He never did confess to suicide.'

Flambeau laid his cigar down. 'You mean,' he said, 'that the writing was forged?'

'No,' said Father Brown. 'Quinton wrote it all right.'

'Well, there you are,' said the aggravated Flambeau; 'Quinton wrote, "I die by my own hand," with his own hand on a plain piece of paper.'

'Of the wrong shape,' said the priest calmly.

'Oh, the shape be damned!' cried Flambeau. 'What has the shape to do with it?'

'There were twenty-three snipped papers,' resumed Brown unmoved, 'and only twenty-two pieces snipped off. Therefore one of the pieces had been destroyed, probably that from the written paper. Does that suggest anything to you?'

A light dawned on Flambeau's face, and he said: 'There was something else written by Quinton, some other words. "They will tell you I die by my own hand," or "Do not believe that——" '

'Hotter, as the children say,' said his friend. 'But the piece was hardly half an inch across; there was no room for one word, let alone five. Can you think of anything hardly bigger than a comma which the man with hell in his heart had to tear away as a testimony against him?'

'I can think of nothing,' said Flambeau at last.

'What about quotation marks?' said the priest, and flung his cigar far into the darkness like a shooting star.

All words had left the other man's mouth, and Father Brown said, like one going back to fundamentals:

'Leonard Quinton was a romancer, and was writing an Oriental romance about wizardry and hypnotism. He——'

At this moment the door opened briskly behind them, and the doctor came out with his hat on. He put a long envelope into the priest's hands.

155

'That's the document you wanted,' he said, 'and I must be getting home. Good night.'

'Good night,' said Father Brown, as the doctor walked briskly to the gate. He had left the front door open, so that a shaft of gaslight fell upon them. In the light of this Brown opened the envelope and read the following words:

'DEAR FATHER BROWN,—*Vicisti Galilæe.*[15] Otherwise, damn your eyes, which are very penetrating ones. Can it be possible that there is something in all that stuff of yours after all?

'I am a man who has ever since boyhood believed in Nature and in all natural functions and instincts, whether men called them moral or immoral. Long before I became a doctor, when I was a schoolboy keeping mice and spiders, I believed that to be a good animal is the best thing in the world. But just now I am shaken; I have believed in Nature; but it seems as if Nature could betray a man. Can there be anything in your bosh? I am really getting morbid.

'I loved Quinton's wife. What was there wrong in that? Nature told me to, and it's love that makes the world go round. I also thought quite sincerely that she would be happier with a clean animal like me than with that tormenting little lunatic. What was there wrong in that? I was only facing facts, like a man of science. She would have been happier.

'According to my own creed I was quite free to kill Quinton,

---

15. *Vicisti Galilæe* is usually written with a comma between the two words. The Latin translates as 'Thou hast conquered, Galilean!' Theodoretus, a fifth-century Greek father of the Church, attributed the remark to the pagan emperor Julian the Apostate when he was dying of wounds in a battle with the Persians. Julian was the last Roman emperor who tried to revive the vanishing polytheism of the empire's Greek heritage.

Algernon Charles Swinburne put the phrase as a motto above his 'Hymn to Proserpine', a poem about the victory of Christianity over paganism. (Proserpine, daughter of Zeus and Demeter, was the wife of Pluto, making her the Queen of Hades.) Chesterton often quoted Swinburne's lilting line: 'Thou hast conquered, O pale Galilean; the world has grown grey from thy breath.'

which was the best thing for everybody, even himself.[16] But as a healthy animal I had no notion of killing myself. I resolved, therefore, that I would never do it until I saw a chance that would leave me scot free. I saw that chance this morning.

'I have been three times, all told, into Quinton's study to-day. The first time I went in he would talk about nothing but the weird tale, called "The Curse of a Saint," which he was writing, which was all about how some Indian hermit made an English colonel kill himself by thinking about him. He showed me the last sheets, and even read me the last paragraph, which was something like this: "The conqueror of the Punjab, a mere yellow skeleton, but still gigantic, managed to lift himself on his elbow and gasp in his nephew's ear: 'I die by my own hand, yet I die murdered! ' " It so happened by one chance out of a hundred, that those last words were written at the top of a new sheet of paper. I left the room, and went out into the garden intoxicated with a frightful opportunity.

'We walked round the house; and two more things happened in my favour. You suspected an Indian, and you found a dagger which the Indian might most probably use. Taking the opportunity to stuff it in my pocket I went back to Quinton's study, locked the door, and gave him his sleeping draught. He was against answering Atkinson at all, but I urged him to call out and quiet the fellow, because I wanted a clear proof that Quinton was alive when I left the room for the second time. Quinton lay down in the conservatory, and I came through the study. I am a quick man with my hands, and in a minute and a half I had done what I wanted to do. I had emptied all the first part of Quinton's romance into the fireplace, where it burnt to ashes. Then I saw that the quotation marks wouldn't do, so I snipped them off, and to make it seem likelier, snipped the whole quire[17] to match. Then I came out with the knowledge that Quinton's confession of suicide lay on the front table, while Quinton lay alive but asleep in the conservatory beyond.

---

16. Dr Harris seems to think that an atheist has no good reason to avoid murdering someone if it is in his own interest. Let's hope Chesterton did not share this absurd belief. One would be hard put to show that among murderers there is a higher proportion of atheists than in the general population.

17. A quire is one twentieth of a ream (500) of identical sheets of paper.

'The last act was a desperate one; you can guess it: I pretended to have seen Quinton dead and rushed to his room. I delayed you with the paper, and, being a quick man with my hands, killed Quinton while you were looking at his confession of suicide. He was half-asleep being drugged, and I put his own hand on the knife and drove it into his body. The knife was of so queer a shape that no one but an operator[18] could have calculated the angle that would reach his heart. I wonder if you noticed this.

'When I had done it, the extraordinary thing happened. Nature deserted me. I felt ill. I felt just as if I had done something wrong. I think my brain is breaking up; I feel some sort of desperate pleasure in thinking I have told the thing to somebody; that I shall not have to be alone with it if I marry and have children. What is the matter with me? . . . Madness . . . or can one have remorse, just as if one were in Byron's poems! I cannot write any more.—JAMES ERSKINE HARRIS.'

Father Brown carefully folded up the letter, and put it in his breast pocket just as there came a loud peal at the gate bell, and the wet waterproofs of several policemen gleamed in the road outside.

### AFTERWORD

In my judgement this is the most unsatisfactory tale in the book. It is not just that the events are wildly implausible—all Father Brown stories are implausible—but that Dr James Harris is totally implausible. Here is an intelligent doctor who talks and acts normally. We are told he is good-tempered. Yet calmly and in cold blood he stabs a patient to death so he can pursue the man's wife. Then, merely because Father Brown, whom he has never met before, requests it, he writes down the details of why and how he committed murder!

Chesterton tried to make the doctor's confessional letter more believable by having him intimate at the end that he is going mad. Why? Because he has discovered, to his amazement, that he feels remorse! It won't do. No one can read the doctor's letter without realizing it was contrived by G.K. solely to bring his story to some kind of end.

---

**18.** The *OED*'s third definition of 'operator' is 'One who performs a surgical operation . . . ' In the story's magazine text the word is 'anatomist'.

Unfortunately, it doesn't even do that. All sorts of loose ends remain dangling. Did Flambeau walk away when Father Brown read the doctor's confession? Presumably he did, because the priest told the doctor that his statement would be confidential, and it is unthinkable that Father Brown would break his word. He would not even show the document to the police. Earlier we were told that everything about the crime eventually became known except for what Mrs Quinton said to Father Brown. Does this mean known to Father Brown only, or to the police as well? Are we to assume the doctor was so overcome with remorse that he would tell the arriving police what he told Father Brown? The story ends without our knowing whether the doctor *ever* openly confessed his crime, although Chesterton's statement that everything became known may have been intended to suggest that the doctor did eventually go to the authorities.

The story contains, however, one subtle aspect worth speculating about. When Father Brown first met Mrs Quinton he intuitively guessed her to be an 'over-driven' woman who 'does her duty for twenty years, and then does something dreadful'. I like to think that Chesterton is hinting delicately that Mrs Quinton had an affair with the doctor, and may even have known of his plans to kill her husband. After Father Brown emerges from his conference with her, looking 'pale and tragic', his first action is to ask the doctor to write down all the details of what had happened. Knowing that what she told the priest would never be disclosed, did Mrs Quinton tell Father Brown about her affair with the doctor and her knowledge or suspicion that he had killed her husband? Did the doctor conclude from Father Brown's pallor, his way of speaking, above all the look in his eyes, that the woman he loved had revealed everything? If so, it would make his quick confession much less unbelievable.

The Oriental dagger had a wrong shape. The sermon paper had a wrong shape. Whatever Mrs Quinton said to Father Brown, and much as I regret saying it, the story has a wrong shape. For me its greatest merit is in the cadences of its descriptions: the wind 'creeping up the dim garden path and shuffling the fallen leaves', and the white lightning that 'opened its enormous eye in one wink' before 'the sky shut up again'.

# 8

# The Sins of Prince Saradine*

WHEN Flambeau took his month's holiday from his office in Westminster[1] he took it in a small sailing-boat, so small that it passed much of its time as a rowing-boat. He took it, moreover, on little rivers in the Eastern counties, rivers so small that the boat looked like a magic boat sailing on land through meadows and cornfields. The vessel was just comfortable for two people; there was room only for necessities, and Flambeau had stocked it with such things as his special philosophy considered necessary. They reduced themselves, apparently, to four essentials: tins of salmon, if he should want to eat; loaded revolvers, if he should want to fight; a bottle of brandy, presumably in case he should faint; and a priest, presumably in case he should die. With this light luggage he crawled down the little Norfolk rivers, intending to reach the Broads[2] at last, but meanwhile delighting in the overhanging gardens and meadows, the mirrored mansions or villages, lingering to fish in the pools and corners, and in some sense hugging the shore.

Like a true philosopher, Flambeau had no aim in his holiday; but, like a true philosopher, he had an excuse. He had a sort of

---

* A prince vanquishes two enemies by an evil scheme based on a trick he had learned from Flambeau, and one that puts him beyond the reach of the law. *Cassell's Magazine* published the story, with pictures by Sidney Lucas, In May 1911.

1. For US readers, Westminster is Britain's equivalent of Washington, DC. A large borough in the centre of London, it contains Westminster Abbey, Westminster Cathedral, New Scotland Yard, Charing Cross, Trafalgar Square, Hyde Park, and the government buildings of Whitehall.

2. The Broads is a low region of marshland, shallow lakes, and lagoons, connected by rivers, in the eastern counties of Norfolk and Suffolk. It is the locale of Sherlock Holmes's case of 'The Gloria Scott'. During the Second World War the name was the butt of many jokes by American soldiers.

half purpose, which he took just so seriously that its success would crown the holiday, but just so lightly that its failure would not spoil it. Years ago, when he had been a king of thieves and the most famous figure in Paris, he had often received wild communications of approval, denunciation, or even love; but one had, somehow, stuck in his memory. It consisted simply of a visiting-card, in an envelope with an English postmark. On the back of the card was written in French and in green ink: 'If you ever retire and become respectable, come and see me. I want to meet you, for I have met all the other great men of my time. That trick of yours of getting one detective to arrest the other was the most splendid scene in French history.' On the front of the card was engraved in the formal fashion, 'Prince Saradine, Reed House, Reed Island,[3] Norfolk.'

He had not troubled much about the prince then, beyond ascertaining that he had been a brilliant and fashionable figure in southern Italy. In his youth, it was said, he had eloped with a married woman of high rank; the escapade was scarcely startling in his social world, but it had clung to men's minds because of an additional tragedy: the alleged suicide of the insulted husband, who appeared to have flung himself over a precipice in Sicily. The prince then lived in Vienna for a time, but his more recent years seemed to have been passed in perpetual and restless travel. But when Flambeau, like the prince himself, had left European celebrity and settled in England, it occurred to him that he might pay a surprise visit to this eminent exile in the Norfolk Broads. Whether he should find the place he had no idea; and, indeed, it was sufficiently small and forgotten. But, as things fell out, he found it much sooner than he expected.

They had moored their boat one night under a bank veiled in high grasses and short pollarded trees.[4] Sleep, after heavy sculling, had come to them early, and by a corresponding accident they awoke before it was light. To speak more strictly, they awoke before it was daylight; for a large lemon moon was only just setting in the forest of high grass above their heads, and the

---

3. Reed Island is an invented name.
4. Pollarded trees are trees that have had their branches cut off to produce a rounded head of young growth. Willows growing on riverbanks are often pollarded to prevent them overhanging the water.

sky was of a vivid violet-blue, nocturnal but bright. Both men had simultaneously a reminiscence of childhood, of the elfin and adventurous time when tall weeds close over us like woods. Standing up thus against the large low moon, the daisies really seemed to be giant daisies, the dandelions to be giant dandelions. Somehow it reminded them of the dado[5] of a nursery wall-paper. The drop of the river-bed sufficed to sink them under the roots of all shrubs and flowers and make them gaze upwards at the grass.

'By Jove!' said Flambeau, 'it's like being in fairyland.'

Father Brown sat bolt upright in the boat and crossed himself. His movement was so abrupt that his friend asked him, with a mild stare, what was the matter.

'The people who wrote the mediæval ballads,' answered the priest, 'knew more about fairies than you do. It isn't only nice things that happen in fairyland.'

'Oh, bosh!' said Flambeau. 'Only nice things could happen under such an innocent moon. I am for pushing on now and seeing what does really come. We may die and rot before we ever see again such a moon or such a mood.'

'All right,' said Father Brown. 'I never said it was always wrong to enter fairyland. I only said it was always dangerous.'

They pushed slowly up the brightening river; the glowing violet of the sky and the pale gold of the moon grew fainter and fainter, and faded into that vast colourless cosmos that precedes the colours of the dawn. When the first faint stripes of red and gold and grey split the horizon from end to end they were broken by the black bulk of a town or village which sat on the river just ahead of them. It was already an easy twilight, in which all things were visible, when they came under the hanging roofs and bridges of this riverside hamlet. The houses, with their long, low, stooping roofs, seemed to come down to drink at the river, like huge grey and red cattle. The broadening and whitening dawn had already turned to working daylight before they saw any living creature on the wharves and bridges of that silent town. Eventually they saw a very placid and prosperous man in his shirt sleeves, with a face as round as the recently sunken moon, and rays of red whisker around the low arc of it, who was leaning on a post above the sluggish tide. By an impulse not to be

_____

5. See Chapter 5, Note 8.

analysed, Flambeau rose to his full height in the swaying boat and shouted at the man to ask if he knew Reed Island or Reed House. The prosperous man's smile grew slightly more expansive, and he simply pointed up the river towards the next bend of it. Flambeau went ahead without further speech.

The boat took many such grassy corners and followed many such reedy and silent reaches of river; but before the search had become monotonous they had swung round a specially sharp angle and come into the silence of a sort of pool or lake, the sight of which instinctively arrested them. For in the middle of this wider piece of water, fringed on every side with rushes, lay a long, low islet, along which ran a long, low house or bungalow built of bamboo or some kind of tough tropic cane. The upstanding rods of bamboo which made the walls were pale yellow, the sloping rods that made the roof were of darker red or brown, otherwise the long house was a thing of repetition and monotony. The early morning breeze rustled the reeds round the island and sang in the strange ribbed house as in a giant pan-pipe.

'By George!' cried Flambeau; 'here is the place, after all! Here is Reed Island, if ever there was one. Here is Reed House, if it is anywhere. I believe that fat man with whiskers was a fairy.'

'Perhaps,' remarked Father Brown impartially. 'If he was, he was a bad fairy.'

But even as he spoke the impetuous Flambeau had run his boat ashore in the rattling reeds, and they stood in the long, quaint islet beside the odd and silent house.

The house stood with its back, as it were, to the river and the only landing-stage; the main entrance was on the other side, and looked down the long island garden. The visitors approached it, therefore, by a small path running round nearly three sides of the house, close under the low eaves. Through three different windows on three different sides they looked in on the same long, well-lit room, panelled in light wood, with a large number of looking-glasses, and laid out as for an elegant lunch. The front door, when they came round to it at last, was flanked by two turquoise-blue flower-pots. It was opened by a butler of the drearier type—long, lean, grey and listless—who murmured that Prince Saradine was from home at present, but was expected hourly; the house being kept ready for him and his guests. The exhibition of the card with the scrawl of green ink awoke a flicker of life in the parchment face of this depressed retainer, and it was with a certain shaky courtesy that he suggested that the strangers should remain. 'His Highness may be here any minute,' he said, 'and would be distressed to have just missed any gentleman he had invited. We have orders always to keep a little cold lunch for him and his friends, and I am sure he would wish it to be offered.'

Moved with curiosity to this minor adventure, Flambeau assented gracefully, and followed the old man, who ushered him ceremoniously into the long, lightly panelled room. There was nothing very notable about it, except the rather unusual alternation of many long, low windows with many long, low oblongs of looking-glass, which gave a singular air of lightness and unsubstantialness to the place. It was somehow like lunching out of doors. One or two pictures of a quiet kind hung in the corners, one a large grey photograph of a very young man in uniform, another a red chalk sketch of two long-haired boys. Asked by Flambeau whether the soldierly person was the prince, the butler answered shortly in the negative; it was the prince's younger brother, Captain Stephen Saradine, he said. And with that the old man seemed to dry up suddenly and lose all taste for conversation.

After lunch had tailed off with exquisite coffee and liqueurs, the guests were introduced to the garden, the library, and the housekeeper—a dark, handsome lady, of no little majesty, and rather like a plutonic Madonna. It appeared that she and the butler were the only survivors of the prince's original foreign *ménage*, all the other servants now in the house being new and collected in Norfolk by the housekeeper. This latter lady went by the name of Mrs Anthony, but she spoke with a slight Italian accent, and Flambeau did not doubt that Anthony was a Norfolk version of some more Latin name. Mr Paul, the butler, also had a faintly foreign air, but he was in tongue and training English, as are many of the most polished men-servants of the cosmopolitan nobility.

Pretty and unique as it was, the place had about it a curious luminous sadness. Hours passed in it like days. The long, well-windowed rooms were full of daylight, but it seemed a dead daylight. And through all other incidental noises, the sound of talk, the clink of glasses, or the passing feet of servants, they could hear on all sides of the house the melancholy noise of the river.

'We have taken a wrong turning, and come to a wrong place,' said Father Brown, looking out of the window at the grey-green sedges and the silver flood. 'Never mind; one can sometimes do good by being the right person in the wrong place.'

Father Brown, though commonly a silent, was an oddly sympathetic little man, and in those few but endless hours he unconsciously sank deeper into the secrets of Reed House than his professional friend. He had that knack of friendly silence which is so essential to gossip; and saying scarcely a word, he probably obtained from his new acquaintances all that in any case they would have told. The butler indeed was naturally uncommunicative. He betrayed a sullen and almost animal affection for his master; who, he said, had been very badly treated. The chief offender seemed to be his highness's brother, whose name alone would lengthen the old man's lantern jaws and pucker his parrot nose into a sneer. Captain Stephen was a ne'er-do-well, apparently, and had drained his benevolent brother of hundreds and thousands; forced him to fly from fashionable life and live quietly in this retreat. That was all Paul, the butler, would say, and Paul was obviously a partisan.

The Italian housekeeper was somewhat more communicative, being, as Brown fancied, somewhat less content. Her tone about her master was faintly acid; though not without a certain awe. Flambeau and his friend were standing in the room of the looking-glasses examining the red sketch of the two boys, when the housekeeper swept in swiftly on some domestic errand. It was a peculiarity of this glittering, glass-panelled place that anyone entering was reflected in four or five mirrors at once;[6] and Father Brown, without turning round, stopped in the middle of a sentence of family criticism. But Flambeau, who had his face close up to the picture, was already saying in a loud voice, 'The brothers Saradine, I suppose. They both look innocent enough. It would be hard to say which is the good brother and which the bad.' Then, realising the lady's presence, he turned the conversation with some triviality, and strolled out into the garden. But Father Brown still gazed steadily at the red crayon sketch; and Mrs Anthony still gazed steadily at Father Brown.

---

**6.** The many mirrors in the house suggest the way in which the identities of persons in the story are mirrored and confused with one another. Mirrors play significant roles in other Father Brown stories, notably 'The Man in the Passage' (*The Wisdom of Father Brown*) and 'The Mirror of the Magistrate' (*The Secret of Father Brown*).

She had large and tragic brown eyes, and her olive face glowed darkly with a curious and painful wonder—as of one doubtful of a stranger's identity or purpose. Whether the little priest's coat and creed touched some southern memories of confession, or whether she fancied he knew more than he did, she said to him in a low voice as to a fellow plotter, 'He is right enough in one way, your friend. He says it would be hard to pick out the good and bad brothers. Oh, it would be hard, it would be mighty hard, to pick out the good one.'

'I don't understand you,' said Father Brown, and began to move away.

The woman took a step nearer to him, with thunderous brows and a sort of savage stoop, like a bull lowering his horns.

'There isn't a good one,' she hissed. 'There was badness enough in the captain taking all that money, but I don't think there was much goodness in the prince giving it. The captain's not the only one with something against him.'

A light dawned on the cleric's averted face, and his mouth formed silently the word 'blackmail.' Even as he did so the woman turned an abrupt white face over her shoulder and almost fell. The door had opened soundlessly and the pale Paul stood like a ghost in the doorway. By the weird trick of the reflecting walls, it seemed as if five Pauls had entered by five doors simultaneously.

'His Highness,' he said, 'has just arrived.'

In the same flash the figure of a man had passed outside the first window, crossing the sunlit pane like a lighted stage. An instant later he passed at the second window and the many mirrors repainted in successive frames the same eagle profile and marching figure. He was erect and alert, but his hair was white and his complexion of an odd ivory yellow. He had that short, curved Roman nose which generally goes with long, lean cheeks and chin, but these were partly masked by moustache and imperial.[7] The moustache was much darker than the beard, giving an effect slightly theatrical, and he was dressed up to the same dashing part, having a white top hat, an orchid in his coat, a yellow

---

7. An imperial is a small portion of beard allowed to grow just below the lower lip, the rest of the beard being shaved off: it is so named because Emperor Napoleon III wore his beard that way.

waistcoat and yellow gloves which he flapped and swung as he walked. When he came round to the front door they heard the stiff Paul open it, and heard the new arrival say cheerfully, 'Well, you see I have come.' The stiff Mr Paul bowed and answered in his inaudible manner; for a few minutes their conversation could not be heard. Then the butler said, 'Everything is at your disposal'; and the glove-flapping Prince Saradine came gaily into the room to greet them. They beheld once more that spectral scene—five princes entering a room with five doors.

The prince put the white hat and yellow gloves on the table and offered his hand quite cordially.

'Delighted to see you here, Mr Flambeau,' he said. 'Know you very well by reputation, if that's not an indiscreet remark.'

'Not at all,' answered Flambeau, laughing. 'I am not sensitive. Very few reputations are gained by unsullied virtue.'

The prince flashed a sharp look at him to see if the retort had any personal point; then he laughed also and offered chairs to everyone, including himself.

'Pleasant little place, this, I think,' he said with a detached air. 'Not much to do, I fear; but the fishing is really good.'

The priest, who was staring at him with the grave stare of a baby, was haunted by some fancy that escaped definition. He looked at the grey, carefully curled hair, yellow white visage, and slim, somewhat foppish figure. These were not unnatural, though perhaps a shade *prononcé*,[8] like the outfit of a figure behind the footlights. The nameless interest lay in something else, in the very framework of the face; Brown was tormented with a half memory of having seen it somewhere before. The man looked like some old friend of his dressed up. Then he suddenly remembered the mirrors, and put his fancy down to some psychological effect of that multiplication of human masks.

Prince Saradine distributed his social attentions between his guests with great gaiety and tact. Finding the detective of a sporting turn and eager to employ his holiday, he guided Flambeau and Flambeau's boat down to the best fishing spot in the stream, and was back in his own canoe in twenty minutes to join Father Brown in the library and plunge equally politely into the priest's

---

8. *Prononcé*: prominent, pronounced.

more philosophic pleasures. He seemed to know a great deal both about the fishing and the books, though of these not the most edifying; he spoke five or six languages, though chiefly the slang of each. He had evidently lived in varied cities and very motley societies, for some of his cheerfullest stories were about gambling hells and opium dens, Australian bushrangers or Italian brigands. Father Brown knew that the once celebrated Saradine had spent his last few years in almost ceaseless travel, but he had not guessed that the travels were so disreputable or so amusing.

Indeed, with all his dignity of a man of the world, Prince Saradine radiated to such sensitive observers as the priest, a certain atmosphere of the restless and even the unreliable. His face was fastidious, but his eye was wild; he had little nervous tricks, like a man shaken by drink or drugs, and he neither had, nor professed to have, his hand on the helm of household affairs. All these were left to the two old servants, especially to the butler, who was plainly the central pillar of the house. Mr Paul, indeed, was not so much a butler as a sort of steward or, even, chamberlain; he dined privately, but with almost as much pomp as his master; he was feared by all the servants; and he consulted with the prince decorously, but somewhat unbendingly—rather as if he were the prince's solicitor. The sombre housekeeper was a mere shadow in comparison; indeed, she seemed to efface herself and wait only on the butler, and Brown heard no more of those volcanic whispers which had half told him of the younger brother who blackmailed the elder. Whether the prince was really being thus bled by the absent captain, he could not be certain, but there was something insecure and secretive about Saradine that made the tale by no means incredible.

When they went once more into the long hall with the windows and the mirrors, yellow evening was dropping over the waters and the willowy banks; and a bittern sounded in the distance like an elf upon his dwarfish drum. The same singular sentiment of some sad and evil fairyland crossed the priest's mind again like a little grey cloud. 'I wish Flambeau were back,' he muttered.

'Do you believe in doom?' asked the restless Prince Saradine suddenly.

'No,' answered his guest. 'I believe in Doomsday.'

The prince turned from the window and stared at him in a

singular manner, his face in shadow against the sunset. 'What do you mean?' he asked.

'I mean that we here are on the wrong side of the tapestry,' answered Father Brown. 'The things that happen here do not seem to mean anything; they mean something somewhere else. Somewhere else retribution will come on the real offender. Here it often seems to fall on the wrong person.'

The prince made an inexplicable noise like an animal; in his shadowed face the eyes were shining queerly. A new and shrewd thought exploded silently in the other's mind. Was there another meaning in Saradine's blend of brilliancy and abruptness? Was the prince—— Was he perfectly sane? He was repeating, 'The wrong person—the wrong person,' many more times than was natural in a social exclamation.

Then Father Brown awoke tardily to a second truth. In the mirrors before him he could see the silent door standing open, and the silent Mr Paul standing in it, with his usual pallid impassiveness.

'I thought it better to announce at once,' he said, with the same stiff respectfulness as of an old family lawyer, 'a boat rowed by six men has come to the landing-stage, and there's a gentleman sitting in the stern.'

'A boat!' repeated the prince; 'a gentleman?' and he rose to his feet.

There was a startled silence punctuated only by the odd noise of the bird in the sedge; and then, before anyone could speak again, a new face and figure passed in profile round the three sunlit windows, as the prince had passed an hour or two before. But except for the accident that both outlines were aquiline, they had little in common. Instead of the new white topper of Saradine, was a black one of antiquated or foreign shape; under it was a young and very solemn face, clean shaven, blue about its resolute chin, and carrying a faint suggestion of the young Napoleon. The association was assisted by something old and odd about the whole get-up, as of a man who had never troubled to change the fashions of his fathers. He had a shabby blue frock coat, a red, soldierly looking waistcoat, and a kind of coarse white trousers common among the early Victorians, but strangely incongruous to-day. From all this old clothes-shop his olive face stood out strangely young and monstrously sincere.

'The deuce!' said Prince Saradine, and clapping on his white hat he went to the front door himself, flinging it open on the sunset garden.

By that time the new-comer and his followers were drawn up on the lawn like a small stage army. The six boatmen had pulled the boat well up on shore, and were guarding it almost menacingly, holding their oars erect like spears. They were swarthy men, and some of them wore earrings. But one of them stood forward beside the olive-faced young man in the red waistcoat, and carried a large black case of unfamiliar form.

'Your name,' said the young man, 'is Saradine?'

Saradine assented rather negligently.

The new-comer had dull, dog-like brown eyes, as different as possible from the restless and glittering grey eyes of the prince. But once again Father Brown was tortured with a sense of having seen somewhere a replica of the face; and once again he remembered the repetitions of the glass-panelled room, and put down the coincidence to that. 'Confound this crystal palace!' he muttered. 'One sees everything too many times. It's like a dream.'

'If you are Prince Saradine,' said the young man, 'I may tell you that my name is Antonelli.'

'Antonelli,' repeated the prince languidly. 'Somehow I remember the name.'

'Permit me to present myself,' said the young Italian.

With his left hand he politely took off his old-fashioned top hat: with his right he caught Prince Saradine so ringing a crack across the face that the white top hat rolled down the steps and one of the blue flower-pots rocked upon its pedestal.

The prince, whatever he was, was evidently not a coward; he sprang at his enemy's throat and almost bore him backwards to the grass. But his enemy extricated himself with a singularly inappropriate air of hurried politeness.

'That is all right,' he said, panting and in halting English. 'I have insulted. I will give satisfaction. Marco, open the case.'

The man beside him with the earrings and the big black case proceeded to unlock it. He took out of it two long Italian rapiers, with splendid steel hilts and blades, which he planted point downwards in the lawn. The strange young man standing facing the entrance with his yellow and vindictive face, the two swords standing up in the turf like two crosses in a cemetery, and the line of the ranked rowers behind, gave it all an odd appearance of being some barbaric court of justice. But everything else was unchanged, so sudden had been the interruption. The sunset gold still glowed on the lawn, and the bittern still boomed as announcing some small but dreadful destiny.

'Prince Saradine,' said the man called Antonelli, 'when I was an infant in the cradle you killed my father and stole my mother; my father was the more fortunate. You did not kill him fairly, as I am going to kill you. You and my wicked mother took him driving to a lonely pass in Sicily, flung him down a cliff, and went on your way. I could imitate you if I chose, but imitating you is too vile. I have followed you all over the world, and you have always fled from me. But this is the end of the world—and of you. I have you now, and I give you the chance you never gave my father. Choose one of those swords.'

Prince Saradine, with contracted brows, seemed to hesitate a moment, but his ears were still singing with the blow, and he sprang forward and snatched at one of the hilts. Father Brown had also sprung forward, striving to compose the dispute; but he soon found his personal presence made matters worse. Saradine was a French freemason and a fierce atheist, and a priest moved him by the law of contraries. And for the other man neither priest nor layman moved him at all. This young man with the Bonaparte face and the brown eyes was something far sterner than a puritan—a pagan. He was a simple slayer from the morning of the earth; a man of the stone age—a man of stone.

One hope remained, the summoning of the household; and Father Brown ran back into the house. He found, however, that all the under servants had been given a holiday ashore by the autocrat Paul, and that only the sombre Mrs Anthony moved uneasily about the long rooms. But the moment she turned a ghastly face upon him, he resolved one of the riddles of the house of mirrors. The heavy brown eyes of Antonelli where the heavy brown eyes of Mrs Anthony; and in a flash he saw half the story.

'Your son is outside,' he said without wasting words; 'either he or the prince will be killed. Where is Mr Paul?'

'He is at the landing-stage,' said the woman faintly. 'He is—he is—signalling for help.'

'Mrs Anthony,' said Father Brown seriously, 'there is no time for nonsense. My friend has his boat down the river fishing. Your son's boat is guarded by your son's men. There is only this one canoe; what is Mr Paul doing with it?'

'Santa Maria! I do not know,' she said; and swooned all her length on the matted floor.

Father Brown lifted her to a sofa, flung a pot of water over her, shouted for help, and then rushed down to the landing-stage of the little island. But the canoe was already in mid-stream, and old Paul was pulling and pushing it up the river with an energy incredible at his years.

'I will save my master,' he cried, his eyes blazing maniacally. 'I will save him yet!'

Father Brown could do nothing but gaze after the boat as it struggled up-stream and pray that the old man might waken the little town in time.

'A duel is bad enough,' he muttered, rubbing up his rough dust-coloured hair,[9] 'but there's something wrong about this duel, even as a duel. I feel it in my bones. But what can it be?'

As he stood staring at the water, a wavering mirror of sunset, he heard from the other end of the island garden a small but unmistakable sound—the cold concussion of steel. He turned his head.

Away on the farthest cape or headland of the long islet, on a strip of turf beyond the last rank of roses, the duellists had already crossed swords. Evening above them was a dome of virgin gold, and, distant as they were, every detail was picked out. They had cast off their coats, but the yellow waistcoat and white hair of Saradine, the red waistcoat and white trousers of Antonelli, glittered in the level light like the colours of the dancing clockwork dolls. The two swords sparkled from point to pommel like two diamond pins. There was something frightful in the two figures appearing so little and so gay. They looked like two butterflies trying to pin each other to a cork.

Father Brown ran as hard as he could, his little legs going like a wheel. But when he came to the field of combat he found he was both too late and too early—too late to stop the strife, under the shadow of the grim Sicilians leaning on their oars, and too early to anticipate any disastrous issue of it. For the two men were

---

9. We learn for the first time that Father Brown's hair is light brown.

singularly well matched, the prince using his skill with a sort of cynical confidence, the Sicilian using his with a murderous care. Few finer fencing matches can ever have been seen in crowded amphitheatres than that which tinkled and sparkled on that forgotten island in the reedy river. The dizzy fight was balanced so long that hope began to revive in the protesting priest; by all common probability Paul must soon come back with the police. It would be some comfort even if Flambeau came back from his fishing, for Flambeau, physically speaking, was worth four other men. But there was no sign of Flambeau, and, what was much queerer, no sign of Paul or the police. No other raft or stick was left to float on; in that lost island in that vast nameless pool, they were cut off as on a rock in the Pacific.

Almost as he had the thought the ringing of the rapiers quickened to a rattle, the prince's arms flew up, and the point shot out behind between his shoulder-blades. He went over with a great whirling movement, almost like one throwing the half of a boy's cart-wheel. The sword flew from his hand like a shooting star, and dived into the distant river. And he himself sank with so earth-shaking a subsidence that he broke a big rose-tree with his body and shook up into the sky a cloud of red earth—like the smoke of some heathen sacrifice. The Sicilian had made blood-offering to the ghost of his father.

The priest was instantly on his knees by the corpse; but only to make too sure that it was a corpse. As he was still trying some last hopeless tests he heard for the first time voices from farther up the river, and saw a police boat shoot up to the landing-stage, with constables and other important people, including the excited Paul. The little priest rose with a distinctly dubious grimace.

'Now, why on earth,' he muttered, 'why on earth couldn't he have come before?'

Some seven minutes later the island was occupied by an invasion of townsfolk and police, and the latter had put their hands on the victorious duellist, ritually reminding him that anything he said might be used against him.

'I shall not say anything,' said the monomaniac, with a wonderful and peaceful face. 'I shall never say anything any more. I am very happy, and I only want to be hanged.'

Then he shut his mouth as they led him away, and it is the

strange but certain truth that he never opened it again in this world, except to say 'Guilty' at his trial.

Father Brown had stared at the suddenly crowded garden, the arrest of the man of blood, the carrying away of the corpse after its examination by the doctor, rather as one watches the breakup of some ugly dream; he was motionless, like a man in a nightmare. He gave his name and address as a witness, but declined their offer of a boat to the shore, and remained alone in the island garden, gazing at the broken rose bush and the whole green theatre of that swift and inexplicable tragedy. The light died along the river; mist rose in the marshy banks; a few belated birds flitted fitfully across.

Stuck stubbornly in his sub-consciousness (which was an unusually lively one) was an unspeakable certainty that there was something still unexplained. This sense that had clung to him all day could not be fully explained by his fancy about 'looking-glass land.' Somehow he had not seen the real story, but some game or masque. And yet people do not get hanged or run through the body for the sake of a charade.

As he sat on the steps of the landing-stage ruminating he grew conscious of the tall, dark streak of a sail coming silently down the shining river, and sprang to his feet with such a back-rush of feeling that he almost wept.

'Flambeau!' he cried, and shook his friend by both hands again and again, much to the astonishment of that sportsman, as he came on shore with his fishing tackle. 'Flambeau,' he said, 'so you're not killed?'

'Killed!' repeated the angler in great astonishment. 'And why should I be killed?'

'Oh, because nearly everybody else is,' said his companion rather wildly. 'Saradine got murdered, and Antonelli wants to be hanged, and his mother's fainted, and I, for one, don't know whether I'm in this world or the next. But, thank God, you're in the same one.' And he took the bewildered Flambeau's arm.

As they turned from the landing-stage they came under the eaves of the low bamboo house, and looked in through one of the windows, as they had done on their first arrival. They beheld a lamp-lit interior well calculated to arrest their eyes. The table in the long dining-room had been laid for dinner when Saradine's destroyer had fallen like a storm-bolt on the island. And the dinner was now in placid progress, for Mrs Anthony sat some-what sullenly at the foot of the table, while at the head of it was Mr Paul, the *major domo*, eating and drinking of the best, his bleared, bluish eyes standing queerly out of his face, his gaunt countenance inscrutable, but by no means devoid of satisfaction.

With a gesture of powerful impatience, Flambeau rattled at the window, wrenched it open, and put an indignant head into the lamp-lit room.

'Well!' he cried. 'I can understand you may need some refresh-ment, but really to steal your master's dinner while he lies mur-dered in the garden——'

'I have stolen a great many things in a long and pleasant life,' replied the strange old gentleman placidly; 'this dinner is one of the few things I have not stolen. This dinner and this house and garden happen to belong to me.'

A thought flashed across Flambeau's face. 'You mean to say,' he began, 'that the will of Prince Saradine——'

'I am Prince Saradine,' said the old man, munching a salted almond.

Father Brown, who was looking at the birds outside, jumped as if he were shot, and put in at the window a pale face like a tur-nip.

'You are *what?*' he repeated in a shrill voice.

'Paul, Prince Saradine, *à vos ordres*,'[10] said the venerable person politely, lifting a glass of sherry. 'I live here very quietly, being a domestic kind of fellow; and for the sake of modesty I am called Mr Paul, to distinguish me from my unfortunate brother Mr Stephen. He died, I hear, recently—in the garden. Of course, it is not my fault if enemies pursue him to this place. It is owing to the regret-table irregularity of his life. He was not a domestic character.'

He relapsed into silence, and continued to gaze at the opposite wall just above the bowed and sombre head of the woman. They saw plainly the family likeness that had haunted them in the dead man. Then his old shoulders began to heave and shake a little, as if he were choking, but his face did not alter.

'My God!'[11] cried Flambeau after a pause, 'he's laughing!'

---

10. *À vos ordres*: at your service.
11. In the magazine version Flambeau's unlikely exclamation is 'Good Heavens!'

'Come away,' said Father Brown, who was quite white. 'Come away from this house of hell. Let us get into an honest boat again.'

Night had sunk on rushes and river by the time they had pushed off from the island, and they went down-stream in the dark, warming themselves with two big cigars that glowed like crimson ships' lanterns. Father Brown took his cigar out of his mouth and said:

'I suppose you can guess the whole story now? After all, it's a primitive story. A man had two enemies. He was a wise man. And so he discovered that two enemies are better than one.'

'I do not follow that,' answered Flambeau.

'Oh, it's really simple,' rejoined his friend. 'Simple, though anything but innocent. Both the Saradines were scamps, but the prince, the elder, was the sort of scamp that gets to the top, and the younger, the captain, was the sort that sinks to the bottom. This squalid officer fell from beggar to blackmailer, and one ugly day he got his hold upon his brother, the prince. Obviously it was for no light matter, for Prince Paul Saradine was frankly 'fast,' and had no reputation to lose as to the mere sins of society. In plain fact, it was a hanging matter, and Stephen literally had a rope round his brother's neck. He had somehow discovered the truth about the Sicilian affair, and could prove that Paul murdered old Antonelli in the mountains. The captain raked in the hush money heavily for ten years, until even the prince's splendid fortune began to look a little foolish.

'But Prince Saradine bore another burden besides his blood-sucking brother. He knew that the son of Antonelli, a mere child at the time of the murder, had been trained in savage Sicilian loyalty, and lived only to avenge his father, not with the gibbet (for he lacked Stephen's legal proof), but with the old weapons of vendetta. The boy had practised arms with a deadly perfection, and about the time that he was old enough to use them Prince Saradine began, as the society papers said, to travel. The fact is that he began to flee for his life, passing from place to place like a hunted criminal; but with one relentless man upon his trail. That was Prince Paul's position, and by no means a pretty one. The more money he spent on eluding Antonelli the less he had to silence Stephen. The more he gave to silence Stephen the less chance there was of finally escaping Antonelli. Then it was that he showed himself a great man—a genius like Napoleon.

'Instead of resisting his two antagonists, he surrended suddenly to both of them. He gave way, like a Japanese wrestler, and his foes fell prostrate before him. He gave up the race round the world, and he gave up his address to young Antonelli; then he gave up everything to his brother. He sent Stephen money enough for smart clothes and easy travel, with a letter saying roughly: "This is all I have left. You have cleaned me out. I still have a little house in Norfolk, with servants and a cellar, and if you want more from me you must take that. Come and take possession if you like, and I will live there quietly as your friend or agent or anything." He knew that the Sicilian had never seen the Saradine brothers save, perhaps, in pictures; he knew they were somewhat alike, both having grey, pointed beards. Then he shaved his own face and waited. The trap worked. The unhappy captain, in his new clothes, entered the house in triumph as a prince, and walked upon the Sicilian's sword.

'There was one hitch, and it is to the honour of human nature. Evil spirits like Saradine often blunder by never expecting the virtues of mankind. He took it for granted that the Italian's blow, when it came, would be dark, violent and nameless, like the blow it avenged; that the victim would be knifed at night, or shot from behind a hedge, and so die without speech. It was a bad minute for Prince Paul when Antonelli's chivalry proposed a formal duel, with all its possible explanations. It was then that I found him putting off in his boat with wild eyes. He was fleeing, bareheaded, in an open boat before Antonelli should learn who he was.

'But, however agitated, he was not hopeless. He knew the adventurer and he knew the fanatic. It was quite probable that Stephen, the adventurer, would hold his tongue, through his mere histrionic pleasure in playing a part, his lust for clinging to his new cosy quarters, his rascal's trust in luck, and his fine fencing. It was certain that Antonelli, the fanatic, would hold his tongue, and be hanged without telling tales of his family. Paul hung about on the river till he knew the fight was over. Then he roused the town, brought the police, saw his two vanquished enemies taken away for ever, and sat down smiling to his dinner.'

'Laughing, God help us!' said Flambeau with a strong shudder. 'Do they get such ideas from Satan?'

'He got that idea from you,' answered the priest.

'God forbid!' ejaculated Flambeau. 'From me? What do you mean?'

The priest pulled a visiting-card from his pocket and held it up in the faint glow of his cigar; it was scrawled with green ink.

'Don't you remember his original invitation to you?' he asked, 'and the compliment to your criminal exploit? "That trick of yours," he says, "of getting one detective to arrest the other?" He has just copied your trick. With an enemy on each side of him, he slipped swiftly out of the way and let them collide and kill each other.'

Flambeau tore Prince Saradine's card from the priest's hands and rent it savagely in small pieces.

'There's the last of that old skull and crossbones,' he said as he scattered the pieces upon the dark and disappearing waves of the stream; 'but I should think it would poison the fishes.'

The last gleam of white card and green ink was drowned and darkened; a faint and vibrant colour as of morning changed the sky, and the moon behind the grasses grew paler. They drifted in silence.

'Father,' said Flambeau suddenly, 'do you think it was all a dream?'

The priest shook his head, whether in dissent or agnosticism, but remained mute. A smell of hawthorn and of orchards came to them through the darkness, telling them that a wind was awake; the next moment it swayed their little boat and swelled their sail, and carried them onward down the winding river to happier places and the homes of harmless men.

# 9

# The Hammer of God*

THE little village of Bohun Beacon[1] was perched on a hill so steep that the tall spire of its church seemed only like the peak of a small mountain. At the foot of the church stood a smithy, generally red with fires and always littered with hammers and scraps of iron; opposite to this, over a rude cross of cobbled paths, was 'The Blue Boar,' the only inn of the place. It was upon this crossway, in the lifting of a leaden and silver daybreak, that two brothers met in the street and spoke; though one was beginning the day and the other finishing it. The Rev. and Hon. Wilfred Bohun was very devout, and was making his way to some austere exercises of prayer or contemplation at dawn. Colonel the Hon. Norman Bohun, his elder brother, was by no means devout, and was sitting in evening dress on the bench outside 'The Blue Boar,' drinking what the philosophic observer was free to regard either as his last glass on Tuesday or his first on Wednesday. The colonel was not particular.

The Bohuns were one of the very few aristocratic families really dating from the Middle Ages, and their pennon had actually seen Palestine. But it is a great mistake to suppose that such houses stand high in chivalric tradition. Few except the poor preserve traditions. Aristocrats live not in traditions but in fashions. The Bohuns had been Mohocks[2] under Queen Anne

---

* The brother of an Anglican priest is killed by a hammer blow on the head, so powerful that only the local blacksmith seems strong enough to have committed the crime. Although the ninth chapter of the book, it was the fourth Father Brown story to be published (the *Storyteller*, December 1910). It has been reprinted in many anthologies.

1. Bohun Beacon is an imaginary town forty miles from Greenford. Father Brown, who seems to move around a lot from parish to parish, has a chapel in the village.

2. According to the *OED* the Mohocks were 'a class of aristocratic ruffians who infested the streets of London' in the early eighteenth century. 'Did I tell you of a race of rakes', Jonathan Swift wrote in his *Journal to Stella*,

and Mashers[3] under Queen Victoria. But like more than one of the really ancient houses, they had rotted in the last two centuries into mere drunkards and dandy degenerates, till there had even come a whisper of insanity. Certainly there was something hardly human about the colonel's wolfish pursuit of pleasure, and his chronic resolution not to go home till morning had a touch of the hideous clarity[4] of insomnia. He was a tall, fine animal, elderly, but with hair still startlingly yellow. He would have looked merely blonde and leonine, but his blue eyes were sunk so deep in his face that they looked black. They were a little too close together. He had very long yellow moustaches; on each side of them a fold or furrow from nostril to jaw, so that a sneer seemed cut into his face. Over his evening clothes he wore a curious pale yellow coat that looked more like a very light dressing gown than an overcoat, and on the back of his head was stuck an extraordinary broad-brimmed hat of a bright green colour, evidently some Oriental curiosity caught up at random. He was proud of appearing in such incongruous attires—proud of the fact that he always made them look congruous.

His brother the curate had also the yellow hair and the elegance, but he was buttoned up to the chin in black, and his face was clean-shaven, cultivated, and a little nervous. He seemed to live for nothing but his religion; but there were some who said (notably the blacksmith, who was a Presbyterian) that it was a love of Gothic architecture rather than of God, and that his haunting of the church like a ghost was only another and purer turn of the almost morbid thirst for beauty which sent his brother raging after women and wine. This charge was doubtful, while the man's practical piety was indubitable. Indeed, the charge was mostly an ignorant misunderstanding of the love of solitude and secret prayer, and was founded on his being often found

'called the Mohocks, that play the devil about this town every night, slit people's noses, and beat them . . . ?' The word derived from the Mohawks, then believed by the English to be a fierce tribe of American Indians.

**3.** The *OED* defines a masher as 'a fop of affected manners and exaggerated style of dress who frequented music-halls and fashionable promenades and who posed as a "lady-killer" '. Introduced from the US, the word became common in England in the 1880s.

**4.** In many later printings of this story the word is altered to 'charity'—clearly a printer's error.

kneeling, not before the altar, but in peculiar places, in the crypts or gallery, or even in the belfry. He was at the moment about to enter the church through the yard of the smithy, but stopped and frowned a little as he saw his brother's cavernous eyes staring in the same direction. On the hypothesis that the colonel was interested in the church he did not waste any speculations. There only remained the blacksmith's shop, and though the blacksmith was a Puritan and none[5] of his people, Wilfred Bohun had heard some scandals about a beautiful and rather celebrated wife. He flung a suspicious look across the shed, and the colonel stood up laughing to speak to him.

'Good morning, Wilfred,' he said. 'Like a good landlord I am watching sleeplessly over my people. I am going to call on the blacksmith.'

Wilfred looked at the ground, and said: 'The blacksmith is out. He is over at Greenford.'[6]

'I know,' answered the other with silent laughter; 'that is why I am calling on him.'

'Norman,' said the cleric, with his eye on a pebble in the road, 'are you ever afraid of thunderbolts?'

'What do you mean?' asked the colonel. 'Is your hobby meteorology?'

'I mean,' said Wilfred, without looking up, 'do you ever think that God might strike you in the street?'

'I beg your pardon,' said the colonel; 'I see your hobby is folklore.'

'I know your hobby is blasphemy,' retorted the religious man, stung in the one live place of his nature. 'But if you do not fear God, you have good reason to fear man.'

The elder raised his eyebrows politely. 'Fear man?' he said.

'Barnes the blacksmith is the biggest and strongest man for forty miles round,' said the clergyman sternly. 'I know you are no coward or weakling, but he could throw you over the wall.'

This struck home, being true, and the lowering line by mouth

---

5. None: not one. The blacksmith does not belong to the town's Anglican church. As we soon learn, his beautiful wife does not belong either. She is a Catholic who attends Father Brown's chapel.

6. Greenford is a suburb a few miles to the west of London.

and nostril darkened and deepened. For a moment he stood with
the heavy sneer on his face. But in an instant Colonel Bohun had
recovered his own cruel good humour and laughed, showing two
dog-like front teeth under his yellow moustache. 'In that case,
my dear Wilfred,' he said quite carelessly, 'it was wise for the last
of the Bohuns to come out partially in armour.'

And he took off the queer round hat covered with green, showing that it was lined within with steel. Wilfred recognised it
indeed as a light Japanese or Chinese helmet torn down from a
trophy that hung in the old family hall.

'It was the first hat to hand,' explained his brother airily;
'always the nearest hat—and the nearest woman.'

'The blacksmith is away at Greenford,' said Wilfred quietly;
'the time of his return is unsettled.'

And with that he turned and went into the church with bowed
head, crossing himself like one who wishes to be quit of an
unclean spirit. He was anxious to forget such grossness in the
cool twilight of his tall Gothic cloisters; but on that morning it
was fated that his still round of religious exercises should be
everywhere arrested by small shocks. As he entered the church,
hitherto always empty at that hour, a kneeling figure rose hastily
to its feet and came towards the full daylight of the doorway.
When the curate saw it he stood still with surprise. For the early
worshipper was none other than the village idiot, a nephew of the
blacksmith, one who neither would nor could care for the church
or for anything else. He was always called 'Mad Joe,' and seemed
to have no other name; he was a dark, strong, slouching lad, with
a heavy white face, dark straight hair. and a mouth always open.
As he passed the priest, his moon-calf countenance gave no hint
of what he had been doing or thinking of. He had never been
known to pray before. What sort of prayers was he saying now?
Extraordinary prayers surely.

Wilfred Bohun stood rooted to the spot long enough to see the
idiot go out into the sunshine, and even to see his dissolute
brother hail him with a sort of avuncular jocularity. The last
thing he saw was the colonel throwing pennies at the open mouth
of Joe, with the serious appearance of trying to hit it.

This ugly sunlight picture of the stupidity and cruelty of the
earth sent the ascetic finally to his prayers for purification and
new thoughts. He went up to a pew in the gallery, which brought

him under a coloured window which he loved and always quieted his spirit; a blue window with an angel carrying lilies. There he began to think less about the half-wit, with his livid face and mouth like a fish. He began to think less of his evil brother, pacing like a lean lion in his horrible hunger. He sank deeper and deeper into those cold and sweet colours of silver blossoms and sapphire sky.

In this place half an hour afterwards he was found by Gibbs, the village cobbler, who had been sent for him in some haste. He got to his feet with promptitude, for he knew that no small matter would have brought Gibbs into such a place at all. The cobbler was, as in many villages, an atheist, and his appearance in church was a shade more extraordinary than Mad Joe's. It was a morning of theological enigmas.

'What is it?' asked Wilfred Bohun rather stiffly, but putting out a trembling hand for his hat.

The atheist spoke in a tone that, coming from him, was quite startlingly respectful, and even, as it were, huskily sympathetic.

'You must excuse me, sir,' he said in a hoarse whisper, 'but we didn't think it right not to let you know at once. I'm afraid a rather dreadful thing has happened, sir. I'm afraid your brother——'

Wilfred clenched his frail hands. 'What devilry has he done now?' he cried in involuntary passion.

'Why, sir,' said the cobbler, coughing, 'I'm afraid he's done nothing, and won't do anything. I'm afraid he's done for. You had really better come down, sir.'

The curate followed the cobbler down a short winding stair, which brought them out at an entrance rather higher than the street. Bohun saw the tragedy in one glance, flat underneath him like a plan. In the yard of the smithy were standing five or six men mostly in black, one in an inspector's uniform. They included the doctor, the Presbyterian minister, and the priest from the Roman Catholic chapel, to which the blacksmith's wife belonged. The latter was speaking to her, indeed, very rapidly, in an undertone, as she, a magnificent woman with red-gold hair, was sobbing blindly on a bench. Between these two groups, and just clear of the main heap of hammers, lay a man in evening dress, spread-eagled and flat on his face. From the height above Wilfred could have sworn to every item of his costume and appearance, down to the Bohun rings upon his fingers; but the skull was only a hideous splash, like a star of blackness and blood.

Wilfred Bohun gave but one glance, and ran down the steps into the yard. The doctor, who was the family physician, saluted him, but he scarcely took any notice. He could only stammer out: 'My brother is dead. What does it mean? What is this horrible mystery?' There was an unhappy silence; and then the cobbler, the most outspoken man present, answered: 'Plenty of horror, sir,' he said, 'but not much mystery.'

'What do you mean?' asked Wilfred, with a white face.

'It's plain enough,' answered Gibbs. 'There is only one man for forty miles round that could have struck such a blow as that, and he's the man that had most reason to.'

'We must not prejudge anything,' put in the doctor, a tall, black-bearded man, rather nervously; 'but it is competent for me to corroborate what Mr Gibbs says about the nature of the blow, sir; it is an incredible blow. Mr Gibbs says that only one man in this district could have done it. I should have said myself that nobody could have done it.'

A shudder of superstition went through the slight figure of the curate. 'I can hardly understand,' he said.

'Mr Bohun,' said the doctor in a low voice, 'metaphors literally fail me. It is inadequate to say that the skull was smashed to bits like an egg-shell. Fragments of bone were driven into the body and the ground like bullets into a mud wall. It was the hand of a giant.'

He was silent a moment, looking grimly through his glasses; then he added: 'The thing has one advantage—that it clears most people of suspicion at one stroke. If you or I or any normally made man in the country were accused of this crime, we should be acquitted as an infant would be acquitted of stealing the Nelson Column.'[7]

---

7. This famous landmark, a statue of the British naval hero Admiral Lord Nelson, is in Trafalgar Square opposite the National Gallery. The fluted column of granite, 145 feet high, supports a bronze statue of Lord Nelson standing with his one arm on a sword. As a result of battle wounds, Nelson lost both his right arm and the sight of his right eye. Here is how Robert Bridges described the statue in a poem:

'That's what I say,' repeated the cobbler obstinately; 'there's only one man that could have done it and he's the man that would have done it. Where's Simeon Barnes, the blacksmith?'

'He's over at Greenford,' faltered the curate.

'More likely over in France,' muttered the cobbler.

'No; he is in neither of those places,' said a small and colourless voice, which came from the little Roman priest who had joined the group. 'As a matter of fact, he is coming up the road at this moment.'

The little priest was not an interesting man to look at, having stubbly brown hair and a round and stolid face. But if he had been as splendid as Apollo no one would have looked at him at that moment. Everyone turned round and peered at the pathway which wound across the plain below, along which was indeed walking, at his own huge stride and with a hammer on his shoulder, Simeon the smith. He was a bony and gigantic man, with deep, dark, sinister eyes and a dark chin beard. He was walking and talking quietly with two other men; and though he was never specially cheerful, he seemed quite at his ease.

'My God!' cried the atheistic cobbler, 'and there's the hammer he did it with.'

'No,' said the inspector, a sensible-looking man with a sandy moustache, speaking for the first time. 'There's the hammer he did it with over there by the church wall. We have left it and the body exactly as they are.'

All glanced round, and the short priest went across and looked down in silence at the tool where it lay. It was one of the smallest and the lightest of the hammers, and would not have caught the eye among the rest; but on the iron edge of it were blood and yellow hair.

After a silence the short priest spoke without looking up, and there was a new note in his dull voice. 'Mr Gibbs was hardly right,' he said, 'in saying that there is no mystery. There is at least the mystery of why so big a man should attempt so big a blow with so little a hammer.'

---

Sailing in the sky
With one arm and one eye.

Four bronze lions guard the base of the column, and on the four sides of the base are bronze reliefs depicting battle scenes.

'Oh, never mind that,' cried Gibbs, in a fever. 'What are we to do with Simeon Barnes?'

'Leave him alone,' said the priest quietly. 'He is coming here of himself. I know those two men with him. They are very good fellows from Greenford, and they have come over about the Presbyterian chapel.'

Even as he spoke the tall smith swung round the corner of the church, and strode into his own yard. Then he stood there quite still, and the hammer fell from his hand. The inspector, who had preserved impenetrable propriety, immediately went up to him.

'I won't ask you, Mr Barnes,' he said, 'whether you know anything about what has happened here. You are not bound to say. I hope you don't know, and that you will be able to prove it. But I must go through the form of arresting you in the King's name for the murder of Colonel Norman Bohun.'

'You are not bound to say anything,' said the cobbler in officious excitement. 'They've got to prove everything. They haven't proved yet that it is Colonel Bohun, with the head all smashed up like that.'

'That won't wash,' said the doctor aside to the priest. 'That's out of the detective stories. I was the colonel's medical man, and I knew his body better than he did. He had very fine hands, but quite peculiar ones. The second and third fingers were the same in length. Oh, that's the colonel right enough.'

As he glanced at the brained corpse upon the ground the iron eyes of the motionless blacksmith followed them and rested there also.

'Is Colonel Bohun dead?' said the smith quite calmly. 'Then he's damned.'

'Don't say anything! Oh, don't say anything,' cried the atheist cobbler, dancing about in an ecstasy of admiration of the English legal system. For no man is such a legalist as the good Secularist.

The blacksmith turned on him over his shoulder the august face of a fanatic.

'It's well for you infidels to dodge like foxes because the world's law favours you,' he said; 'but God guards His own in His pocket, as you shall see this day.'

Then he pointed to the colonel and said: 'When did this dog die in his sins?'

'Moderate your language,' said the doctor.

'Moderate the Bible's language, and I'll moderate mine. When did he die?'

'I saw him alive at six o'clock this morning,' stammered Wilfred Bohun.

'God is good,' said the smith. 'Mr Inspector, I have not the slightest objection to being arrested. It is you who may object to arresting me. I don't mind leaving the court without a stain on my character. You do mind perhaps leaving the court with a bad set-back in your career.'

The solid inspector for the first time looked at the blacksmith with a lively eye; as did everybody else, except the short, strange priest, who was still looking down at the little hammer that had dealt the dreadful blow.

'There are two men standing outside this shop,' went on the blacksmith with ponderous lucidity, 'good tradesmen in Greenford whom you all know, who will swear that they saw me from before midnight till daybreak and long after in the committee-room of our Revival Mission, which sits all night, we save souls so fast. In Greenford itself twenty people could swear to me for all that time. If I were a heathen, Mr Inspector, I would let you walk on to your downfall. But as a Christian man I feel bound to give you your chance, and ask you whether you will hear my alibi now or in court.'

The inspector seemed for the first time disturbed, and said, 'Of course I should be glad to clear you altogether now.'

The smith walked out of his yard with the same long and easy stride, and returned to his two friends from Greenford, who were indeed friends of nearly everyone present. Each of them said a few words which no one ever thought of disbelieving. When they had spoken, the innocence of Simeon stood up as solid as the great church above them.

One of those silences struck the group which are more strange and insufferable than any speech. Madly, in order to make conversation, the curate said to the Catholic priest:

'You seem very much interested in that hammer, Father Brown.'

'Yes, I am,' said Father Brown; 'why is it such a small hammer?'

The doctor swung round on him.

'By George, that's true,' he cried; 'who would use a little hammer with ten larger hammers lying about?'

Then he lowered his voice in the curate's ear and said: 'Only the kind of person that can't lift a large hammer. It is not a question of force or courage between the sexes. It's a question of lifting power in the shoulders. A bold woman could commit ten murders with a light hammer and never turn a hair. She could not kill a beetle with a heavy one.'

Wilfred Bohun was staring at him with a sort of hypnotised horror, while Father Brown listened with his head a little on one side, really interested and attentive. The doctor went on with more hissing emphasis:

'Why do these idiots always assume that the only person who hates the wife's lover is the wife's husband? Nine times out of ten the person who most hates the wife's lover is the wife. Who knows what insolence or treachery he had shown her—look there?'

He made a momentary gesture towards the red-haired woman on the bench. She had lifted her head at last and the tears were drying on her splendid face. But the eyes were fixed on the corpse with an electric glare that had in it something of idiocy.

The Rev. Wilfred Bohun made a limp gesture as if waving away all desire to know; but Father Brown, dusting off his sleeve some ashes blown from the furnace, spoke in his indifferent way.

'You are like so many doctors,' he said; 'your mental science is really suggestive. It is your physical science that is utterly impossible. I agree that the woman wants to kill the co-respondent much more than the petitioner does. And I agree that a woman will always pick up a small hammer instead of a big one. But the difficulty is one of physical impossibility. No woman ever born could have smashed a man's skull out flat like that.' Then he added reflectively, after a pause: 'These people haven't grasped the whole of it. The man was actually wearing an iron helmet, and the blow scattered it like broken glass. Look at that woman. Look at her arms.'

Silence held them all up again, and then the doctor said rather sulkily: 'Well, I may be wrong; there are objections to everything. But I stick to the main point. No man but an idiot would pick up that little hammer if he could use a big hammer.'

With that the lean and quivering hands of Wilfred Bohun went up to his head and seemed to clutch his scanty yellow hair. After an instant they dropped, and he cried: 'That was the word I wanted; you have said the word.'

Then he continued, mastering his discomposure: 'The words you said were, "No man but an idiot would pick up the small hammer."'

'Yes,' said the doctor. 'Well?'

'Well,' said the curate, 'no man but an idiot did.' The rest stared at him with eyes arrested and riveted, and he went on in a febrile and feminine agitation.

'I am a priest,' he cried unsteadily, 'and a priest should be no shedder of blood. I—I mean that he should bring no one to the gallows. And I thank God that I see the criminal clearly now—because he is a criminal who cannot be brought to the gallows.'

'You will not denounce him?' inquired the doctor.

'He would not be hanged if I did denounce him,' answered Wilfred with a wild but curiously happy smile. 'When I went into the church this morning I found a madman praying there—that poor Joe, who has been wrong all his life. God knows what he prayed; but with such strange folk it is not incredible to suppose that their prayers are all upside down. Very likely a lunatic would pray before killing a man. When I last saw poor Joe he was with my brother. My brother was mocking him.'

'By Jove!' cried the doctor, 'this is talking at last. But how do you explain——'

The Rev. Wilfred was almost trembling with the excitement of his own glimpse of the truth. 'Don't you see; don't you see,' he cried feverishly; 'that is the only theory that covers both the queer things, that answers both the riddles. The two riddles are the little hammer and the big blow. The smith might have struck the big blow, but would not have chosen the little hammer. His wife would have chosen the little hammer, but she could not have struck the big blow. But the madman might have done both. As for the little hammer—why, he was mad and might have picked up anything. And for the big blow, have you never heard, doctor, that a maniac in his paroxysm may have the strength of ten men?'

The doctor drew a deep breath and then said, 'By golly, I believe you've got it.'

Father Brown had fixed his eyes on the speaker so long and

steadily as to prove that his large grey, ox-like eyes were not quite so insignificant as the rest of his face. When silence had fallen he said with marked respect: 'Mr Bohun, yours is the only theory yet propounded which holds water every way and is essentially unassailable. I think, therefore, that you deserve to be told, on my positive knowledge, that it is not the true one.' And with that the odd[8] little man walked away and stared again at the hammer.

'That fellow seems to know more than he ought to,' whispered the doctor peevishly to Wilfred. 'Those popish priests are deucedly sly.'

'No, no,' said Bohun, with a sort of wild fatigue. 'It was the lunatic. It was the lunatic.'

The group of the two clerics and the doctor had fallen away from the more official group containing the inspector and the man he had arrested. Now, however, that their own party had broken up, they heard voices from the others. The priest looked up quietly and then looked down again as he heard the blacksmith say in a loud voice:

'I hope I've convinced you, Mr Inspector. I'm a strong man, as you say, but I couldn't have flung my hammer bang here from Greenford. My hammer hasn't got wings that it should come flying half a mile over hedges and fields.'

The inspector laughed amicably and said: 'No, I think you can be considered out of it, though it's one of the rummiest coincidences I ever saw. I can only ask you to give us all the assistance you can in finding a man as big and strong as yourself. By George! you might be useful, if only to hold him! I suppose you yourself have no guess at the man?'

'I may have a guess,' said the pale smith, 'but it is not at a man.' Then, seeing the scared eyes turn towards his wife on the

---

**8.** As in an earlier instance (see Chapter 2, Note 11), the magazine text has the word 'old'. Nowhere in the canon do we learn Father Brown's age or date of birth. In 'The Worst Crime in the World' (*The Secret of Father Brown*) the little priest tries to jump a wide moat. Although he falls into the water, he later remarks that an 'old man' would have been unable even to attempt the leap—a fact that convinces Father Brown an eighty-year-old suspect could not be guilty of a crime. Unfortunately, the chronology of the Father Brown stories is seldom clear, so we don't know at what time in the priest's life this story took place.

bench, he put his huge hand on her shoulder and said: 'Nor a woman either.'

'What do you mean?' asked the inspector jocularly. 'You don't think cows use hammers, do you?'

'I think no thing of flesh held that hammer,' said the blacksmith in a stifled voice; 'mortally speaking, I think the man died alone.'

Wilfred made a sudden forward movement and peered at him with burning eyes.

'Do you mean to say, Barnes,' came the sharp voice of the cobbler, 'that the hammer jumped up of itself and knocked the man down?'

'Oh, you gentlemen may stare and snigger,' cried Simeon; 'you clergymen who tell us on Sunday in what a stillness the Lord smote Sennacherib.[9] I believe that One who walks invisible in every house defended the honour of mine, and laid the defiler dead before the door of it. I believe the force in that blow was just the force there is in earthquakes, and no force less.'

Wilfred said, with a voice utterly undescribable: 'I told Norman myself to beware of the thunderbolt.'

'That agent is outside my jurisdiction,' said the inspector with a slight smile.

'You are not outside His,' answered the smith; 'see you to it,' and, turning his broad back, he went into the house.

The shaken Wilfred was led away by Father Brown, who had an easy and friendly way with him. 'Let us get out of this horrid place, Mr Bohun,' he said. 'May I look inside your church? I hear it's one of the oldest in England. We take some interest, you know,' he added with a comical grimace, 'in old English churches.'

---

9. Sennacherib was an Assyrian king who built a mighty palace at Nineveh, and was murdered (perhaps by his sons) in 681 BC. When Sennacherib tried to take Jerusalem, 'the Lord sent an angel, which cut off all the mighty men of valour, and the leaders and captains in the camp of the king of Assyria. So he returned with shame of face to his own land. And when he was come into the house of his god, they that came forth of his own bowels slew him there with the sword' (2 Chronicles 32:21). This Old Testament account was the basis of Lord Byron's popular poem, 'The Destruction of Sennacherib'.

Wilfred Bohun did not smile, for humour was never his strong point. But he nodded rather eagerly, being only too ready to explain the Gothic splendours to someone more likely to be sympathetic than the Presbyterian blacksmith or the atheist cobbler.

'By all means,' he said, 'let us go in at this side.' And he led the way into the high side entrance at the top of the flight of steps. Father Brown was mounting the first step to follow him when he felt a hand on his shoulder, and turned to behold the dark, thin figure of the doctor, his face darker yet with suspicion.

'Sir,' said the physician harshly, 'you appear to know some secrets in this black business. May I ask if you are going to keep them to yourself?'

'Why, doctor,' answered the priest, smiling quite pleasantly, 'there is one very good reason why a man of my trade should keep things to himself when he is not sure of them, and that is that it is so constantly his duty to keep them to himself when he is sure of them. But if you think I have been discourteously reticent with you or anyone, I will go to the extreme limit of my custom. I will give you two very large hints.'

'Well, sir?' said the doctor gloomily.

'First,' said Father Brown quietly, 'the thing is quite in your own province. It is a matter of physical science. The blacksmith is mistaken, not perhaps in saying that the blow was divine, but certainly in saying that it came by a miracle. It was no miracle, doctor, except in so far as man is himself a miracle, with his strange and wicked and yet half-heroic heart. The force that smashed that skull was a force well known to scientists—one of the most frequently debated of the laws of nature.'

The doctor, who was looking at him with frowning intentness, only said: 'And the other hint?'

'The other hint is this,' said the priest. 'Do you remember the blacksmith, though he believes in miracles, talking scornfully of the impossible fairy tale that his hammer had wings and flew half a mile across country?'

'Yes,' said the doctor, 'I remember that.'

'Well,' added Father Brown, with a broad smile, 'that fairy tale was the nearest thing to the real truth that has been said to-day.' And with that he turned his back and stumped up the steps after the curate.

The Reverend Wilfred, who had been waiting for him, pale

and impatient, as if this little delay were the last straw for his nerves, led him immediately to his favourite corner of the church, that part of the gallery closest to the carved roof and lit by the wonderful window with the angel. The little Latin priest explored and admired everything exhaustively, talking cheerfully but in a low voice all the time. When in the course of his investigation he found the side exit and the winding stair down which Wilfred had rushed to find his brother dead, Father Brown ran not down but up, with the agility of a monkey, and his clear voice came from an outer platform above.

'Come up here, Mr Bohun,' he called. 'The air will do you good.'

Bohun followed him, and came out on a kind of stone gallery or balcony outside the building, from which one could see the illimitable plain in which their small hill stood, wooded away to the purple horizon and dotted with villages and farms. Clear and square, but quite small beneath them, was the blacksmith's yard, where the inspector still stood taking notes and the corpse still lay like a smashed fly.

'Might be the map of the world, mightn't it?' said Father Brown.

'Yes,' said Bohun very gravely, and nodded his head.

Immediately beneath and about them the lines of the Gothic building plunged outwards into the void with a sickening swiftness akin to suicide. There is that element of Titan energy in the architecture of the Middle Ages that, from whatever aspect it be seen, it always seems to be rushing away, like the strong back of some maddened horse. This church was hewn out of ancient and silent stone, bearded with old fungoids and stained with the nests of birds.[10] And yet, when they saw it from below, it sprang like a fountain at the stars; and when they saw it, as now, from above, it poured like a cataract into a voiceless pit. For these two men on the tower were left alone with the most terrible aspect of the Gothic; the monstrous foreshortening and disproportion, the dizzy perspectives, the glimpses of great things small and small things great; a topsy-turvydom of stone in the mid-air. Details of

---

10. This marvellous paragraph, in which Chesterton so beautifully conveys the essence of Gothic architecture, is not in the original magazine version. G.K. added the passage to the book's first English edition.

stone, enormous by their proximity, were relieved against a pattern of fields and farms, pygmy in their distance. A carved bird or beast at a corner seemed like some vast walking or flying dragon wasting the pastures and villages below. The whole atmosphere was dizzy and dangerous, as if men were upheld in air amid the gyrating wings of colossal genii; and the whole of that old church, as tall and rich as a cathedral, seemed to sit upon the sunlit country like a cloud-burst.

'I think there is something rather dangerous about standing on these high places even to pray,' said Father Brown. 'Heights were made to be looked at, not to be looked from.'

'Do you mean that one may fall over?' asked Wilfred.

'I mean that one's soul may fall if one's body doesn't,' said the other priest.

'I scarcely understand you,' remarked Bohun indistinctly.

'Look at that blacksmith, for instance,' went on Father Brown calmly; 'a good man, but not a Christian[11]—hard, imperious, unforgiving. Well, his Scotch religion was made up by men who prayed on hills and high crags, and learnt to look down on the world more than to look up at heaven. Humility is the mother of giants. One sees great things from the valley; only small things from the peak.'

'But he—he didn't do it,' said Bohun tremulously.

'No,' said the other in an odd voice; 'we know he didn't do it.'

After a moment he resumed, looking tranquilly out over the plain with his pale grey eyes. 'I knew a man,' he said, 'who began by worshipping with others before the altar, but who grew fond of high and lonely places to pray from, corners or niches in the belfry or the spire. And once in one of those dizzy places, where the whole world seemed to turn under him like a wheel, his brain turned also, and he fancied he was God. So that though he was a good man, he committed a great crime.'

---

**11.** Father Brown is capable of wise and beautiful remarks, and also remarks that are foolish and ugly. This is one the ugliest. Because the blacksmith is a Scottish Presbyterian, Father Brown does not consider him a Christian! Let us give the priest the benefit of doubt and assume that what he really means is that the smith is not a *good* Christian, as one might say that Torquemada was not a good Christian. (See Chapter 12, Note 3.)

Wilfred's face was turned away, but his bony hands turned blue and white as they tightened on the parapet of stone.

'He thought it was given to *him* to judge the world and strike down the sinner. He would never have had such a thought if he had been kneeling with other men upon a floor. But he saw all men walking about like insects. He saw one especially strutting just below him, insolent and evident by a bright green hat—a poisonous insect.'

Rooks cawed round the corners of the belfry; but there was no other sound till Father Brown went on.

'This also tempted him, that he had in his hand one of the most awful engines of nature; I mean gravitation, that mad and quickening rush by which all earth's creatures fly back to her heart when released. See, the inspector is strutting just below us in the smithy. If I were to toss a pebble over this parapet it would be something like a bullet by the time it struck him. If I were to drop a hammer—even a small hammer——'

Wilfred Bohun threw one leg over the parapet, and Father Brown had him in a minute by the collar.

'Not by that door,' he said quite gently; 'that door leads to hell.'

Bohun staggered back against the wall, and stared at him with frightful eyes.

'How do you know all this?' he cried. 'Are you a devil?'

'I am a man,' answered Father Brown gravely; 'and therefore have all devils in my heart.[12] Listen to me,' he said after a short pause. 'I know what you did—at least, I can guess the great part of it. When you left your brother you were racked with unrighteous rage to the extent even that you snatched up a small hammer, half inclined to kill him with his foulness on his mouth. Recoiling, you thrust it under your buttoned coat instead, and rushed into the church. You pray wildly in many places, under the angel window, upon the platform above, and on a higher platform still, from which you could see the colonel's Eastern hat

12. Father Brown's statement is often cited by critics of the mystery story. As Chesterton frequently reminds us, one secret of the priest's success in solving crimes is his ability to get inside a criminal's mind by empathizing with his evil motives.

like the back of a green beetle crawling about. Then something snapped in your soul, and you let God's thunderbolt fall.'

Wilfred put a weak hand to his head, and asked in a low voice: 'How did you know that his hat looked like a green beetle?'

'Oh, that,' said the other with the shadow of a smile, 'that was common sense. But hear me further. I say I know all this; but no one else shall know it. The next step is for you; I shall take no more steps; I will seal this with the seal of confession. If you ask me why, there are many reasons, and only one that concerns you. I leave things to you because you have not yet gone very far wrong, as assassins go. You did not help to fix the crime on the smith when it was easy; or on his wife, when that was easy. You tried to fix it on the imbecile because you knew that he could not suffer. That was one of the gleams that it is my business to find in assassins. And now come down into the village, and go your own way as free as the wind; for I have said my last word.'

They went down the winding stairs in utter silence, and came out into the sunlight by the smithy. Wilfred Bohun carefully unlatched the wooden gate of the yard, and going up to the inspector, said: 'I wish to give myself up; I have killed my brother.'

### AFTERWORD

It is, of course, as unlikely anyone could drop a hammer from so high a place, and have it hit a man's head, as it is that a 'devout' cleric (as G.K. describes him) would murder his own brother. No matter. We are in Chesterton's world of bizarre semi-fantasy where improbable events are as commonplace as improbable characters.

# 10

# The Eye of Apollo*

THAT singular smoky sparkle, at once a confusion and a transparency, which is the strange secret of the Thames, was changing more and more from its grey to its glittering extreme as the sun climbed to the zenith over Westminster, and two men crossed Westminster Bridge. One man was very tall and the other very short; they might even have been fantastically compared to the arrogant clock-tower of Parliament and the humbler humped shoulders of the Abbey, for the short man was in clerical dress. The official description of the tall man was M. Hercule Flambeau,[1] private detective, and he was going to his new offices in a new pile of flats facing the Abbey entrance. The official description of the short man was the Rev J. Brown,[2] attached to St.

---

* A disciple of a sun-worshipping humbug prophet dies in a fall down an elevator shaft. Was it accident or murder? The story (which first appeared in *Cassell's Magazine*, March 1911, with Sidney Lucas illustrations) is a strong indictment of religious cults that deny the reality of illness and evil.

1. This is the first time we are told Flambeau's first name. Perhaps it too is assumed. In Chapter 8 we learned that his office is in Westminster—now we can place it in an apartment building that faces the entrance of Westminster Abbey. Eventually Flambeau marries a Spanish lady and retires to a castle in Spain where, resuming his real family name of Duroc, he raises a large family. (See 'The Secret of Father Brown' in the book of the same title.)

2. How the J. got into the British first edition is a capital mystery. There is no mention of it in the magazine version, and it was removed from later printings of the book, presumably with Chesterton's approval. (Removing the J., by the way, creates a solecism. No one in England would write 'the Reverend Brown'.) It has been suggested that when Chesterton reworked the opening of this story for the book (see this chapter's afterword) he may have intended to honour Father John O'Connor, the original Father Brown, by giving his priest the first name of John. But this is pure speculation. The mystery deepens when we come upon the name Paul in the next story.

In a memorable paper, 'Some Notes on a Meeting at Chisham' (read at a Chicago meeting of the Baker Street Irregulars in 1947), Robert Bayer made a strong case for the appearance of Sherlock Holmes in 'The Man with Two

Francis Xavier's Church, Camberwell,[3] and he was coming from a Camberwell death-bed to see the new offices of his friend.

The building was American in its sky-scraping altitude, and American also in the oiled elaboration of its machinery of telephones and lifts. But it was barely finished and still understaffed; only three tenants had moved in; the office just above Flambeau was occupied, as also was the office just below him; the two floors above that and the three floors below were entirely bare. But the first glance at the new tower of flats caught something much more arresting. Save for a few relics of scaffolding, the one glaring object was erected outside the office just above Flambeau's. It was an enormous gilt effigy of the human eye, surrounded with rays of gold, and taking up as much room as two or three of the office windows.

'What on earth is that?' asked Father Brown, and stood still.

'Oh, a new religion,' said Flambeau, laughing; 'one of those new religions that forgive your sins by saying you never had any. Rather like Christian Science, I should think.[4] The fact is that a fellow calling himself Kalon (I don't know what his name is,

Beards' (*The Secret of Father Brown*). While working on a review of a recent reprinting of this paper (my review appeared in *Baker Street Miscellanea*, Winter 1984) I thought to check the Holmes canon to see if it contains a reference to a J. Brown. It does! In 'The Adventure of the Six Napoleons' there is a Joshua Brown, of Chiswick, who buys one of the six plaster busts of Napoleon, and who aids Holmes in solving the crime. I argue that this was none other than a young Father Brown, not yet a man of the cloth, but working independently of Holmes as an amateur detective.

Watson may have purposely concealed the fact that Joshua Brown later became the famous detective priest. Years later, Chesterton returned the favour by not identifying Holmes as the detective who failed to solve a case by his usual methods, whereas Father Brown's intuitive methods succeeded. It seems entirely possible that England's two greatest detectives collaborated twice on remarkable cases.

3. Father Brown has moved again, this time to a parish in south London: Camberwell is in the borough of Southwark. In Holmes's 'Case of Identity' a Mary Sutherland lives at 31 Lyon Place in Camberwell, and one of Watson's many untold stories (it is mentioned in 'The Five Orange Pips') is 'The Camberwell Poisoning Case'.

4. Chesterton understandably despised Christian Science. He considered it a foggy denial of both science and Christianity, and closely related to the naïve optimism of American capitalism. See his essays on Christian Science in *The Uses of Diversity* and *All is Grist*.

except that it can't be that) has taken the flat just above me. I have two lady typewriters[5] underneath me, and this enthusiastic old humbug on top. He calls himself the New Priest of Apollo, and he worships the sun.'

'Let him look out,' said Father Brown. 'The sun was the cruellest of all the gods. But what does that monstrous eye mean?'

'As I understand it, it is a theory of theirs,' answered Flambeau, 'that a man can endure anything if his mind is quite steady. Their two great symbols are the sun and the open eye; for they say that if a man were really healthy he could stare at the sun.'

'If a man were really healthy,' said Father Brown, 'he would not bother to stare at it.'

'Well, that's all I can tell you about the new religion,' went on Flambeau carelessly. 'It claims, of course, that it can cure all physical diseases.'

'Can it cure the one spiritual disease?' asked Father Brown, with a serious curiosity.

'And what is the one spiritual disease?' asked Flambeau, smiling.

'Oh, thinking one is quite well,' said his friend.

Flambeau was more interested in the quiet little office below him than in the flamboyant temple above. He was a lucid Southerner, incapable of conceiving himself as anything but a Catholic or an atheist; and new religions of a bright and pallid sort were not much in his line. But humanity was always in his line, especially when it was good-looking; moreover, the ladies downstairs were characters in their way. The office was kept by two sisters, both slight and dark, one of them tall and striking. She had a dark, eager and aquiline profile, and was one of those women whom one always thinks of in profile, as of the clean-cut edge of some weapon. She seemed to cleave her way through life. She had eyes of startling brilliancy, but it was the brilliancy of steel rather than of diamonds; and her straight, slim figure was a shade too stiff for its grace. Her younger sister was like her shortened shadow, a little greyer, paler, and more insignificant.

---

**5.** At the time G.K. wrote, typists in both England and the US were called typewriters.

They both wore a business-like black, with little masculine cuffs and collars. There are thousands of such curt, strenuous ladies in the offices of London, but the interest of these lay rather in their real than their apparent position.

For Pauline Stacey, the elder, was actually the heiress of a crest and half a county, as well as great wealth; she had been brought up in castles and gardens, before a frigid fierceness (peculiar to the modern woman) had driven her to what she considered a harsher and a higher existence. She had not, indeed, surrendered her money; in that there would have been a romantic or monkish abandon quite alien to her masterful utilitarianism. She held her wealth, she would say, for use upon practical social objects. Part of it she had put into her business, the nucleus of a model typewriting emporium; part of it was distributed in various leagues and causes for the advancement of such work among women. How far Joan, her sister and partner, shared this slightly prosaic idealism no one could be very sure. But she followed her leader with a dog-like affection which was somehow more attractive, with its touch of tragedy, than the hard, high spirits of the elder. For Pauline Stacey had nothing to say to tragedy; she was understood to deny its existence.

Her rigid rapidity and cold impatience had amused Flambeau very much on the first occasion of his entering the flats. He had lingered outside the lift in the entrance hall waiting for the lift-boy, who generally conducts strangers to the various floors. But this bright-eyed falcon of a girl had openly refused to endure such official delay. She said sharply that she knew all about the lift, and was not dependent on boys—or on men either. Though her flat was only three floors above, she managed in the few seconds of ascent to give Flambeau a great many of her fundamental views in an off-hand manner; they were to the general effect that she was a modern working woman and loved modern working machinery. Her bright black eyes blazed with abstract anger against those who rebuke mechanic science and ask for the return of romance. Everyone, she said, ought to be able to manage machines, just as she could manage the lift. She seemed almost to resent the fact of Flambeau opening the lift-door for her; and that gentleman went up to his own apartments smiling with somewhat mingled feelings at the memory of such spit-fire self-dependence.

She certainly had a temper, of a snappy, practical sort; the gestures of her thin, elegant hands were abrupt or even destructive. Once Flambeau entered her office on some typewriting business, and found she had just flung a pair of spectacles belonging to her sister into the middle of the floor and stamped on them. She was already in the rapids of an ethical tirade about the 'sickly medical notions' and the morbid admission of weakness implied in such an apparatus. She dared her sister to bring such artificial, unhealthy rubbish into the place again. She asked if she was expected to wear wooden legs or false hair or glass eyes; and as she spoke her eyes sparkled like the terrible crystal.

Flambeau, quite bewildered with this fanaticism, could not refrain from asking Miss Pauline (with direct French logic) why a pair of spectacles was a more morbid sign of weakness than a lift, and why, if science might help us in the one effort, it might not help us in the other.

'That is *so* different,' said Pauline Stacey, loftily. 'Batteries and motors and all those things are marks of the force of man—yes, Mr Flambeau, and the force of woman, too! We shall take our turn at these great engines that devour distance and defy time. That is high and splendid—that is really science. But these nasty props and plasters the doctors sell—why, they are just badges of poltroonery. Doctors stick on legs and arms as if we were born cripples and sick slaves. But I was free-born, Mr Flambeau! People only think they need these things because they have been trained in fear instead of being trained in power and courage, just as the silly nurses tell children not to stare at the sun, and so they can't do it without blinking. But why among the stars should there be one star I may not see? The sun is not my master, and I will open my eyes and stare at him whenever I choose.'[6]

***

6. The last two sentences of this paragraph do not appear in the magazine text. The paragraph originally ended with: 'But I am above the sun. I am immortal: and I will open my eyes and stare at it whenever I choose.'

It is hard to believe, but Dr William Horatio Bates, in his classic work of crank science *The Cure of Imperfect Sight by Treatment Without Glasses*, recommended the practice of looking directly at the sun for brief periods. This section of his book was wisely excised from editions published after his death. Like Kalon and Pauline Stacey, Bates firmly believed that all spectacles were crutches that should be thrown away. It is a measure of Aldous

'Your eyes,' said Flambeau, with a foreign bow, 'will dazzle the sun.' He took pleasure in complimenting this strange stiff beauty, partly because it threw her a little off her balance. But as he went upstairs to his floor he drew a deep breath and whistled, saying to himself: 'So she has got into the hands of that conjuror upstairs with his golden eye.' For, little as he knew or cared about the new religion of Kalon, he had heard of his special notion about sun-gazing.[7]

He soon discovered that the spiritual bond between the floors above and below him was close and increasing. The man who called himself Kalon was a magnificent creature, worthy, in a physical sense, to be the pontiff of Apollo. He was nearly as tall even as Flambeau, and very much better looking, with a golden beard, strong blue eyes, and a mane flung back like a lion's. In

---

Huxley's ignorance of ophthalmology that he wrote an entire book, *The Art of Seeing*, in defence of Bates's quackery. (You'll find the lurid details in my *Fads and Fallacies in the Name of Science*.)

Gustav Theodor Fechner, a nineteenth-century German psychologist and philosopher, was blinded for years as a result of staring at the sun to investigate after-image effects on the retina. He never fully recovered his sight, though he claimed it was partly restored after prayer and meditation. He believed that his restored sight enabled him to see force-fields surrounding plants and animals. (In Fechner's panpsychic metaphysics, plants have a low-order consciousness, as do the Earth, planets, Sun, and other stars.)

You might be tempted to suppose that Chesterton's Kalon and the cult of Apollo are wild caricatures of modern cults and their charismatic leaders. Not so. The civilized world still swarms with cults built around money-grubbing charlatans who purvey doctrines more fantastic than Kalon's—witness Scientology for example, or the recent claims of Transcendental Meditation. In 1977 Bobbs-Merrill published *Project X: The Search for the Secrets of Immortality*, by occult journalist Gene Savoy. Influenced by Fechner's metaphysics, Savoy recommends letting sunlight enter the body through the eyes, allowing its cosmic energies to make the body healthier and longer lived. Perhaps Savoy also came under the influence of Kalon! Bobbs-Merrill should have been ashamed to publish this book, but at least they had the sense to print a warning in the front: 'Neither the author nor the publisher assume any responsibility whatsoever for any possible harm that may result from the indiscriminate use, application, or misuse by the reader of the techniques described.'

7. In the magazine text, the last part of this sentence reads: 'he had heard that its great type of the real impotence of evil was this strength of the eye to meet the sun'.

structure he was the blonde beast of Nietzsche, but all this animal beauty was heightened, brightened and softened by genuine
intellect and spirituality. If he looked like one of the great Saxon
kings, he looked like one of the kings that were also saints. And
this despite the cockney incongruity of his surroundings; the fact
that he had an office half-way up a building in Victoria Street;
that the clerk (a commonplace youth in cuffs and collars) sat in
the outer room, between him and the corridor; that his name was
on a brass plate, and the gilt emblem of his creed hung above his
street, like the advertisement of an oculist. All this vulgarity
could not take away from the man called Kalon the vivid
oppression and inspiration that came from his soul and body.
When all was said, a man in the presence of this quack did feel in
the presence of a great man. Even in the loose jacket-suit of linen
that he wore as a workshop dress in his office he was a fascinating
and formidable figure; and when robed in the white vestments
and crowned with the golden circlet, in which he daily saluted
the sun, he really looked so splendid that the laughter of the
street people sometimes died suddenly on their lips. For three
times in the day the new sun-worshipper went out on his little
balcony, in the face of all Westminster, to say some litany to his
shining lord: once at daybreak, once at sunset, and once at the
shock of noon. And it was while the shock of noon still shook
faintly from the towers of Parliament and parish church that
Father Brown, the friend of Flambeau, first looked up and saw
the white priest of Apollo.[8]

Flambeau had seen quite enough of these daily salutations of
Phœbus, and plunged into the porch of the tall building without
even looking for his clerical friend to follow. But Father Brown,
whether from a professional interest in ritual or a strong individual interest in tomfoolery, stopped and stared up at the balcony
of the sun-worshipper, just as he might have stopped and stared
up at a Punch and Judy. Kalon the Prophet was already erect,
with argent garments and uplifted hands, and the sound of his
strangely penetrating voice could be heard all the way down the

---

**8.** In *Cassell's Magazine* the next paragraph is preceded by the following
sentence: 'He had crossed Westminster Bridge with Flambeau, coming from
the South London slum in which he was now officiating, in order to see his
friend's new business apartments.'

busy street uttering his solar litany. He was already in the middle
of it; his eyes were fixed upon the flaming disc. It is doubtful if he
saw anything or anyone on this earth; it is substantially certain
that he did not see a stunted, round-faced priest who, in the
crowd below, looked up at him with blinking eyes. That was perhaps the most startling difference between even these two far
divided men. Father Brown could not look at anything without
blinking; but the priest of Apollo could look on the blaze at noon
without a quiver of the eyelid.

'O sun,' cried the prophet, 'O star that art too great to be
allowed among the stars! O fountain that flowest quietly in that
secret spot that is called space. White father of all white unwearied things, white flames and white flowers and white peaks.[9]
Father, who art more innocent than all thy most innocent and
quiet children; primal purity, into the peace of which——'

A rush and crash like the reversed rush of a rocket was cloven
with a strident and incessant yelling. Five people rushed into the
gate of the mansions as three people rushed out, and for an
instant they all deafened each other. The sense of some utterly
abrupt horror seemed for a moment to fill half the street with bad
news—bad news that was all the worse because no one knew
what it was. Two figures remained still after the crash of commo-
tion: the fair priest of Apollo on the balcony above, and the ugly
priest of Christ below him.

At last the tall figure and titanic energy of Flambeau appeared
in the doorway of the mansions and dominated the little mob.
Talking at the top of his voice like a fog-horn, he told somebody
or anybody to go for a surgeon; and as he turned back into the
dark and thronged entrance his friend Father Brown slipped in
insignificantly after him. Even as he ducked and dived through
the crowd he could still hear the magnificent melody and monotony of the solar priest still calling on the happy god who is the
friend of fountains and flowers.

Father Brown found Flambeau and some six other people
standing round the enclosed space into which the lift commonly
descended. But the lift had not descended. Something else had
descended; something that ought to have come by a lift.

---

**9.** In the magazine, this sentence reads: 'White Father of all white
unwearied things, white clouds and white flowers and white birds.'

For the last four minutes Flambeau had looked down on it; had seen the brained and bleeding figure of that beautiful woman who denied the existence of tragedy.[10] He had never had the slightest doubt that it was Pauline Stacey; and, though he had sent for a doctor, he had not the slightest doubt that she was dead.

He could not remember for certain whether he had liked her or disliked her; there was so much both to like and dislike. But she had been a person to him, and the unbearable pathos of details and habit stabbed him with all the small daggers of bereavement. He remembered her pretty face and priggish speeches with a sudden secret vividness which is all the bitterness of death. In an instant, like a bolt from the blue, like a thunderbolt from nowhere, that beautiful and defiant body had been dashed down the open well of the lift to death at the bottom. Was it suicide? With so insolent an optimist it seemed impossible. Was it murder? But who was there in those hardly inhabited flats to murder anybody? In a rush of raucous words, which he meant to be strong and suddenly found weak, he asked where was that fellow Kalon. A voice, habitually heavy, quiet and full, assured him that Kalon for the last fifteen minutes had been away up on his balcony worshippng his god. When Flambeau heard the voice, and felt the hand of Father Brown, he turned his swarthy face and said abruptly:

'Then, if he has been up there all the time, who can have done it?'

'Perhaps,' said the other, 'we might go upstairs and find out. We have half an hour before the police will move.'

Leaving the body of the slain heiress in charge of the surgeons, Flambeau dashed up the stairs to the typewriting office, found it utterly empty, and then dashed up to his own. Having entered that, he abruptly returned with a new and white face to his friend.

'Her sister,' he said, with an unpleasant seriousness, 'her sister seems to have gone out for a walk.'

Father Brown nodded. 'Or, she may have gone up to the office of that sun man,' he said. 'If I were you I should just verify that,

---

10. The magazine text is: 'the brained and bleeding figure of the most beautiful woman in Westminster'.

and then let us all talk it over in your office. No,' he added suddenly, as if remembering something, 'shall I ever get over that
stupidity of mine? Of course, in their office downstairs.'

Flambeau stared; but he followed the little father downstairs to
the empty flat of the Staceys, where that impenetrable pastor
took a large red-leather chair in the very entrance, from which he
could see the stairs and landings, and waited. He did not wait
very long. In about four minutes three figures descended the
stairs, alike only in their solemnity. The first was Joan Stacey,
the sister of the dead woman—evidently she *had* been upstairs in
the temporary temple of Apollo; the second was the priest of
Apollo himself, his litany finished, sweeping down the empty
stairs in utter magnificence—something in his white robes, beard
and parted hair had the look of Doré's Christ[11] leaving the Pre-
torium; the third was Flambeau, black browed and somewhat
bewildered.

Miss Joan Stacey, dark, with a drawn face and hair prematurely touched with grey, walked straight to her own desk and set
out her papers with a practical flap. The mere action rallied
everyone else to sanity. If Miss Joan Stacey was a criminal, she
was a cool one. Father Brown regarded her for some time with an
odd little smile, and then, without taking his eyes off her,
addressed himself to somebody else.

'Prophet,' he said, presumably addressing Kalon, 'I wish you
would tell me a lot about your religion.'

'I shall be proud to do it,' said Kalon, inclining his still
crowned head, 'but I am not sure that I understand.'

'Why, it's like this,' said Father Brown, in his frankly doubtful
way: 'We are taught that if a man has really bad first principles,
that must be partly his fault. But, for all that, we can make some
difference between a man who insults his quite clear conscience
and a man with a conscience more or less clouded with sophis-
tries. Now, do you really think that murder is wrong at all?'

'Is this an accusation?' asked Kalon very quietly.

'No,' answered Brown, equally gently, 'it is the speech for the
defence.'

---

11. This is a reference to one of the pictures in a popular book of Bible
illustrations by the French artist Paul Gustave Doré.

In the long and startled stillness of the room the prophet of Apollo slowly rose; and really it was like the rising of the sun. He filled that room with his light and life in such a manner that a man felt he could as easily have filled Salisbury Plain.[12] His robed form seemed to hang the whole room with classic draperies; his epic gesture seemed to extend it into grander perspectives, till the little black figure of the modern cleric seemed to be a fault and an intrusion, a round, black blot upon some splendour of Hellas.

'We meet at last, Caiaphas,'[13] said the prophet. 'Your church and mine are the only realities on this earth. I adore the sun, and you the darkening of the sun; you are the priest of the dying and I of the living God. Your present work of suspicion and slander is worthy of your coat and creed. All your church is but a black police; you are only spies and detectives seeking to tear from men confessions of guilt, whether by treachery or torture. You would convict men of crime, I would convict them of innocence. You would convince them of sin, I would convince them of virtue.

'Reader of the books of evil, one more word before I blow away your baseless nightmares for ever. Not even faintly could you understand how little I care whether you can convict me or no. The things you call disgrace and horrible hanging are to me no more than an ogre in a child's toybook to a man once grown up. You said you were offering the speech for the defence. I care so little for the cloudland of this life that I will offer you the speech for the prosecution. There is but one thing that can be said against me in this matter, and I will say it myself. The woman that is dead was my love and my bride; not after such manner as your tin chapels call lawful, but by a law purer and sterner than you will ever understand. She and I walked another world from yours, and trod palaces of crystal while you were plodding through tunnels and corridors of brick. Well, I know that policemen, theological and otherwise, always fancy that where there

---

12. Salisbury Plain is a large chalk plateau in Wiltshire, north of Salisbury. The remains of many ancient monuments are there, including the famous Stonehenge.

13. Caiaphas was the high priest who presided over the council that condemned Jesus.

has been love there must soon be hatred; so there you have the first point made for the prosecution. But the second point is stronger; I do not grudge it you. Not only is it true that Pauline loved me, but it is also true that this very morning, before she died, she wrote at that table a will leaving me and my new church half a million. Come, where are the handcuffs? Do you suppose I care what foolish things you do with me? Penal servitude will only be like waiting for her at a wayside station. The gallows will only be going to her in a headlong car.'

He spoke with the brain-shaking authority of an orator, and Flambeau and Joan Stacey stared at him in an amazed admiration. Father Brown's face seemed to express nothing but extreme distress; he looked at the ground with one wrinkle of pain across his forehead. The prophet of the sun leaned easily against the mantelpiece and resumed:

'In a few words I have put before you the whole case against me—the only possible case against me. In fewer words still I will blow it to pieces, so that not a trace of it remains. As to whether I have committed this crime, the truth is in one sentence: I could not have committed this crime. Pauline Stacey fell from this floor to the ground at five minutes past twelve. A hundred people will go into the witness-box and say that I was standing out upon the balcony of my own rooms above from just before the stroke of noon to a quarter-past—the usual period of my public prayers. My clerk (a respectable youth from Clapham, with no sort of connection with me) will swear that he sat in my outer office all the morning, and that no communication passed through. He will swear that I arrived a full ten minutes before the hour, fifteen minutes before any whisper of the accident, and that I did not leave the office or the balcony all that time. No one ever had so complete an alibi; I could subpœna half Westminster. I think you had better put the handcuffs away again. The case is at an end.

'But last of all, that no breath of this idiotic suspicion remain in the air, I will tell you all you want to know. I believe I do know how my unhappy friend came by her death. You can, if you choose, blame me for it, or my faith and philosophy at least; but you certainly cannot lock me up. It is well known to all students of the higher truths that certain adepts and *illuminati* have in history attained the power of levitation—that is, of being self-sustained upon the empty air.[14] It is but a part of that general conquest of matter which is the main element in our occult wisdom. Poor Pauline was of an impulsive and ambitious temper. I think, to tell the truth, she thought herself somewhat deeper in the mysteries than she was; and she has often said to me, as we went down in the lift together, that if one's will were strong enough, one could float down as harmlessly as a feather. I solemnly believe that in some ecstasy of noble thoughts she attempted the miracle. Her will, or faith, must have failed her at the crucial instant, and the lower law of matter had its horrible revenge. There is the whole story, gentlemen, very sad and, as you think, very presumptuous and wicked, but certainly not criminal or in any way connected with me. In the shorthand of the police-courts, you had better call it suicide. I shall always call it heroic failure for the advance of science and the slow scaling of heaven.'

It was the first time Flambeau had ever seen Father Brown vanquished. He still sat looking at the ground, with a painful and corrugated brow, as if in shame. It was impossible to avoid the feeling which the prophet's winged words had fanned, that here was a sullen, professional suspecter of men overwhelmed by a prouder and purer spirit of natural liberty and health. At last he said, blinking as if in bodily distress: 'Well, if that is so, sir, you need do no more than take the testamentary paper you spoke of and go. I wonder where the poor lady left it.'

'It will be over there on her desk by the door, I think,' said Kalon, with that massive innocence of manner that seemed to acquit him wholly. 'She told me specially she would write it this morning, and I actually saw her writing as I went up in the lift to my own room.'

---

**14.** Today's popular cult of Transcendental Meditation (TM) now claims that with sufficient training (for which of course the *illuminati* pay a whopping fee) you can learn to levitate and to make yourself invisible. The cult distributes literature showing disciples meditating in a lotus position, seemingly suspended in mid-air. Critics contend that the floaters are bouncing on a bed, the picture having been snapped at the top of a bounce. A friend suggests a better theory. The meditator is not levitating at all. She is being held in the air by an invisible TMer.

'Was her door open then?' asked the priest, with his eye on a corner of the matting.

'Yes,' said Kalon calmly.

'Ah! it has been open ever since,' said the other, and resumed his silent study of the mat.

'There is a paper over here,' said the grim Miss Joan, in a somewhat singular voice. She had passed over to her sister's desk by the doorway, and was holding a sheet of blue foolscap in her hand. There was a sour smile on her face that seemed unfit for such a scene or occasion, and Flambeau looked at her with a darkening brow.

Kalon the prophet stood away from the paper with that royal unconsciousness that had carried him through. But Flambeau took it out of the lady's hand, and read it with the utmost amazement. It did, indeed, begin in the formal manner of a will, but after the words 'I give and bequeath all of which I die possessed' the writing abruptly stopped with a set of scratches, and there was no trace of the name of any legatee. Flambeau, in wonder, handed this truncated testament to his clerical friend, who glanced at it and silently gave it to the priest of the sun.

An instant afterwards that pontiff, in his splendid sweeping draperies, had crossed the room in two great strides, and was towering over Joan Stacey, his blue eyes standing from his head.

'What monkey tricks have you been playing here?' he cried. 'That's not all Pauline wrote.'

They were startled to hear him speak in quite a new voice, with a Yankee shrillness in it; all his grandeur and good English had fallen from him like a cloak.

'That is the only thing on her desk,' said Joan, and confronted him steadily with the same smile of evil favour.

Of a sudden the man broke out into blasphemies and cataracts of incredulous words. There was something shocking about the dropping of his mask; it was like a man's real face falling off.

'See here!' he cried in broad American, when he was breathless with cursing, 'I may be an adventurer, but I guess you're a murderess. Yes, gentlemen, here's your death explained, and without any levitation. The poor girl is writing a will in my favour; her cursed sister comes in, struggles for the pen, drags her to the well, and throws her down before she can finish it. Sakes![15] I reckon we want the handcuffs after all.'

'As you have truly remarked,' replied Joan, with ugly calm, 'your clerk is a very respectable young man, who knows the nature of an oath; and he will swear in any court that I was up in your office arranging some typewriting work for five minutes before and five minutes after my sister fell. Mr Flambeau will tell you that he found me there.'

There was a silence.

'Why, then,' cried Flambeau, 'Pauline was alone when she fell, and it was suicide!'

'She was alone when she fell,' said Father Brown, 'but it was not suicide.'

'Then how did she die?' asked Flambeau impatiently.

'She was murdered.'

'But she was all alone,' objected the detective.

'She was murdered when she was all alone,' answered the priest.

All the rest stared at him, but he remained sitting in the same old dejected attitude, with a wrinkle in his round forehead and an appearance of impersonal shame and sorrow; his voice was colourless and sad.

'What I want to know,' cried Kalon, with an oath, 'is when the police are coming for this bloody and wicked sister. She's killed her flesh and blood; she's robbed me of half a million that was just as sacredly mine as——'

'Come, come, prophet,' interrupted Flambeau, with a kind of sneer; 'remember that all this world is a cloudland.'

The hierophant of the sun-god made an effort to climb back on to his pedestal. 'It is not the mere money,' he cried, 'though that would equip the cause throughout the world. It is also my beloved one's wishes. To Pauline all this was holy. In Pauline's eyes——'

Father Brown suddenly sprang erect, so that his chair fell over flat behind him. He was deathly pale, yet he seemed fired with a hope. His eyes shone.

15. Chesterton was never very good when he tried, as he did on rare occasions, to inject American slang into dialogue.

'That's it!' he cried in a clear voice. 'That's the way to begin. In Pauline's eyes——'

The tall prophet retreated before the tiny priest in an almost mad disorder. 'What do you mean? How dare you?' he cried repeatedly.

'In Pauline's eyes,' repeated the priest, his own shining more and more. 'Go on—in God's name, go on. The foulest crime the fiends ever prompted feels lighter after confession; and I implore you to confess. Go on, go on—in Pauline's eyes——'

'Let me go, you devil!' thundered Kalon, struggling like a giant in bonds. 'Who are you, you cursed spy, to weave your spider's webs round me, and peep and peer? Let me go.'

'Shall I stop him?' asked Flambeau, bounding towards the exit, for Kalon had already thrown the door wide open.

'No; let him pass,' said Father Brown, with a strange deep sigh that seemed to come from the depths of the universe. 'Let Cain pass by, for he belongs to God.'

There was a long-drawn silence in the room when he had left it, which was to Flambeau's fierce wits one long agony of interrogation. Miss Joan Stacey very coolly tidied up the papers on her desk.

'Father,' said Flambeau at last, 'it is my duty, not my curiosity only—it is my duty to find out, if I can, who committed the crime.'

'Which crime?' asked Father Brown.

'The one we are dealing with, of course,' replied his impatient friend.

'We are dealing with two crimes,' said Brown, 'crimes of very different weight—and by very different criminals.'

Miss Joan Stacey, having collected and put away her papers, proceeded to lock up her drawer. Father Brown went on, noticing her as little as she noticed him.

'The two crimes,' he observed, 'were committed against the same weakness of the same person, in a struggle for her money. The author of the larger crime found himself thwarted by the smaller crime; the author of the smaller crime got the money.'

'Oh, don't go on like a lecturer,' groaned Flambeau; 'put it in a few words.'

'I can put it in one word,' answered his friend.

Miss Joan Stacey skewered her business-like black hat on to her head with a business-like black frown before a little mirror, and, as the conversation proceeded, took her handbag and umbrella in an unhurried style, and left the room.

'The truth is in one word, and a short one,' said Father Brown. 'Pauline Stacey was blind.'[16]

'Blind!' repeated Flambeau, and rose slowly to his whole huge stature.

'She was subject to it by blood,' Brown proceeded. 'Her sister would have started eyeglasses if Pauline would have let her; but it was her special philosophy or fad that one must not encourage such diseases by yielding to them. She would not admit the cloud; or she tried to dispel it by will. So her eyes got worse and worse with straining; but the worst strain was to come. It came with this precious prophet, or whatever he calls himself, who taught her to stare at the hot sun with the naked eye. It was called accepting Apollo. Oh, if these new pagans would only be old pagans, they would be a little wiser! The old pagans knew that mere naked Nature-worship must have a cruel side. They knew that the eye of Apollo can blast and blind.'

There was a pause, and the priest went on in a gentle and even broken voice. 'Whether or no that devil deliberately made her blind, there is no doubt that he deliberately killed her through her blindness. The very simplicity of the crime is sickening. You know he and she went up and down in those lifts without official help; you know also how smoothly and silently the lifts slide. Kalon brought the lift to the girl's landing, and saw her, through the open door, writing in her slow, sightless way the will she had promised him. He called out to her cheerily that he had the lift ready for her, and she was to come out when she was ready. Then he pressed a button and shot soundlessly up to his own floor, walked through his own office, out on to his own balcony, and was safely praying before the crowded street when the poor girl,

---

16. The story is more plausible if 'blind' is taken to mean that Pauline Stacey was only partially blind. Staring at the sun could easily have permanently injured her retinas, yet left her with enough vision, like poor old Fechner, to get about fairly well without others realizing how weak her sight was.

having finished her work, ran gaily out to where lover and lift were to receive her, and stepped——'

'Don't!' cried Flambeau.

'He ought to have got half a million by pressing that button,' continued the little father, in the colourless voice in which he talked of such horrors. 'But that went smash. It went smash because there happened to be another person who also wanted the money, and who also knew the secret about poor Pauline's sight. There was one thing about that will that I think nobody noticed: although it was unfinished and without a signature, the other Miss Stacey and some servant of hers had already signed it as witnesses. Joan had signed first, saying Pauline could finish it later, with a typical feminine contempt for legal forms. Therefore, Joan wanted her sister to sign the will without real witnesses. Why? I thought of the blindness, and felt sure she had wanted Pauline to sign in solitude because she had wanted her not to sign at all.

'People like the Staceys always use fountain pens; but this was specially natural to Pauline. By habit and her strong will and memory she could still write almost as well as if she saw; but she could not tell when her pen needed dipping. Therefore, her fountain pens were carefully filled by her sister—all except this fountain pen. This was carefully *not* filled by her sister; the remains of the ink held out for a few lines and then failed altogether. And the prophet lost five hundred thousand pounds and committed one of the most brutal and brilliant murders in human history for nothing.'

Flambeau went to the open door and heard the official police ascending the stairs. He turned and said: 'You must have followed everything devilish close to have traced the crime to Kalon in ten minutes.'[17]

Father Brown gave a sort of start.

'Oh! to him,' he said. 'No; I had to follow rather close to find

---

17. This paragraph was heavily edited for the book. Originally it read: 'Flambeau was leaning back in his chair and looking at his friend with a queer and wondering expression. "You must have followed everything that has happened here devilish closely", he said, "to have traced the crime to Kalon at all." '

out about Miss Joan and the fountain pen. But I knew Kalon was the criminal before I came into the front door.'

'You must be joking!' cried Flambeau.

'I'm quite serious,' answered the priest. 'I tell you I knew he had done it, even before I knew what he had done.'

'But why?'

'These pagan stoics,' said Brown reflectively, 'always fail by their strength. There came a crash and a scream down the street, and the priest of Apollo did not start or look round. I did not know what it was. But I knew that he was expecting it.'

## AFTERWORD

For reasons I do not know, this story differs more from its original magazine version than any other story in the book. A long beginning section of four paragraphs was omitted, replaced by a completely new opening paragraph, and there are more than a hundred spots in the tale where words were dropped, new words added, and sentences omitted, added, or altered. In my notes I have indicated only the most significant changes.

The original opening is worth reprinting in full because it provides important information not otherwise available. We learn for instance that Flambeau began his detective business in Hampstead. We learn that Kalon's career was undamaged by his murder of Pauline Stacey— the American charlatan later acquired a million followers in Central America!

The excised opening paragraphs follow:

When Flambeau applied his talents to the capturing of spoilers instead of the capturing of spoil, it was not remarkable that he should meet with considerable success. He was even in the habit of lightly asserting that the trades of thief and detective were so like each other that he hardly knew the difference. In truth, however, from having been a highly unscrupulous bandit, he became a particularly scrupulous inquirer, and would touch no business except what was worthy of an old family solicitor. Hence his cases, though quaint, and sometimes serious, were seldom squalid, and sometimes brought him into intellectual atmospheres, too, seldom associated with the police.

One of the strangest of such occurrences was that accident or violence, or whatever it was, that left (as some think) a faint fleck upon the splendour of the new religion now so fashionable in London and New York; I mean the religion founded by that remarkable man Kalon, who called himself the New Priest of Apollo. With the tenets and subsequent history of this gospel of Greek ideality we are not much concerned. It was one of the many new religions of the twentieth century that taught a superior innocence of sin and pain; and seemed devised not so much to lighten the troubles of the unfortunate, as to complete the satisfaction of the lucky. Its principal symbols were the Sun and the Open Eye; its priests professed (as a type of their strength and knowledge) that they could gaze unblinking at the sun at noon. It was, they said, a morbid human superstition that such fires are not to be endured; the fountain of light cannot blind us. Kalon, the founder, is now a pope of whole prairies full of villages in Central America, with a church of many million souls. But these incidents occurred earlier in his career, when he was not so successful, though, perhaps, equally conspicuous.

After his first successes in Hampstead, Flambeau had moved into ampler offices in Westminster. The building was a new pile of flats within sight of the Abbey; the official machinery of the mansions was in the swiftest and most American style, but not fully completed; the service was still understaffed, and only three tenants, including Flambeau, had managed to move into the flats. Outside, save for the remains of a scaffolding, the one conspicuous object was an enormous effigy of the human eye, surrounded by rays of gold, erected over the balcony and office of the New Priest of Apollo.

Immediately under this modern and official Delphi were Flambeau's chambers, modestly marked as those of an inquiry agent; immediately under that was the office of two lady typewriters. The ground floor and the rest of the house were empty.

I must add a word of caution in case anyone reading this book is foolish enough to experiment with sun gazing. Contrary to Kalon, Bates, and Huxley, damage to the eyes can be irreparable. Even during a total eclipse of the sun, retinas can be injured by ultraviolet radiation. It is not enough to view a solar eclipse, total or otherwise, through sun glasses or dark film because the ultraviolet radiation gets through. One is advised to turn one's back to the sun and watch the progress of the eclipse by means of a lens or pinhole that throws the sun's image on a sheet of cardboard.

# The Sign of the Broken Sword*

THE thousand arms of the forest were grey, and its million fingers silver. In a sky of dark green-blue-like slate the stars were bleak and brilliant like splintered ice. All that thickly wooded and sparsely tenanted countryside was stiff with a bitter and brittle frost. The black hollows between the trunks of the trees looked like bottomless, black caverns of that heartless Scandinavian hell, a hell of incalculable cold. Even the square stone tower of the church looked northern to the point of heathenry, as if it were some barbaric tower among the sea rocks of Iceland. It was a queer night for anyone to explore a churchyard. But, on the other hand, perhaps it was worth exploring.

It rose abruptly out of the ashen wastes of forest in a sort of hump or shoulder of green turf that looked grey in the starlight. Most of the graves were on a slant, and the path leading up to the church was as steep as a staircase. On the top of the hill, in the one flat and prominent place, was the monument for which the place was famous. It contrasted strangely with the featureless graves all round, for it was the work of one of the greatest sculptors of modern Europe; and yet his fame was at once forgotten in the fame of the man whose image he had made. It showed, by touches of the small silver pencil of starlight, the massive metal figure of a soldier recumbent, the strong hands sealed in an everlasting worship, the great head pillowed upon a gun. The venerable face was bearded, or rather whiskered, in the old, heavy

---

* Never before in detective fiction had a murderer tried to conceal his crime by so evil a means as in this wild tale. The historical events, reconstructed by Father Brown, involve a strange battle in Brazil during which a British regiment is decimated and its general killed. The plot is complicated. You may have to reread the story carefully to understand all its subtle and sordid details. It was first published in the *Storyteller* (February 1911).

Colonel Newcome fashion.[1] The uniform, though suggested with
the few strokes of simplicity, was that of modern war. By his right
side lay a sword, of which the tip was broken off; on the left side
lay a Bible. On glowing summer afternoons wagonettes[2] came
full of Americans and cultured suburbans to see the sepulchre;
but even then they felt the vast forest land with its one dumpy
dome of churchyard and church as a place oddly dumb and neglected. In this freezing darkness of mid-winter one would think
he might be left alone with the stars. Nevertheless, in the stillness
of those stiff woods a wooden gate creaked, and two dim figures
dressed in black climbed up the little path to the tomb.

So faint was that frigid starlight that nothing could have been
traced about them except that while they both wore black, one
man was enormously big, and the other (perhaps by contrast)
almost startlingly small. They went up to the great graven tomb
of the historic warrior, and stood for a few minutes staring at it.
There was no human, perhaps no living, thing for a wide circle;
and a morbid fancy might well have wondered if they were
human themselves. In any case, the beginning of their conversation might have seemed strange. After the first silence the small
man said to the other:

'Where does a wise man hide a pebble?'

And the tall man answered in a low voice: 'On the beach.'

The small man nodded, and after a short silence said: 'Where
does a wise man hide a leaf?'

And the other answered: 'In the forest.'

There was another stillness, and then the tall man resumed:
'Do you mean that when a wise man has to hide a real diamond
he has been known to hide it among sham ones?'[3]

---

1. Colonel Newcome is a character in William Makepeace Thackeray's
novel *The Newcomes*. The Colonel is a British army officer, kind and lovable,
who returns to London after a distinguished service in India. Like other
English officers of his day, his bushy moustache is continuous with his side
whiskers. The novel ends tragically with the Colonel's loss of fortune and
death in an almshouse.

2. Wagonettes were small four-wheel carriages, open at the sides, with a
bench along each side on which three or four passengers could sit facing
inward. They served as horse-drawn omnibuses.

3. Flambeau is recalling the incidents of 'The Flying Stars' (Chapter 4).

'No, no,' said the little man with a laugh, 'we will let bygones be bygones.'

He stamped his cold feet for a second or two, and then said: 'I'm not thinking of that at all, but of something else; something rather peculiar. Just strike a match, will you?'

The big man fumbled in his pocket, and soon a scratch and a flare painted gold the whole flat side of the monument. On it was cut in black letters the well-known words which so many Americans had reverently read: 'Sacred to the Memory of General Sir Arthur St. Clare, Hero and Martyr, who Always Vanquished his Enemies and Always Spared Them, and Was Treacherously Slain by Them At Last. May God in Whom he Trusted both Reward and Revenge him.'

The match burnt the big man's fingers, blackened, and dropped. He was about to strike another, but his small companion stopped him. 'That's all right, Flambeau, old man; I saw what I wanted. Or, rather, I didn't see what I didn't want. And now we must walk a mile and a half along the road to the next inn, and I will try to tell you all about it. For Heaven knows a man should have fire and ale when he dares tell such a story.'

They descended the precipitous path, they re-latched the rusty gate, and set off at a stamping, ringing walk down the frozen forest road. They had gone a full quarter of a mile before the smaller man spoke again. He said: 'Yes; the wise man hides a pebble on the beach. But what does he do if there is no beach? Do you know anything of that great St. Clare trouble?'

'I know nothing about English generals, Father Brown,' answered the large man, laughing, 'though a little about English policemen. I only know that you have dragged me a precious long dance to all the shrines of this fellow, whoever he is. One would think he got buried in six different places. I've seen a memorial to General St. Clare in Westminster Abbey. I've seen a ramping equestrian statue[4] of General St. Clare on the Embankment.[5] I've seen a medallion of General St. Clare in the street he

---

4. A ramping horse is one with its forelegs raised as if about to attack.

5. On each side of the Thames, as it flows through London, is the Thames Embankment—a system of stone walls, paved roads, and walkways. Sir Christopher Wren proposed the costly project in 1666 to protect the city from the river's encroaching mud and sewage, but it took centuries to

was born in, and another in the street he lived in; and now you drag me after dark to his coffin in the village churchyard.[6] I am beginning to be a bit tired of his magnificent personality, especially as I don't in the least know who he was. What are you hunting for in all these crypts and effigies?'

'I am only looking for one word,' said Father Brown. 'A word that isn't there.'

'Well,' asked Flambeau; 'are you going to tell me anything about it?'

'I must divide it into two parts,' remarked the priest. 'First there is what everybody knows; and then there is what I know. Now, what everybody knows is short and plain enough. It is also entirely wrong.'

'Right you are,' said the big man called Flambeau cheerfully. 'Let's begin at the wrong end. Let's begin with what everybody knows, which isn't true.'

'If not wholly untrue, it is at least very inadequate,' continued Brown; 'for in point of fact, all that the public knows amounts precisely to this: The public knows that Arthur St. Clare was a great and successful English general. It knows that after splendid yet careful campaigns both in India and Africa he was in command against Brazil when the great Brazilian patriot Olivier issued his ultimatum. It knows that on that occasion St. Clare with a very small force attacked Olivier with a very large one, and was captured after heroic resistance. And it knows that after his capture, and to the abhorrence of the civilised world, St. Clare was hanged on the nearest tree. He was found swinging there after the Brazilians had retired, with his broken sword hung round his neck.'

'And that popular story is untrue?' suggested Flambeau.

---

complete. The Embankment on the north side of the Thames is called the Victoria Embankment; on the south side, the Albert Embankment.

Cleopatra's Needle is an obelisk on the Victoria Embankment close to Waterloo Bridge. It was near this bridge that John Openshaw was tossed into the Thames in Sherlock Holmes's case of 'The Five Orange Pips'.

**6.** Flambeau's remarks inform us that General St. Clare was born in the Iceland village where he lived for a time, and is now buried in the town's Protestant churchyard. Why Iceland? Chesterton surely chose it because its 'hell of incalculable cold' (as it is called in the story's first paragraph) suggests (see Note 13) the ice at the bottom of Dante's hell where the souls of traitors are tormented.

'No,' said his friend quietly, 'that story is quite true, so far as it goes.'

'Well, I think it goes far enough!' said Flambeau; 'but if the popular story is true, what is the mystery?'

They had passed many hundreds of grey and ghostly trees before the little priest answered. Then he bit his finger reflectively and said: 'Why, the mystery is a mystery of psychology. Or, rather, it is a mystery of two psychologies. In that Brazilian business two of the most famous men of modern history acted flat against their characters. Mind you, Olivier and St. Clare were both heroes—the old thing, and no mistake; it was like the fight between Hector and Achilles. Now, what would you say to an affair in which Achilles was timid and Hector was treacherous?'

'Go on,' said the large man impatiently as the other bit his finger again.

'Sir Arthur St. Clare was a soldier of the old religious type— the type that saved us during the Mutiny,'[7] continued Brown. 'He was always more for duty than for dash; and with all his personal courage was decidedly a prudent commander, particularly indignant at any needless waste of soldiers. Yet in this last battle he attempted something that a baby could see was absurd. One need not be a strategist to see it was as wild as wind; just as one need not be a strategist to keep out of the way of a motor-bus. Well, that is the first mystery; what had become of the English general's head? The second riddle is, what had become of the Brazilian general's heart? President Olivier might be called a visionary or a nuisance; but even his enemies admitted that he was magnanimous to the point of knight errantry. Almost every other prisoner he had ever captured had been set free or even loaded with benefits. Men who had really wronged him came away touched by his simplicity and sweetness. Why the deuce

---

7. Father Brown is referring to the great Indian Mutiny of 1857, also called the Sepoy Rebellion. The Bengal army in central India, under the control of England's East India Company, mutinied for a variety of reasons. The revolt was put down by British troops with considerable loss of life, and control of India was taken over by the Crown. The sepoys (native soldiers) were inflamed by their belief that British cartridges were being greased with unclean animal oils, a practice violating tenets of their Brahmin faith. For the sad, bizarre details of this crisis in the history of British imperialism, see 'Indian Mutiny' in the *Encyclopaedia Britannica* (14th edition).

should he diabolically revenge himself only once in his life; and then for the one particular blow that could not have hurt him? Well, there you have it. One of the wisest men in the world acted like an idiot for no reason. One of the best men in the world acted like a fiend for no reason. That's the long and the short of it; and I leave it to you, my boy.'

'No, you don't,' said the other with a snort. 'I leave it to you; and you jolly well tell me all about it.'

'Well,' resumed Father Brown, 'it's not fair to say that the public impression is just what I've said, without adding that two things have happened since. I can't say they threw a new light; for nobody can make sense of them. But they threw a new kind of darkness; they threw the darkness in new directions. The first was this. The family physician of the St. Clares quarrelled with that family, and began publishing a violent series of articles, in which he said that the late general was a religious maniac; but as far as the tale went, this seemed to mean little more than a religious man. Anyhow, the story fizzled out. Everyone knew, of course, that St. Clare had some of the eccentricities of puritan piety. The second incident was much more arresting. In the luckless and unsupported regiment which made that rash attempt at the Black River[8] there was a certain Captain Keith, who was at that time engaged to St. Clare's daughter, and who afterwards married her. He was one of those who were captured by Olivier, and, like all the rest except the general, appears to have been bounteously treated and promptly set free. Some twenty years afterwards this man, then Lieutenant-Colonel Keith, published a sort of autobiography called "A British Officer in Burmah and Brazil." In the place where the reader looks eagerly for some account of the mystery of St. Clare's disaster may be found the following words: "Everywhere else in this book I have narrated things exactly as they occurred, holding as I do the old-fashioned opinion that the glory of England is old enough to take care of itself. The exception I shall make is in this matter of the defeat by the Black River; and my reasons, though private, are honourable

---

8. Chesterton may have made up the name Black River, but there is a Rio Prêto (Portuguese for Black River) in Brazil that rises east of Brasilia, flows down beside the Serra do Rio Prêto, and eventually runs into the Rio São Francisco.

and compelling. I will, however, add this in justice to the memories of two distinguished men. General St. Clare has been accused of incapacity on this occasion; I can at least testify that this action, properly understood, was one of the most brilliant and sagacious of his life. President Olivier by similar report is charged with savage injustice. I think it due to the honour of an enemy to say that he acted on this occasion with even more than his characteristic good feeling. To put the matter popularly, I can assure my countrymen that St. Clare was by no means such a fool nor Olivier such a brute as he looked. This is all I have to say; nor shall any earthly consideration induce me to add a word to it." '

A large frozen moon like a lustrous snowball began to show through the tangle of twigs in front of them, and by its light the narrator had been able to refresh his memory of Captain Keith's text from a scrap of printed paper. As he folded it up and put it back in his pocket Flambeau threw up his hand with a French gesture.

'Wait a bit, wait a bit,' he cried excitedly. 'I believe I can guess it at the first go.'

He strode on, breathing hard, his black head and bull neck forward, like a man winning a walking race. The little priest, amused and interested, had some trouble in trotting beside him. Just before them the trees fell back a little to left and right, and the road swept downwards across a clear, moonlit valley, till it dived again like a rabbit into the wall of another wood. The entrance to the farther forest looked small and round, like the black hole of a remote railway tunnel. But it was within some hundred yards, and gaped like a cavern before Flambeau spoke again.

'I've got it,' he cried at last, slapping his thigh with his great hand. 'Four minutes' thinking, and I can tell your whole story myself.'

'All right,' assented his friend. 'You tell it.'

Flambeau lifted his head, but lowered his voice.

'General Sir Arthur St. Clare,' he said, 'came of a family in which madness was hereditary; and his whole aim was to keep this from his daughter, and even, if possible, from his future son-in-law. Rightly or wrongly, he thought the final collapse was close, and resolved on suicide. Yet ordinary suicide would blazen the very idea he dreaded. As the campaign approached the clouds came thicker on his brain; and at last in a mad moment he sacrificed his public duty to his private. He rushed rashly into battle, hoping to fall by the first shot. When he found that he had only attained capture and discredit, the sealed bomb in his brain burst, and he broke his own sword and hanged himself.'

He stared firmly at the grey façade of forest in front of him, with the one black gap in it, like the mouth of the grave, into which their path plunged. Perhaps something menacing in the road thus suddenly swallowed reinforced his vivid vision of the tragedy, for he shuddered.

'A horrid story,' he said.

'A horrid story,' repeated the priest with bent head. 'But not the real story.'

Then he threw back his head with a sort of despair and cried: 'Oh, I wish it had been.'

The tall Flambeau faced round and stared at him.

'Yours is a clean story,' cried Father Brown, deeply moved. 'A sweet, pure, honest story, as open and white as that moon. Madness and despair are innocent enough. There are worse things, Flambeau.'

Flambeau looked up wildly at the moon thus invoked; and from where he stood one black tree-bough curved across it exactly like a devil's horn.

'Father—father,' cried Flambeau with the French gesture and stepping yet more rapidly forward, 'do you mean it was worse than that?'

'Worse than that,' said the other[9] like a grave echo. And they plunged into the black cloister of the woodland, which ran by them in a dim tapestry of trunks, like one of the dark corridors in a dream.

They were soon in the most secret entrails of the wood, and felt close about them foliage that they could not see, when the priest said again:

---

**9.** In the *Storyteller* this appears as 'said Paul'. No one knows if 'Paul' was in Chesterton's original manuscript, or whether it was somehow a printer's error. The British first edition changed it to 'the other', and the American first edition has it 'the priest'.

'Where does a wise man hide a leaf? In the forest. But what does he do if there is no forest?'

'Well, well,' cried Flambeau irritably, 'what does he do?'

'He grows a forest to hide it in,' said the priest in an obscure voice. 'A fearful sin.'

'Look here,' cried his friend impatiently, for the dark wood and the dark sayings got a little on his nerves; 'will you tell me this story or not? What other evidence is there to go on?'

'There are three more bits of evidence,' said the other, 'that I have dug up in holes and corners; and I will give them in logical rather than chronological order. First of all, of course, our authority for the issue and event of the battle is in Olivier's own dispatches, which are lucid enough. He was entrenched with two or three regiments on the heights that swept down to the Black River, on the other side of which was lower and more marshy ground. Beyond this again was gently rising country, on which was the first English outpost, supported by others which lay, however, considerably in its rear. The British forces as a whole were greatly superior in numbers; but this particular regiment was just far enough from its base to make Olivier consider the project of crossing the river to cut it off. By sunset, however, he had decided to retain his own position, which was a specially strong one. At daybreak next morning he was thunderstruck to see that this stray handful of English, entirely unsupported from their rear, had flung themselves across the river, half by a bridge to the right, and the other half by a ford higher up, and were massed upon the marshy bank below him.

'That they should attempt an attack with such numbers against such a position was incredible enough; but Olivier noticed something yet more extraordinary. For instead of attempting to seize more solid ground, this mad regiment, having put the river in its rear by one wild charge, did nothing more, but stuck there in the mire like flies in treacle. Needless to say, the Brazilians blew great gaps in them with artillery, which they could only return with spirited but lessening rifle fire. Yet they never broke; and Olivier's curt account ends with a strong tribute of admiration for the mystic valour of these imbeciles. "Our line then advanced finally," writes Olivier, "and drove them into the river; we captured General St. Clare himself and several other officers. The colonel and the major had both fallen in the battle. I cannot resist saying that few finer sights can have been seen in history than the last stand of this extraordinary regiment; wounded officers picking up the rifles of dead soldiers, and the general himself facing us on horseback bareheaded and with a broken sword." On what happened to the general afterwards Olivier is as silent as Captain Keith.'

'Well,' grunted Flambeau, 'get on to the next bit of evidence.'

'The next evidence,' said Father Brown, 'took some time to find, but it will not take long to tell. I found at last in an almshouse down in the Lincolnshire Fens[10] an old soldier who not only was wounded at the Black River, but had actually knelt beside the colonel of the regiment when he died. This latter was a certain Colonel Clancy, a big bull of an Irishman; and it would seem that he died almost as much of rage as of bullets. He, at any rate, was not responsible for that ridiculous raid; it must have been imposed on him by the general. His last edifying words, according to my informant, were these: "And there goes the damned old donkey with the end of his sword knocked off. I wish it was his head." You will remark that everyone seems to have noticed this detail about the broken sword blade, though most people regard it somewhat more reverently than did the late Colonel Clancy. And now for the third fragment.'

Their path through the woodland began to go upward, and the speaker paused a little for breath before he went on. Then he continued in the same business-like tone:

'Only a month or two ago a certain Brazilian official died in England, having quarrelled with Olivier and left his country. He was a well-known figure both here and on the Continent, a Spaniard named Espado; I knew him myself, a yellow-faced old dandy, with a hooked nose. For various private reasons I had permission to see the documents he had left; he was a Catholic, of course, and I had been with him towards the end. There was nothing of his that lit up any corner of the black St. Clare busi-

---

10. The Lincolnshire Fens is a large flat marshy area where several rivers empty into The Wash, a bay of the North Sea on England's east coast. The Fens extend through several counties, one of which is Lincolnshire. The region was originally swampland until a series of drainages and embankments, initiated by the Romans, finally made the area suitable for cultivation.

ness, except five or six common exercise books filled with the diary of some English soldier. I can only suppose that it was found by the Brazilians on one of those that fell. Anyhow, it stopped abruptly the night before the battle.

'But the account of that last day in the poor fellow's life was certainly worth reading. I have it on me; but it's too dark to read it here, and I will give you a résumé. The first part of that entry is full of jokes, evidently flung about among the men, about somebody called the Vulture. It does not seem as if this person, whoever he was, was one of themselves, nor even an Englishman; neither is he exactly spoken of as one of the enemy. It sounds rather as if he were some local go-between and non-combatant; perhaps a guide or a journalist. He has been closeted with old Colonel Clancy; but is more often seen talking to the major. Indeed, the major is somewhat prominent in this soldier's narrative; a lean, dark-haired man, apparently, of the name of Murray—a north of Ireland man and a Puritan. There are continual jests about the contrast between this Ulsterman's austerity and the conviviality of Colonel Clancy. There is also some joke about the Vulture wearing bright-coloured clothes.

'But all these levities are scattered by what may well be called the note of a bugle. Behind the English camp and almost parallel to the river ran one of the few great roads of that district. Westward the road curved round towards the river, which it crossed by the bridge before mentioned. To the east the road swept backwards into the wilds, and some two miles along it was the next English outpost. From this direction there came along the road that evening a glitter and clatter of light cavalry, in which even the simple diarist could recognise with astonishment the general with his staff. He rode the great white horse which you have seen so often in illustrated papers and Academy pictures; and you may be sure that the salute they gave him was not merely ceremonial. He, at least, wasted no time on ceremony, but, springing from the saddle immediately, mixed with the group of officers, and fell into emphatic though confidential speech. What struck our friend the diarist most was his special disposition to discuss matters with Major Murray; but, indeed, such a selection, so long as it was not marked, was in no way unnatural. The two men were made for sympathy; they were men who "read their Bibles"; they were both the old Evangelical type of officer.

However this may be, it is certain that when the general mounted again he was still talking earnestly to Murray; and that as he walked his horse slowly down the road towards the river, the tall Ulsterman still walked by his bridle rein in earnest debate. The soldiers watched the two until they vanished behind a clump of trees where the road turned towards the river. The colonel had gone back to his tent, and the men to their pickets; the man with the diary lingered for another four minutes, and saw a marvellous sight.

'The great white horse which had marched slowly down the road, as it had marched in so many processions, flew back, galloping up the road towards them as if it were mad to win a race. At first they thought it had run away with the man on its back; but they soon saw that the general, a fine rider, was himself urging it to full speed. Horse and man swept up to them like a whirlwind; and then, reining up the reeling charger, the general turned on them a face like flame, and called for the colonel like the trumpet that wakes the dead.

'I conceive that all the earthquake events of that catastrophe tumbled on top of each other rather like lumber in the minds of men such as our friend with the diary. With the dazed excitement of a dream, they found themselves falling—literally falling—into their ranks, and learned that an attack was to be led at once across the river. The general and the major, it was said, had found out something at the bridge, and there was only just time to strike for life. The major had gone back at once to call up the reserve along the road behind; it was doubtful if even with that prompt appeal help could reach them in time. But they must pass the stream that night, and seize the heights by morning. It is with the very stir and throb of that romantic nocturnal march that the diary suddenly ends.'

Father Brown had mounted ahead; for the woodland path grew smaller, steeper, and more twisted, till they felt as if they were ascending a winding staircase. The priest's voice came from above out of the darkness.

'There was one other little and enormous thing. When the general urged them to their chivalric charge he half drew his sword from the scabbard; and then, as if ashamed of such melodrama, thrust it back again. The sword again, you see.'

A half-light broke through the network of boughs above them, flinging the ghost of a net about their feet; for they were mounting again to the faint luminosity of the naked night. Flambeau felt truth all round him as an atmosphere, but not as an idea. He answered with bewildered brain:

'Well, what's the matter with the sword? Officers generally have swords, don't they?'

'They are not often mentioned in modern war,' said the other dispassionately; 'but in this affair one falls over the blessed sword everywhere.'

'Well, what is there in that?' growled Flambeau; 'it was a two-pence coloured sort of incident;[11] the old man's blade breaking in his last battle. Anyone might bet the papers would get hold of it, as they have. On all these tombs and things it's shown broken at the point. I hope you haven't dragged me through this Polar expedition merely because two men with an eye for a picture saw St. Clare's broken sword.'

'No,' cried Father Brown, with a sharp voice like a pistol shot; 'but who saw his unbroken sword?'

'What do you mean?' cried the other, and stood still under the stars. They had come abruptly out of the grey gates of the wood.

'I say, who saw his unbroken sword?' repeated Father Brown obstinately. 'Not the writer of the diary, anyhow; the general sheathed it in time.'

Flambeau looked about him in the moonlight, as a man struck blind might look in the sun; and his friend went on for the first time with eagerness:

'Flambeau,' he cried, 'I cannot prove it, even after hunting through the tombs. But I am sure of it. Let me add just one more tiny fact that tips the whole thing over. The colonel, by a strange chance, was one of the first struck by a bullet. He was struck long before the troops came to close quarters. But he saw St. Clare's sword broken. Why was it broken? How was it broken? My friend, it was broken before the battle.'

'Oh!' said his friend, with a sort of forlorn jocularity; 'and pray where is the other piece?'

---

11. Flambeau means by this a paltry incident.

'I can tell you,' said the priest promptly. 'In the north-east corner of the cemetery of the Protestant Cathedral at Belfast.'

'Indeed?' inquired the other. 'Have you looked for it?'

'I couldn't,' replied Brown, with frank regret. 'There's a great marble monument on top of it; a monument to the heroic Major Murray, who fell fighting gloriously at the famous Battle of the Black River.'

Flambeau seemed suddenly galvanised into existence. 'You mean,' he cried hoarsely, 'that General St. Clare hated Murray, and murdered him on the field of battle because——'

'You are still full of good and pure thoughts,' said the other. 'It was worse than that.'

'Well,' said the large man, 'my stock of evil imagination is used up.'

The priest seemed really doubtful where to begin, and at last he said again:

'Where would a wise man hide a leaf? In the forest.'

The other did not answer.

'If there were no forest, he would make a forest. And if he wished to hide a dead leaf, he would make a dead forest.'

There was still no reply, and the priest added still more mildly and quietly:

'And if a man had to hide a dead body, he would make a field of dead bodies to hide it in.'

Flambeau began to stamp forward with an intolerance of delay in time or space; but Father Brown went on as if he were continuing the last sentence:

'Sir Arthur St. Clare, as I have already said, was a man who read his Bible. That was what was the matter with *him*. When will people understand that it is useless for a man to read his Bible unless he also reads everybody else's Bible? A printer reads a Bible for misprints. A Mormon reads his Bible, and finds polygamy; a Christian Scientist reads his, and finds we have no arms and legs. St. Clare was an old Anglo-Indian Protestant soldier. Now, just think what that might mean; and, for Heaven's sake, don't cant about it. It might mean a man physically formidable living under a tropic sun in an Oriental society, and soaking himself without sense or guidance in an Oriental book. Of course, he read the Old Testament rather than the New. Of course, he found in the Old Testament anything that he wanted—lust, tyranny, treason. Oh, I dare say he was honest, as you call it. But what is the good of a man being honest in his worship of dishonesty?

'In each of the hot and secret countries to which that man went he kept a harem, he tortured witnesses, he amassed shameful gold; but certainly he would have said with steady eyes that he did it to the glory of the Lord. My own theology is sufficiently expressed by asking which Lord? Anyhow, there is this about such evil, that it opens door after door in hell, and always into smaller and smaller chambers. This is the real case against crime, that a man does not become wilder and wilder, but only meaner and meaner. St. Clare was soon suffocated by difficulties of bribery and blackmail; and needed more and more cash. And by the time of the Battle of the Black River he had fallen from world to world to that place which Dante makes the lowest floor of the universe.'

'What do you mean?' asked his friend again.

'I mean *that*,' retorted the cleric, and suddenly pointed at a puddle sealed with ice that shone in the moon. 'Do you remember whom Dante put in the last circle of ice?'

'The traitors,' said Flambeau, and shuddered. As he looked around at the inhuman landscape of trees, with taunting and almost obscene[12] outlines, he could almost fancy he was Dante, and the priest with the rivulet of a voice was, indeed, a Virgil leading him through a land of eternal sins.[13]

The voice went on: 'Olivier, as you know, was quixotic and would not permit a secret service and spies. The thing, however, was done, like many other things, behind his back. It was managed by my old friend Espado; he was the bright-clad fop, whose hook nose got him called the Vulture. Posing as a sort of philanthropist at the front, he felt his way through the English Army, and at last got his fingers on its one corrupt man—please God!—and that man at the top. St. Clare was in foul need of money, and mountains of it. The discredited family doctor was threatening those extraordinary exposures that afterwards began

---

12. The word is 'obscure' in the magazine version.
13. Virgil is Dante's guide through the lowest circle of ice where a three-headed Satan is entrapped.

and were broken off; tales of monstrous and prehistoric things in Park Lane;[14] things done by an English Evangelical that smelt like human sacrifice and hordes of slaves. Money was wanted, too, for his daughter's dowry; for to him the fame of wealth was as sweet as wealth itself. He snapped the last thread, whispered the word to Brazil, and wealth poured in from the enemies of England. But another man had talked to Espado the Vulture as well as he. Somehow the dark, grim young major from Ulster had guessed the hideous truth; and when they walked slowly together down that road towards the bridge Murray was telling the general that he must resign instantly, or be court-martialled and shot. The general temporised with him till they came to the fringe of tropic trees by the bridge; and there by the singing river and the sunlit palms (for I can see the picture) the general drew his sabre and plunged it through the body of the major.'

The wintry road curved over a ridge in cutting frost, with cruel black shapes of bush and thicket; but Flambeau fancied that he saw beyond it faintly the edge of an aureole[15] that was not starlight and moonlight, but some fire such as is made by men. He watched it as the tale drew to its close.

'St. Clare was a hell-hound, but he was a hound of breed. Never, I'll swear, was he so lucid and so strong as when poor Murray lay a cold lump at his feet. Never in all his triumphs, as Captain Keith said truly, was the great man so great as he was in this last world-despised defeat. He looked coolly at his weapon to wipe off the blood; he saw the point he had planted between his victim's shoulders had broken off in the body. He saw quite calmly, as through a club window-pane, all that must follow. He saw that men must find the unaccountable corpse; must extract the unaccountable sword-point; must notice the unaccountable broken sword—or absence of sword. He had killed, but not silenced. But his imperious intellect rose against the facer; there was one way yet. He could make the corpse less unaccountable. He could create a hill of corpses to cover this one. In twenty

14. Park Lane, a street bordering the eastern boundary of Hyde Park, was and is an expensive, exclusive street, a fact that makes St. Clare's monstrous life-style all the more shocking.

15. Flambeau is seeing the firelight of the village inn toward which he and Father Brown are trudging.

minutes eight hundred English soldiers were marching down to their death.'

The warmer glow behind the black winter wood grew richer and brighter, and Flambeau strode on to reach it. Father Brown also quickened his stride; but he seemed merely absorbed in his tale.

'Such was the valour of that English thousand, and such the genius of their commander, that if they had at once attacked the hill, even their mad march might have met some luck. But the evil mind that played with them like pawns had other aims and reasons. They must remain in the marshes by the bridge at least till British corpses should be a common sight there. Then for the last grand scene; the silver-haired soldier-saint would give up his shattered sword to save further slaughter. Oh, it was well organised for an impromptu. But I think (I cannot prove), I think that it was while they stuck there in the bloody mire that someone doubted—and someone guessed.'

He was mute a moment, and then said: 'There is a voice from nowhere that tells me the man who guessed was the lover . . . the man to wed the old man's child.'

'But what about Olivier and the hanging?' asked Flambeau.

'Olivier, partly from chivalry, partly from policy, seldom encumbered his march with captives,' explained the narrator. 'He released everybody in most cases. He released everybody in this case'

'Everybody but the general,' said the tall man.

'Everybody,' said the priest.

Flambeau knitted his black brows. 'I don't grasp it all yet,' he said.

'There is another picture, Flambeau,' said Brown in his more mystical undertone. 'I can't prove it; but I can do more—I can see it. There is a camp breaking up on the bare, torrid hills at morning, and Brazilian uniforms massed in blocks and columns to march. There is the red shirt and long black beard of Olivier, which blows as he stands, his broad-brimmed hat in his hand. He is saying farewell to the great enemy he is setting free—the simple, snow-headed English veteran, who thanks him in the name of his men. The English remnant stand behind at attention; beside them are stores and vehicles for the retreat. The drums roll; the Brazilians are moving; the English are still like statues. So they abide till the last hum and flash of the enemy have faded from the tropic horizon. Then they alter their postures all at once, like dead men coming to life; they turn their fifty faces upon the general—faces not to be forgotten.'

Flambeau gave a great jump. 'Ah,' he cried. 'You don't mean——'

'Yes,' said Father Brown in a deep, moving voice. 'It was an English hand that put the rope round St. Clare's neck; I believe the hand that put the ring on his daughter's finger. They were English hands that dragged him up to the tree of shame; the hands of men that had adored him and followed him to victory. And they were English souls (God pardon and endure us all!) who stared at him swinging in that foreign sun on the green gallows of palm, and prayed in their hatred that he might drop off it into hell.'

As the two topped the ridge there burst on them the strong scarlet light of a red-curtained English inn. It stood sideways in the road, as if standing aside in the amplitude of hospitality. Its three doors stood open with invitation; and even where they stood they could hear the hum and laughter of humanity happy for a night.

'I need not tell you more,' said Father Brown. 'They tried him in the wilderness and destroyed him; and then, for the honour of England and of his daughter, they took an oath to seal up for ever the story of the traitor's purse and the assassin's sword blade. Perhaps—Heaven help them—they tried to forget it. Let us try to forget it, anyhow; here is our inn.'

'With all my heart,' said Flambeau, and was just striding into the bright, noisy bar when he stepped back and almost fell on the road.

'Look there, in the devil's name!' he cried, and pointed rigidly at the square wooden sign that overhung the road. It showed dimly the crude shape of a sabre hilt and a shortened blade; and was inscribed in false archaic lettering, 'The Sign of the Broken Sword.'

'Were you not prepared?' asked Father Brown gently. 'He is the god of this country; half the inns and parks and streets are named after him and his story.'

'I thought we had done with the leper,' cried Flambeau, and spat on the road.

234

'You will never have done with him in England,' said the priest, looking down, 'while brass is strong and stone abides. His marble statues will erect the souls of proud, innocent boys for centuries, his village tomb will smell of loyalty as of lilies. Millions who never knew him shall love him like a father—this man whom the last few that knew him dealt with like dung. He shall be a saint; and the truth shall never be told of him, because I have made up my mind at last. There is so much good and evil in breaking secrets, that I put my conduct to a test. All these newspapers will perish; the anti-Brazil boom[16] is already over; Olivier is already honoured everywhere. But I told myself that if anywhere, by name, in metal or marble that will endure like the pyramids, Colonel Clancy, or Captain Keith, or President Olivier, or any innocent man was wrongly blamed, then I would speak. If it were only that St. Clare was wrongly praised, I would be silent. And I will.'

They plunged into the red-curtained tavern, which was not only cosy, but even luxurious inside. On a table stood a silver model of the tomb of St. Clare, the silver head bowed, the silver sword broken. On the walls were coloured photographs of the same scene, and of the system of wagonettes that took tourists to see it. They sat down on the comfortable padded benches.

'Come, it's cold,' cried Father Brown; 'let's have some wine or beer.'

'Or brandy,' said Flambeau.

### AFTERWORD

'Father Brown and the Historian', by Melvin Cherno, who teaches history at the University of Virginia (*The Chesterton Review*, May 1984), contains an illuminating discussion of Chesterton's story. The historian's

---

**16.** British aggression against Brazil was confined to the late sixteenth century, after which the struggle for Brazil was mostly between Portugal, France, and Holland. However, in about 1900 a bitter boundary dispute broke out between Britain and Brazil over the southern border of British Guiana. Presumably it was during this period that General St. Clare was in charge of the regiment that was defeated by the Brazilian army led by the imaginary Olivier. The border dispute was settled in 1904, after which the anti-Brazilian sentiment in England, mentioned by Father Brown, quickly faded.

art, Cherno writes, is very much like Father Brown's reconstruction of the general's crime—a mixture of cold deduction and subjective intuition. When the priest tells Flambeau that he cannot prove his hypothesis, yet he is sure of it, he is saying something that all historians will understand. Cherno sees Father Brown's reconstruction of what happened as 'a most admirable performance, one that would have a graduate history seminar ebullient with admiration for a professor carrying his students with him in the exciting process of discovery'.

Chesterton wrote some history, but it is usually considered mostly rather pedestrian patriotic propaganda and historians would never recommend it. Similarly, they may avoid putting on their reading lists the historical parts of his more political works. His historical speculation—his article on Don John of Austria and Mary Queen of Scots, in *If: Or History Rewritten*—is probably more worthy of respect. But his real insight into the study of past human affairs is in these accounts of Father Brown's prowess in unraveling murky relationships and questionable behaviour. Father Brown knows everything that historians usually spend a lifetime learning—that things are seldom what they seem, that people almost never act as one might expect them to, that deeply felt emotions (wounded pride, for example) are more likely to be the sources of anti-social behaviour than calculated doctrinaire forethought. Never ruffled, never out to prove his preconceived hunches or theories correct, never closed to new revelations of human perversity, Father Brown instructs us while he entertains us and makes us aware of the fact that, when it comes to understanding human affairs, there is only one method, the method of sympathetic intuition combined with hard-headed precision. We historians may not pick up a Father Brown volume to learn more about our own work, but we cannot lay one down without having done so.

Father Brown plays the historian again in 'The Fairy Tale of Father Brown' (*The Wisdom of Father Brown*). After Flambeau gives him the details of a twenty-year-old murder mystery in Germany, the priest responds with what he calls a 'fairy story'—a shrewd, highly convincing solution of the mystery.

In 1984 my good friend of high-school days in Tulsa, Oklahoma, John Bennett Shaw (I mention his Chesterton collection in Chapter 6, Note 3) unearthed the typescript of a previously unknown Chesterton essay titled 'The Historical Detective Story'. The essay's theme is that one way to inject new life into the mystery tale, which G.K. saw as bogged down by repetition of the same tired old clues and gimmicks, is to write stories about historical mysteries of past times.

For the detective tale is almost the only decently moral tale that is still being told. It is only in blood and thunder stories that there is anything so Christian as blood crying out for justice to the thunder of the judgment; and the shocker is now the only novel that is not shocking.

I suggest that we try to do a little more with what may be called the Historical Detective Story. The play of masks and faces and the mysterious heart of man would be just the same; but we could use a hundred variations, and some emancipations, touching the externals of the action . . . I do not of course mean that we should turn all our detective-dramas into costume plays; I only mean that if we did so now and then, for a change, we should find some new liberties as well as some new limitations.

The next passage is a surprising revelation about the origin of the story you have just read:

> If I may be pardoned another piece of egotism, I may say that I once wrote a short story called 'The Sign of the Broken Sword'. It is, as a modern military episode, very melodramatic and improbable, for the simple reason that I originally planned out the plot as that of some medieval skirmish, with spear and battle-axe, and then translated it back into modern life in order to make it contemporary with one whom Mrs Helen Parry Eden, I think, very truly described as 'that officious little loafer', Father Brown.

It is good to have the name of the lady who made this oftenquoted remark. In his autobiography Chesterton refers to her only as 'a very charming Catholic lady I know', who 'once paid my detective priest the appropriate compliment of saying, "I am very fond of that officious little loafer." ' Helen Parry Eden, in case you are wondering who she was, wrote a book of verse called *Bread and Circuses*. Chesterton praises the book and quotes two poems from it in the first essay of *The Uses of Diversity*. The views of her father, Judge Edward Abbott Parry, are discussed in another essay in the same volume.

# The Three Tools of Death*

BOTH by calling and conviction Father Brown knew better than most of us that every man is dignified when he is dead. But even he felt a pang of incongruity when he was knocked up at daybreak and told that Sir Aaron Armstrong had been murdered. There was something absurd and unseemly about secret violence in connection with so entirely entertaining and popular a figure. For Sir Aaron Armstrong was entertaining to the point of being comic; and popular in such a manner as to be almost legendary. It was like hearing that Sunny Jim had hanged himself;[1] or that Mr Pickwick had died in Hanwell.[2] For though Sir Aaron was a philanthropist, and thus dealt with the darker side of our society, he prided himself on dealing with it in the brightest possible

---

* Too many instruments of death—a noose, a knife, a pistol—lead Father Brown to suspect the strange truth about how a philanthropist died. *Cassell's Magazine* printed the story in its July 1911 issue, with art by Sidney Lucas.

1. We all know who Mr Pickwick is, but who is Sunny Jim? Admittedly peripheral, the story of Sunny Jim provides such a fascinating glimpse into a forgotten corner of Edwardian life that I think it deserves considerable space.

It all began in the US in 1902 when the Force Food Company launched an advertising campaign to promote Force, a whole-wheat-flake breakfast cereal. A young woman named Minnie Maude Hanff, who wrote verse for children, was hired to produce jingles for the new cereal. She and her illustrator Dorothy Fricken, then still in high school, created a grouchy gentleman named Jim Dumps. Hanff's first and best known jingle described Dumps's transformation from a man in the dumps to a man with a sunny disposition:

> Jim Dumps was a most unfriendly man,
> Who lived his life on the hermit plan;
> In his gloomy way he'd gone through life,
> And made the most of woe and strife;
> Till Force one day was served to him—
> Since then they've called him 'Sunny Jim'.

Full-page ads in Sunday newspapers depicted Sunny Jim as a plump little man with, curiously, a pigtail. Hundreds of new jingles followed, such as this one (I quote from Stephen Fox's *The Mirror Makers*, a lively history of American advertising):

Jim Dumps a little girl possessed,
Whom loss of appetite distressed;
'I des' tan't eat!' the child would scream;
Jim fixed a dish of Force and cream—
She tasted it—then, joy for him—
She begged for more from 'Sunny Jim'.

According to Fox, a mammoth likeness of Sunny Jim 'adorned the sides of two eleven-storey buildings in New York. Songs, musical comedies, and vaudeville skits were written about him. Anybody with a cheery personality and the name of James risked being called Sunny Jim.' He became almost as well known to US children as Santa Claus.

Strangely, Sunny Jim's popularity failed to move the product, and the happy little man was abandoned in less than two years. Other characters replaced him on the US advertising landscape, such as Phoebe Snow who rode the Lakawanna Railroad without getting her white clothes sooty, and such later characters as the black chef of Cream of Wheat, the Arrow Collar Man, and Aunt Jemima.

Force was introduced in England in 1903, where Sunny Jim soon became an even more famous personage than he had been in the US. A Sunny Jim rag doll went on sale in England at about the time Chesterton began writing his first Father Brown tales. There have since been at least seven different versions of the doll, almost all identical, that are now prized collectables. The doll is sixteen inches tall. Sunny is a Regency gentleman with powdered white hair, pigtail, red tailcoat, high wing collar, bow tie, and a monocle. He holds a box of Force and a wooden spoon.

Until the start of the Second World War the cereal was imported into England from Canada and the United States, but the war cut off the supply. Force was reintroduced in England in 1955. A. W. Campbell, a correspondent in Edinburgh who was the first to help me track down Sunny Jim, found the cereal on sale in 1985 in an Edinburgh health food shop. The box gives a capsule history of Sunny Jim, and for £1.40 offers a 'fine quality tea towel' on which an advertising poster from the 1920s is reproduced. It shows Sunny Jim and two children leaping over a fence. Below the picture is one of the jingles used in British advertising since 1903:

High o'er the fence
Leaps Sunny Jim.
Force is the food
That raises him.

On an impulse I checked a *Concordance of Finnegans Wake*. Sure enough, Sunny Jim turns up in Joyce's work in two spots: as Sunny Twimjim on page 211 (line 6) and Sunny Sim on page 305 (line 5).

**2.** The Hanwell Lunatic Asylum, on Uxbridge Road in Hanwell, a London suburb, was established in 1831 for the paupers of Middlesex County. The institution has now become St. Bernard's Hospital.

style. His political and social speeches were cataracts of anecdotes and 'loud laughter'; his bodily health was of a bursting sort; his ethics were all optimism; and he dealt with the Drink problem (his favourite topic) with that immortal or even monotonous gaiety which is so often a mark of the prosperous total abstainer.

The established story of his conversion was familiar on the more puritanic platforms and pulpits, how he had been, when only a boy, drawn away from Scotch theology to Scotch whisky, and how he had risen out of both and become (as he modestly put it) what he was. Yet his wide white beard, cherubic face, and sparkling spectacles, at the numberless dinners and congresses where they appeared, made it hard to believe, somehow, that he had ever been anything so morbid as either a dram-drinker or a Calvinist.[3] He was, one felt, the most seriously merry of all the sons of men.

He had lived on the rural skirt of Hampstead in a handsome house, high but not broad, a modern and prosaic tower. The narrowest of its narrow sides overhung the steep green bank of a railway, and was shaken by passing trains. Sir Aaron Armstrong, as he boisterously explained, had no nerves. But if the train had often given a shock to the house, that morning the tables were turned, and it was the house that gave a shock to the train.

The engine slowed down and stopped just beyond that point where an angle of the house impinged upon the sharp slope of turf. The arrest of most mechanical things must be slow; but the living cause of this had been very rapid. A man clad completely in black, even (it was remembered) to the dreadful detail of black gloves, appeared on the ridge above the engine, and waved his black hands like some sable windmill. This in itself would hardly have stopped even a lingering train. But there came out of him a cry which was talked of afterwards as something utterly unnatural and new. It was one of those shouts that are horridly dis-

---

3. Chesterton had little use for Scotch Presbyterianism, as we saw in Chapter 9 (see Note 11). A good summary of G.K.'s reasons for disliking John Calvin and John Knox will be found in the chapter on 'The Idols of Scotland' in *The Thing*. One of Max Beerbohm's cartoons of Chesterton depicts Hilaire Belloc converting G.K. from the errors of Calvinism.

tinct even when we cannot hear what is shouted. The word in this case was 'Murder!'

But the engine-driver swears he would have pulled up just the same if he had heard only the dreadful and definite accent and not the word.

The train once arrested, the most superficial stare could take in many features of the tragedy. The man in black on the green bank was Sir Aaron Armstrong's man-servant Magnus. The baronet in his optimism had often laughed at the black gloves of this dismal attendant; but no one was likely to laugh at him just now.

So soon as an inquirer or two had stepped off the line and across the smoky hedge, they saw, rolled down almost to the bottom of the bank, the body of an old man in a yellow dressing-gown with a very vivid scarlet lining. A scrap of rope seemed caught about his leg, entangled presumably in a struggle. There was a smear or so of blood, though very little; but the body was bent or broken into a posture impossible to any living thing. It was Sir Aaron Armstrong. A few more bewildered moments brought out a big fair-bearded man, whom some travellers could salute as the dead man's secretary, Patrick Royce, once well known in Bohemian society and even famous in the Bohemian arts. In a manner more vague, but even more convincing, he echoed the agony of the servant. By the time the third figure of that household, Alice Armstrong, daughter of the dead man, had come already tottering and wavering into the garden, the engine-driver had put a stop to his stoppage. The whistle had blown and the train had panted on to get help from the next station.

Father Brown had been thus rapidly summoned at the request of Patrick Royce, the big ex-Bohemian secretary. Royce was an Irishman by birth; and that casual kind of Catholic that never remembers his religion until he is really in a hole. But Royce's request might have been less promptly complied with if one of the official detectives had not been a friend and admirer of the unofficial Flambeau; and it was impossible to be a friend of Flambeau without hearing numberless stories about Father Brown. Hence, while the young detective (whose name was Merton) led the little priest across the fields to the railway, their talk was more confidential than could be expected between two total strangers.

'As far as I can see,' said Mr Merton candidly, 'there is no sense to be made of it at all. There is nobody one can suspect. Magnus is a solemn old fool; far too much of a fool to be an assassin. Royce has been the baronet's best friend for years; and his daughter undoubtedly adored him. Besides, it's all too absurd. Who would kill such a cheery old chap as Armstrong? Who could dip his hands in the gore of an after-dinner speaker? It would be like killing Father Christmas.'[4]

'Yes, it was a cheery house,' assented Father Brown. 'It was a cheery house while he was alive. Do you think it will be cheery now he is dead?'

Merton started a little and regarded his companion with an enlivened eye. 'Now he is dead?' he repeated.

'Yes,' continued the priest stolidly, '*he* was cheerful. But did he communicate his cheerfulness? Frankly, was anyone else in the house cheerful but he?'

A window in Merton's mind let in that strange light of surprise in which we see for the first time things we have known all along. He had often been to the Armstrongs', on little police jobs of the philanthropist; and, now he came to think of it, it was in itself a depressing house. The rooms were very high and very cold; the decoration mean and provincial; the draughty corridors were lit by electricity that was bleaker than moonlight. And though the old man's scarlet face and silver beard had blazed like a bonfire in each room or passage in turn, it did not leave any warmth behind it. Doubtless this spectral discomfort in the place was partly due to the very vitality and exuberance of its owner; he needed no stoves or lamps, he would say, but carried his own warmth with him. But when Merton recalled the other inmates, he was compelled to confess that they also were as shadows of their lord. The moody man-servant, with his monstrous black gloves, was almost a nightmare; Royce, the secretary, was solid enough, a big bull of a man, in tweeds, with a short beard; but the straw-coloured beard was startlingly salted with grey like the tweeds, and the broad forehead was barred with premature wrinkles. He was good-natured enough also, but it was a sad sort

---

4. Some American readers may need to be told that Father Christmas is the British equivalent of Santa Claus. One of Chesterton's best-loved essays is about the rumoured death of Father Christmas (*Tremendous Trifles*).

of good-nature, almost a heart-broken sort—he had the general air of being some sort of failure in life. As for Armstrong's daughter, it was almost incredible that she was his daughter; she was so pallid in colour and sensitive in outline. She was graceful, but there was a quiver in the very shape of her that was like the lines of an aspen. Merton had sometimes wondered if she had learnt to quail at the crash of the passing trains.

'You see,' said Father Brown, blinking modestly, 'I'm not sure that the Armstrong cheerfulness is so very cheerful—for other people. You say that nobody could kill such a happy old man, but I'm not sure; *ne nos inducas in tentationem.*[5] If ever I murdered somebody,' he added quite simply, 'I dare say it might be an Optimist.'

'Why?' cried Merton, amused. 'Do you think people dislike cheerfulness?'

'People like frequent laughter,' answered Father Brown, 'but I don't think they like a permanent smile. Cheerfulness without humour is a very trying thing."

They walked some way in silence along the windy grassy bank by the rail, and just as they came under the far-flung shadow of the tall Armstrong house, Father Brown said suddenly, like a man throwing away a troublesome thought rather than offering it seriously: 'Of course, drink is neither good nor bad in itself. But I can't help sometimes feeling that men like Armstrong want an occasional glass of wine, to sadden them.'

Merton's official superior, a grizzled and capable detective named Gilder, was standing on the green bank waiting for the coroner, talking to Patrick Royce, whose big shoulders and bristly beard and hair towered above him. This was the more noticeable because Royce walked always with a sort of powerful stoop, and seemed to be going about his small clerical and dom-estic duties in a heavy and humbled style, like a buffalo drawing a go-cart.

He raised his head with unusual pleasure at the sight of the priest, and took him a few paces apart. Meanwhile Merton was addressing the older detective respectfully indeed, but not with-out a certain boyish impatience.

5. 'Lead us not into temptation', from the Latin version of the Lord's Prayer.

'Well, Mr Gilder, have you got much farther with the mystery?'

'There is no mystery,' replied Gilder, as he looked under dreamy eyelids at the rooks.[6]

'Well, there is for me, at any rate,' said Merton, smiling.

'It is simple enough, my boy,' observed the senior investigator, stroking his grey, pointed beard. 'Three minutes after you'd gone for Mr Royce's parson the whole thing came out. You know that pasty-faced servant in the black gloves who stopped the train?'

'I should know him anywhere. Somehow he rather gave me the creeps.'

'Well,' drawled Gilder, 'when the train had gone on again, that man had gone too. Rather a cool criminal, don't you think, to escape by the very train that went off for the police?'

'You're pretty sure, I suppose,' remarked the young man, 'that he really did kill his master?'

'Yes, my son, I'm pretty sure,' replied Gilder drily, 'for the trifling reason that he has gone off with twenty thousand pounds in papers that were in his master's desk. No, the only thing worth calling a difficulty is how he killed him. The skull seems broken as with some big weapon, but there's no weapon at all lying about, and the murderer would have found it awkward to carry it away, unless the weapon was too small to be noticed.'

'Perhaps the weapon was too big to be noticed,'[7] said the priest, with an odd little giggle.

Gilder looked round at this wild remark, and rather sternly asked Brown what he meant.

'Silly way of putting it, I know,' said Father Brown apologetically. 'Sounds like a fairy tale. But poor Armstrong was killed with a giant's club, a great green club, too big to be seen, and

---

6. The rook is an entirely black variety of European crow, smaller than a raven and a trifle larger than a jackdaw. A sociable bird, it nests in what are called 'rookeries'—large colonies in the upper branches of clumps of trees. Rooks are mentioned earlier, on page 195.

7. In 'The Purloined Letter' Poe's detective C. Auguste Dupin likens the problem of finding the missing letter to a map game in which one player picks out a name on the map and challenges his opponent to find it. Novices usually select minutely lettered names, Dupin explains, but the adept picks a name with such large letters that it escapes notice by being 'excessively obvious'. The murder weapon in this story, like the murderer in 'The Invisible Man', proves to be too big to be seen.

which we call the earth. He was broken against this green bank we are standing on.'

'How do you mean?' asked the detective quickly.

Father Brown turned his moon face up to the narrow façade of the house and blinked hopelessly up. Following his eyes, they saw that right at the top of this otherwise blind back quarter of the building, an attic window stood open.

'Don't you see,' he explained, pointing a little awkwardly like a child, 'he was thrown down from there?'

Gilder frowningly scrutinised the window, and then said: 'Well, it is certainly possible. But I don't see why you are so sure about it.'

Brown opened his grey eyes wide. 'Why,' he said, 'there's a bit of rope round the dead man's leg. Don't you see that other bit of rope up there caught at the corner of the window?'[8]

At that height the thing looked like the faintest particle of dust or hair, but the shrewd old investigator was satisfied. 'You're quite right, sir,' he said to Father Brown; 'that is certainly one to you.'

Almost as he spoke a special train with one carriage took the curve of the line on their left, and, stopping, disgorged another group of policemen, in whose midst was the hangdog visage of Magnus, the absconded servant.

'By Jove! they've got him,' cried Gilder, and stepped forward with quite a new alertness.

'Have you got the money?' he cried to the first policeman.

The man looked him in the face with a rather curious expression and said: 'No.' Then he added: 'At least, not here.'

'Which is the inspector, please?' asked the man called Magnus.

When he spoke everyone instantly understood how this voice had stopped a train. He was a dull-looking man with flat black hair, a colourless face, and a faint suggestion of the East in the level slits in his eyes and mouth. His blood and name, indeed, had remained dubious, ever since Sir Aaron had 'rescued' him

---

8. How could a near-sighted Father Brown, not wearing glasses, see a bit of rope at the corner of a high window? Squinting might enable him to see it, but we are told that the priest 'blinked hopelessly up' and later 'opened his grey eyes wide'. Perhaps he had started wearing glasses, but Chesterton neglected to mention them.

from a waitership in a London restaurant, and (as some said) from more infamous things. But his voice was as vivid as his face was dead. Whether through exactitude in a foreign language, or in deference to his master (who had been somewhat deaf), Magnus's tones had a peculiarly ringing and piercing quality, and the whole group quite jumped when he spoke.

'I always knew this would happen,' he said aloud with brazen blandness. 'My poor old master made game of me for wearing black; but I always said I should be ready for his funeral.'

And he made a momentary movement with his two dark-gloved hands.

'Sergeant,' said Inspector Gilder, eyeing the black hands with wrath, 'aren't you putting the bracelets on this fellow; he looks pretty dangerous.'

'Well, sir,' said the sergeant, with the same odd look of wonder, 'I don't know that we can.'

'What do you mean?' asked the other sharply. 'Haven't you arrested him?'

A faint scorn widened the slit-like mouth, and the whistle of an approaching train seemed oddly to echo the mockery.

'We arrested him,' replied the sergeant gravely, 'just as he was coming out of the police station at Highgate,[9] where he had deposited all his master's money in the care of Inspector Robinson.'

Gilder looked at the man-servant in utter amazement. 'Why on earth did you do that?' he asked of Magnus.

'To keep it safe from the criminal, of course,' replied that person placidly.

'Surely,' said Gilder, 'Sir Aaron's money might have been safely left with Sir Aaron's family.'

The tail of his sentence was drowned in the roar of the train as it went rocking and clanking; but through all the hell of noises to which that unhappy house was periodically subject, they could hear the syllables of Magnus's answer, in all their bell-like distinctness: 'I have no reason to feel confidence in Sir Aaron's family.'

All the motionless men had the ghostly sensation of the pres-

---

9. Highgate is a northern suburb of London. Samuel Coleridge and Andrew Marvell were among its famous literary residents.

ence of some new person; and Merton was scarcely surprised when he looked up and saw the pale face of Armstrong's daughter over Father Brown's shoulder. She was still young and beautiful in a silvery style, but her hair was of so dusty and hueless a brown that in some shadows it seemed to have turned totally grey.

'Be careful what you say,' said Royce gruffly, 'you'll frighten Miss Armstrong.'

'I hope so,' said the man with the clear voice.

As the woman winced and everyone else wondered, he went on: 'I am somewhat used to Miss Armstrong's tremors. I have seen her trembling off and on for years. And some said she was shaking with cold and some she was shaking with fear, but I know she was shaking with hate and wicked anger—fiends that have had their feast this morning. She would have been away by now with her lover and all the money but for me. Ever since my poor old master prevented her from marrying that tipsy blackguard——'

'Stop,' said Gilder very sternly. 'We have nothing to do with your family fancies or suspicions. Unless you have some practical evidence, your mere opinions——'

'Oh! I'll give you practical evidence,' cut in Magnus, in his hacking accent. 'You'll have to subpoena me, Mr Inspector, and I shall have to tell the truth. And the truth is this: An instant after the old man was pitched bleeding out of the window, I ran into the attic, and found his daughter swooning on the floor with a red dagger still in her hand. Allow me to hand that also to the proper authorities.' He took from his tail-pocket a long horn-hilted knife with a red smear on it, and handed it politely to the sergeant. Then he stood back again, and his slits of eyes almost faded from his face in one fat Chinese sneer.[10]

---

10. The sad fact is that in all of Chesterton's fiction I cannot recall an episode in which a Jew, black, or Oriental appears in a favourable light. Particularly deplorable remarks about blacks, especially on the part of Flambeau, can be found in 'The God of the Gongs' (*The Wisdom of Father Brown*). Much of the blame can be assigned to the prevailing culture of England, and to the baleful influence of Belloc, but it is a great pity that G.K., a man of deep and genuine piety, could not rise above such prejudices to the level of Jesus's teachings. (See Chapter 4, Note 1.)

Merton felt an almost bodily sickness at the sight of him; and he muttered to Gilder: 'Surely you would take Miss Armstrong's word against his?'

Father Brown suddenly lifted a face so absurdly fresh that it looked somehow as if he had just washed it. 'Yes,' he said, radiating innocence, 'but is Miss Armstrong's word against his?'

The girl uttered a startled, singular little cry; everyone looked at her. Her figure was rigid as if paralysed; only her face within its frame of faint brown hair was alive with an appalling surprise. She stood like one of a sudden lassooed and throttled.

'This man,' said Mr Gilder gravely, 'actually says that you were found grasping a knife, insensible, after the murder.'

'He says the truth,' answered Alice.

The next fact of which they were conscious was that Patrick Royce strode with his great stooping head into their ring and uttered the singular words: 'Well, if I've got to go, I'll have a bit of pleasure first.'

His huge shoulder heaved and he sent an iron fist smash into Magnus's bland Mongolian visage, laying him on the lawn as flat as a starfish. Two or three of the police instantly put their hands on Royce; but to the rest it seemed as if all reason had broken up and the universe were turning into a brainless harlequinade.

'None of that, Mr Royce,' Gilder had called out authoritatively. 'I shall arrest you for assault.'

'No, you won't,' answered the secretary in a voice like an iron gong, 'you will arrest me for murder.'

Gilder threw an alarmed glance at the man knocked down; but since that outraged person was already sitting up and wiping a little blood off a substantially uninjured face, he only said shortly: 'What do you mean?'

'It is quite true, as this fellow says,' explained Royce, 'that Miss Armstrong fainted with a knife in her hand. But she had not snatched the knife to attack her father, but to defend him.'

'To defend him,' repeated Gilder gravely. 'Against whom?'

'Against me,' answered the secretary.

Alice looked at him with a complex and baffling face; then she said in a low voice: 'After it all, I am still glad you are brave.'

'Come upstairs,' said Patrick Royce heavily, 'and I will show you the whole cursed thing.'

The attic, which was the secretary's private place (and rather a small cell for so large a hermit), had indeed all the vestiges of a violent drama. Near the centre of the floor lay a large revolver as if flung away; nearer to the left was rolled a whisky bottle, open but not quite empty. The cloth of the little table lay dragged and trampled, and a length of cord, like that found on the corpse, was cast wildly across the window-sill. Two vases were smashed on the mantelpiece and one on the carpet.

'I was drunk,' said Royce; and this simplicity in the prematurely battered man somehow had the pathos of the first sin of a baby.

'You all know about me,' he continued huskily; 'everybody knows how my story began, and it may as well end like that too. I was called a clever man once, and might have been a happy one; Armstrong saved the remains of a brain and body from the taverns, and was always kind to me in his own way, poor fellow! Only he wouldn't let me marry Alice here; and it will always be said that he was right enough. Well, you can form your own conclusions, and you won't want me to go into details. That is my whisky bottle half emptied in the corner; that is my revolver quite emptied on the carpet. It was the rope from my box that was found on the corpse, and it was from my window the corpse was thrown. You need not set detectives to grub up my tragedy; it is a common enough weed in this world. I give myself to the gallows; and, by God, that is enough!'

At a sufficiently delicate sign, the police gathered round the large man to lead him away; but their unobtrusiveness was somewhat staggered by the remarkable appearance of Father Brown, who was on his hands and knees on the carpet in the doorway, as if engaged in some kind of undignified prayers. Being a person utterly insensible to the social figure he cut, he remained in this posture, but turned a bright round face up at the company, presenting the appearance of a quadruped with a very comic human head.

'I say,' he said good-naturedly, 'this really won't do at all, you know. At the beginning you said we'd found no weapon. But now we're finding too many; there's the knife to stab, and the rope to strangle, and the pistol to shoot; and after all he broke his neck by falling out of a window! It won't do. It's not economical.' And he shook his head at the ground as a horse does grazing.

Inspector Gilder had opened his mouth with serious intentions, but before he could speak the grotesque figure on the floor had gone on quite volubly.

'And now three quite impossible things. First, these holes in the carpet, where the six bullets have gone in. Why on earth should anybody fire at the carpet? A drunken man lets fly at his enemy's head, the thing that's grinning at him. He doesn't pick a quarrel with his feet, or lay siege to his slippers. And then there's the rope'—and having done with the carpet the speaker lifted his hands and put them in his pockets, but continued unaffectedly on his knees—'in what conceivable intoxication would anybody try to put a rope round a man's neck and finally put it round his leg? Royce, anyhow, was not so drunk as that, or he would be sleeping like a log by now. And, plainest of all, the whisky bottle. You suggest a dipsomaniac fought for the whisky bottle, and then having won, rolled it away in a corner, spilling one half and leaving the other. That is the very last thing a dipsomaniac would do.'

He scrambled awkwardly to his feet, and said to the self-accused murderer in tones of limpid penitence: 'I'm awfully sorry, my dear sir, but your tale is really rubbish.'

'Sir,' said Alice Armstrong in a low tone to the priest, 'can I speak to you alone for a moment?'

This request forced the communicative cleric out of the gangway, and before he could speak in the next room, the girl was talking with strange incisiveness.

'You are a clever man,' she said, 'and you are trying to save Patrick, I know. But it's no use. The core of all this is black, and the more things you find out the more there will be against the miserable man I love.'

'Why?' asked Brown, looking at her steadily.

'Because,' she answered equally steadily, 'I saw him commit the crime myself.'

'Ah!' said the unmoved Brown, 'and what did he do?'

'I was in this room next to them,' she explained; 'both doors were closed, but I suddenly heard a voice, such as I had never heard on earth, roaring 'Hell, hell, hell,' again and again, and then the two doors shook with the first explosion of the revolver. Thrice again the thing banged before I got the two doors open and found the room full of smoke; but the pistol was smoking in my poor, mad Patrick's hand; and I saw him fire the last murderous volley with my own eyes. Then he leapt on my father, who was clinging in terror to the window-sill, and, grappling, tried to strangle him with the rope, which he threw over his head, but which slipped over his struggling shoulders to his feet. Then it tightened round one leg and Patrick dragged him along like a maniac. I snatched a knife from the mat, and, rushing between them, managed to cut the rope before I fainted.'

'I see,' said Father Brown, with the same wooden civility. 'Thank you.'

As the girl collapsed under her memories, the priest passed stiffly into the next room, where he found Gilder and Merton alone with Patrick Royce, who sat in a chair, handcuffed. There he said to the Inspector submissively:

'Might I say a word to the prisoner in your presence; and might he take off those funny cuffs for a minute?'

'He is a very powerful man,' said Merton in an undertone. 'Why do you want them taken off?'

'Why, I thought,' replied the priest humbly, 'that perhaps I might have the very great honour of shaking hands with him.'

Both detectives stared, and Father Brown added: 'Won't you tell them about it, sir?'

The man on the chair shook his tousled head, and the priest turned impatiently.

'Then I will,' he said. 'Private lives are more important than public reputations. I am going to save the living, and let the dead bury their dead.'[11]

He went to the fatal window, and blinked out of it as he went on talking.

'I told you that in this case there were too many weapons and only one death. I tell you now that they were not weapons, and were not used to cause death. All those grisly tools, the noose, the bloody knife, the exploding pistol, were instruments of a curious mercy. They were not used to kill Sir Aaron, but to save him.'

'To save him!' repeated Gilder. 'And from what?'

'From himself,' said Father Brown. 'He was a suicidal maniac.'

'*What?*' cried Merton in an incredulous tone. 'And the Religion of Cheerfulness——'

---

11. Father Brown is quoting Jesus (John 8: 22; Luke 9: 60).

'It is a cruel religion,' said the priest, looking out of the window. 'Why couldn't they let him weep a little, like his fathers before him? His plans stiffened, his views grew cold; behind that merry mask was the empty mind of the atheist. At last, to keep up his hilarious public level, he fell back on that dram-drinking he had abandoned long ago. But there is this horror about alcoholism in a sincere teetotaler: that he pictures and expects that psychological inferno from which he has warned others. It leapt upon poor Armstrong prematurely, and by this morning he was in such a case that he sat here and cried he was in hell, in so crazy a voice that his daughter did not know it. He was mad for death, and with the monkey tricks of the mad he had scattered round him death in many shapes—a running noose and his friend's revolver and a knife. Royce entered accidentally and acted in a flash. He flung the knife on the mat behind him, snatched up the revolver, and having no time to unload it, emptied it shot after shot all over the floor. The suicide saw a fourth shape of death, and made a dash for the window. The rescuer did the only thing he could—ran after him with the rope and tried to tie him hand and foot. Then it was that the unlucky girl ran in, and misunderstanding the struggle, strove to slash her father free. At first she only slashed poor Royce's knuckles, from which has come all the little blood in this affair. But, of course, you noticed that he left blood, but no wound, on that servant's face? Only before the poor woman swooned, she did hack her father loose, so that he went crashing through that window into eternity.'

There was a long stillness slowly broken by the metallic noises of Gilder unlocking the handcuffs of Patrick Royce, to whom he said: 'I think I should have told the truth, sir. You and the young lady are worth more than Armstrong's obituary notices.'

'Confound Armstrong's notices,' cried Royce roughly. 'Don't you see it was because she mustn't know?'

'Mustn't know what?' asked Merton.

'Why, that she killed her father, you fool!' roared the other. 'He'd have been alive now but for her. It might craze her to know that.'

'No, I don't think it would,' remarked Father Brown, as he picked up his hat. 'I rather think I should tell her. Even the most murderous blunders don't poison life like sins; anyhow, I think you may both be the happier now. I've got to go back to the Deaf School.'

As he went out on to the gusty grass an acquaintance from Highgate stopped him and said:

'The Coroner has arrived. The inquiry is just going to begin.'

'I've got to get back to the Deaf School,' said Father Brown. 'I'm sorry I can't stop for the inquiry.'[12]

## AFTERWORD

Chesterton was fond of the notion that one may appear to commit a crime when actually acting from the highest moral motives. Four of his best mystery stories, in the collection titled *Four Faultless Felons*, are based on this theme.

---

**12.** Father Brown's remark provides an appropriate ending for the book. The priest has no interest in the mundane details of police work or the legal outcomes of a crime. Once a mystery is solved, he is off to what he considers more important matters.

# BIBLIOGRAPHY

Five collections of Father Brown stories were published during Chesterton's lifetime: twelve stories in each of the first two books, eight in the third, ten in the fourth, and eight in the fifth, making fifty in all. At least three other stories about the priest are known that were not in any of the five books.

The earliest of the three appeared in an obscure British fiction magazine called *The Premier* (November 1914). The preceding issue had contained a story by Sir Max Pemberton in which a crime is left unsolved. At the end of the story the editors added the following note:

> Proofs of the above mystery story have been sent to Mr G. K. Chesterton, the creator of that famous detective of fiction, 'Father Brown'.
>
> This is quite a new idea of story-telling, and Mr Chesterton has entered into the spirit of the scheme with characteristic enthusiasm. His, or, rather, 'Father Brown's', solution of The Donnington Affair will be embodied in a complete story which will appear in next month's *Premier*.

Father Brown's complicated solution, which Chesterton tells in first person, is titled 'Father Brown and the Donnington Affair'. The two stories, Pemberton's and Chesterton's sequel, were reprinted in *The Chesterton Review*, Winter 1981. Comments by a reader, on the priest's solution of the crime, are in the Spring issue.

Chesterton's last Father Brown story, 'The Vampire of the Village', was published in England in *The Strand* (August 1936), a month or so after the author's death on 14 June. I first heard of this 'missing Father Brown' in 1943 when I was in the navy. My friend John Bennett Shaw, then still building his fabulous Chesterton collection (Shaw now owns the world's largest collection of Sherlockiana), had come across a reprint of the tale in, of all places, a 1939 Sunday edition of *The Chicago Tribune*. I wrote a letter about Shaw's discovery to Frederick Dannay, who was half of the writing team known as Ellery Queen. I assumed Dannay knew of the story, but wrote to propose that he reprint it in *Ellery Queen's Mystery Magazine*, which he edited.

'You're dead wrong', Dannay replied, '—it's *not* old stuff to me! In fact, I know of no Father Brown story by Chesterton that has not appeared in book form. I am writing to the *Chicago Tribune* at once . . . If such a story exists—a Father Brown not included in any of Chesterton's books—I should be willing to publish it in my magazine sight unseen!'

Dannay was unable to obtain permission to reprint the story in his magazine, but he did obtain rights to put it in a book. The story saw its first book publication in *Twentieth Century Detective Stories* (World, 1948), edited by Dannay. It has since been added to two one-volume collected editions of the five Father Brown books.

Apparently there is a 53rd Father Brown story that exists only in manuscript. I have been unable to learn the name of its owner, but I am told he is not yet willing to allow the story's publication.

There have been two Father Brown motion pictures in English (I am uninformed about foreign films), and two television series based on Chesterton's stories about the priest. Walter Connolly starred in the American movie, *Father Brown, Detective*, issued by Paramount in 1934. In 1954 England's Columbia Pictures produced *Father Brown*, with Alec Guinness in the title tole and Peter Finch playing Flambeau. The plot was based mainly on 'The Blue Cross'.

Although Guinness believed he was miscast as the priest, the picture marked a turning point in his life. Here is how the event is told in *Alec Guinness: A Celebration* (London: Pavilion Books, 1984), by John Russell Taylor:

Guinness has often spoken of an uncomfortable void in the centre of his life. Whether his religious beliefs are sufficient to fill this completely is a moot point. But at least in Roman Catholicism he seems to have found something which brings him a certain tranquility, in which his intellect and his instinct can be satisfactorily held in balance. It seems highly appropriate that, though he took some two years of thought and study to convince himself, the first step on the road to belief was purely instinctive. He once told an interviewer that the turning point came when he was making *Father Brown* in France, near Macon, and one night was walking back to his lodgings still wearing his priest's costume: 'It was absolutely dark. I heard little footsteps running after me. Suddenly I felt my hand taken by a seven-year-old boy, who walked with me all the way back to the village swinging my hand and chattering. I only caught little bits of what he was saying. I didn't dare utter a word in case I frightened him with a foreign accent or my clumsy French. I remained absolutely silent, and eventually he squeezed my hand and disappeared, and I thought it was simply marvellous that a child in that kind of dark, in a dark lane, will run up to a man because he's dressed as a priest. And it totally changed my attitude . . . I don't base my religion on that. But it's the attitude. No, I think it's marvellous that a small boy has confidence . . . I've always looked back on it as a magic moment . . .'

A short time after this experience, Guinness was received into the Catholic Church as a convert.

Kenneth More was Father Brown in a BBC television series of twelve episodes that played in England in 1973, and many years later in the United States as part of the Public Broadcasting System's 'Mystery!' series. A new series of seven Father Brown stories, all from *The Innocence*, was produced for BBC Radio in 1984 with Andrew Sachs taking the role of the priest. All twelve stories in *The Innocence of Father Brown*, read by Richard Green, were placed on eight one-hour cassette tapes in 1984. They are currently available from Books on Tape, Box 7900, Newport Beach, California 92660.

The following bibliography, compiled by William White, of Oakland University, Rochester, Michigan, appeared in *The Armchair Detective* (Summer 1983). Professor White has kindly given permission to reprint it here in a slightly updated form.

# G. K. CHESTERTON'S FATHER BROWN:
# A BIBLIOGRAPHY

by WILLIAM WHITE

Some bibliographies start from scratch, but a lot of them have been more or less lifted—that's a euphemism for stolen—from others. This one, of G. K. Chesterton's wonderful priest Father Brown, would not have been possible without books by the late John Sullivan: *G. K. Chesterton: A Bibliography* (London: University of London Press Ltd., 1958), *Chesterton Continued: A Bibliographical Supplement* (London: University of London Press Ltd., 1968), and *Chesterton Three: A Bibliographical Postscript* (Bedford: Vintage Publications, 1980).

I am especially grateful for the section on translations, and, if the material is occasionally incomplete, it's because John Sullivan is no longer in London to answer my queries. All G.K.C. enthusiasts will miss him. As for the list of secondary sources of chapters in books about Chesterton and the articles, which is the first list on such Father Brown material, I make no claims for its completeness. (Reviews of Father Brown books have been excluded.) Without the use of a major university or research library here in Florida, where it has been compiled, it's just about as full as I've been able to make it. I hope readers of *The Armchair Detective* will find it of some use and value.

### FIRST EDITIONS

*The Innocence of Father Brown.* London [etc.]: Cassell and Company, Ltd., 1911. Reprinted from *Cassell's Magazine* and the *Storyteller*. American edition—New York: John Lane Co., 1911.

*The Wisdom of Father Brown.* London [etc.]: Cassell and Company, Ltd., 1914. Reprinted from *Pall Mall Magazine*. American edition—New York: John Lane Co., 1915.

*The Incredulity of Father Brown.* London [etc.]: Cassell and Company, Ltd., 1926. Reprinted from *Cassell's Magazine* and *Nash's Pall Mall Magazine*. American edition—New York: Dodd, Mead, 1926.

*The Secret of Father Brown.* London [etc.]: Cassell and Company, 1927. Reprinted from *Cassell's Magazine* and the *Storyteller*. American edition—New York: Harper and Brothers, 1927.

*The Scandal of Father Brown.* London [etc.]: Cassell and Company Ltd., 1935. Reprinted from the *Storyteller*. American edition—New York: Dodd, Mead, 1935.

### SELECTIONS AND COLLECTIONS

*The Father Brown Stories.* London [etc.]: Cassell and Company, Ltd., 1929. New edition, to include *The Scandal of Father Brown*, 1947. American edition (as *The Father Brown Omnibus*)—New York: Dodd, Mead, 1933. 'The Vampire of the Village' was added to the 1951 American printing and to the 1953 English printing.

*Pocket Book of Father Brown.* New York: Pocket Books, 1943. Philadelphia: The Blakiston Co., 1943. [17 Father Brown stories]
*The Amazing Adventures of Father Brown.* A Dell Mystery. New York: Dell Publishing Co., 1954 [10 stories from 4 Father Brown books] Reprinted 1961 as *Ten Adventures of Father Brown,* introduction by Anthony Boucher.
*Father Brown: Selected Stories.* Introduction by Ronald Knox. World's Classics, No. 547. London: Oxford University Press, 1955.
*The First Book of Father Brown.* Edited for schools by Andrew Scotland. London: Cassell. Silver Circle Readers, 1958. [3 stories] *The Second Book of Father Brown.* [3 stories] *The Third Book of Father Brown.* [3 more stories] *The Fourth Book of Father Brown.* [3 more stories]
*Father Brown Stories.* London: Folio Society, 1959. [14 stories from 5 Father Brown books]
*Father Brown Mystery Stories.* Selected, with an Introduction, by Raymond T. Bond. New York: Dodd, Mead, 1962.

CURRENT EDITIONS

*The Penguin Complete Father Brown.* Harmondsworth, Middlesex, England; New York [etc.]: Penguin Books, 1981. 718 pp.
*The Innocence of Father Brown.* Harmondsworth, Middlesex, England; New York [etc.]: Penguin Books, 1982. 248 pp.
*The Wisdom of Father Brown.* Harmondsworth, Middlesex, England; New York [etc.]: Penguin Books, 1982. 200 pp.
*The Incredulity of Father Brown.* Harmondsworth, Middlesex, England; New York [etc.]: Penguin Books, 1982. 192 pp.
*The Secret of Father Brown.* Harmondsworth, Middlesex, England; New York [etc.]: Penguin Books, 1982. 176 pp.
*The Scandal of Father Brown.* Harmondsworth, Middlesex, England; New York [etc.]: Penguin Books, 1982. 175 pp. [Includes 'The Vampire of the Village'. All of these Father Brown volumes were issued in a similar format, with a portrait of Kenneth More on the front cover, and the legend: 'A Father Brown Mystery, Now a *Mystery* Television Presentation'.]


TRANSLATIONS

Czech

*Prostotota otce Browna [The Innocence of Father Brown].* Translated by A. L. Striz. Stará Rise: M. Floriánová, 1915.
*Nevinnost otce Browna [The Innocence of Father Brown].* Translated by Ivan Schulz. Praha: A. Srdce, 1915.
*Moudrost otce Browna [The Wisdom of Father Brown].* Translated by V. Gach. Praha: Rozmach, 1924.
*Neduvera otce Browna [The Incredulity of Father Brown].* Translated by Stasa Jilovská. Praha: F. Borovy, 1927.
*Tajemstvi otce Browna [The Secret of Father Brown].* Translated by Rudolf Uhl. Praha: J. Albert, 1947.

*Pribehy otce Browna [The Father Brown Stories]*. Translated by J. Z. Novak. Introduction by Jaroslav Hornát. Praha: SNKLHU, 1960. [13 stories]
*Providky otce Browna* [8 stories from *The Innocence of Father Brown*]. Translated by A. Hartmanová. Praha: SNDK, 1966.
*Pochybnosti otce Browna* [9 Father Brown stories]. Praha: Vysehrad, 1974.

Danish

*Fader Browns Historier [The Innocence of Father Brown]*. Edited by Kaj Nielsen and Marie Fergo. Copenhagen: Dansk Bog Klub, P.H. Fergos Forlag, 1939. 3rd Printing 1945. [Note: Later editions give Marie Fergo as sole translator].
*Den kloge Fader Brown [The Wisdom of Father Brown]*. Translated by Henning Kehler. Copenhagen: Frimodt, 1946.
*Den vantro Fader Brown [The Incredulity of Father Brown]*. Translated by Henning Kehler. Copenhagen: Frimodt, 1947.
*Fader Browns Hemmelighed [The Secret of Father Brown]*. Translated by Henning Kehler. Copenhagen: Frimodt, 1948.
*Fader Brown gør Skandale [The Scandal of Father Brown]*. Translated by Henning Kehler. Copenhagen: Frimodt, 1949.
*Fader Browns Mestersktykker* [? Father Brown Stories]. Selected, with an Introduction, by Tage la Cour. Translated by Marie Fergo and Henning Kehler, Copenhagen: Carit Anderson, 1958.

Dutch

*The Innocence of Father Brown*. Translated by N. H. M. Zwager. Groningen: J. B. Wolters, 1929 [Edited for schools]
*Avonturen van Father Brown [The Father Brown Stories]*. Translated by G. Bomans *et al.* Bossum, Paul Brand. Antwerp: Sheed and Ward, 1951. [2 volumes]
*Father Brown Hondt Zich van den Domme [The Innocence of Father Brown]*. Translated by A. A. O. Arens, A. F. C. Brosens *et al.* Antwerp: Het Spectrum, 1958.
*De Wijsheid van Father Brown [The Wisdom of Father Brown]*. Translated by E. Brongersma and A. Noorbeek. Antwerp: Prisma-Boeken, 1960.
*Het Geheim van Father Brown [The Secret of Father Brown]*. Translated by E. Santen and E. Brongersma. Utrecht/Antwerp: Prisma-Boeken, 1961.
*Father Brown Laat Zich mit Foppen [The Incredulity of Father Brown]*. Translated by E. Santen and R. Mon-Timmermans. Urecht/Antwerp: Prisma-Boeken, 1961.

Esperanto

*La Naiveco de Pastro Brown [The Innocence of Father Brown]*. Translated by Cecil Bean. Rickmansworth, Herts: Esperanto Publishing Co., 1937.

French

*La Clairvoyance du Père Brown [The Innocence of Father Brown]*. Translated by Emile Cammaerts. Paris: Perrin, 1919.

*Le Secret du Père Brown [The Secret of Father Brown]*. Translated by Mme. F. Maury. Paris: Gallimard, 1929.
*L'Incrédulité du Père Brown [The Incredulity of Father Brown]*. Translated by Mme. F. Maury. Paris: Gallimard, 1932.
*La Sagesse du Père Brown [The Wisdom of Father Brown]*. Translated by Y. André. Paris: Gallimard, 1936.
*Le Livre Maudit* ['The Blast of the Book', from *The Scandal of Father Brown*]. Translated by J. Fournier-Pargoire. Paris: Editions du Bateau Ivre, 1946.

Gaelic

*The Innocence of Father Brown*. Translated by Seán O'Liatáin. Dublin: Government Printing Office, 1937.

German

*Des Paradies der Diebe* ['The Paradise of Thieves' and other stories from *The Wisdom of Father Brown*]. Translated by C. Meitner. Munich: Musarion, 1927.
*Die verdachtigen Schritte [The Innocence of Father Brown]*. Translated by H. M. von Lama. Munich: Kasel, 1927.
*Ein Pfeil von Himmel: Kriminalerzahlüngen* ['The Arrow of Heaven' and 5 other Father Brown stories]. Translated by D. S. Kellner. Berlin: Die Schmiede, 1927.
*Das Geheimnis des Pater Brown [The Secret of Father Brown]*. Translated by R. Nutt. Frankfurt and Hamburg: Fischer Bücherei, 1928.
*Wer war der Täter? [The Scandal of Father Brown]*. Translated by K. Demmer. Vienna: Amandus, 1948.
*Das Geheimnis des Pater Brown [The Secret of Father Brown]*. Translated by A. P. Zeller. Munich: Droemer, 1958.

Hebrew

*The Innocence of Father Brown*, 1960.

Hungarian

*The Wisdom of Father Brown*. Translated by Franklin-Tarsulat, 1936.
*A Jambor Brown Atya [The Innocence of Father Brown]*. Translated by T. Bartos. Budapest: Europa, 1958.

Italian

*Il Candore di Padre Brown [The Innocence of Father Brown]*. Translated by R. Constanzi. Milan: Rizzoli, 1930.
*Il Segreto di Padre Brown [The Secret of Father Brown]*. Translated by I. Lori. Milan: Bietti, 1931.
*Lo Scandalo di Padre Brown [The Scandal of Father Brown]*. Translated by E. Pivetti. Milan: Garzanti, 1949.
*La Saggezza di Padre Brown [The Wisdom of Father Brown]*. Translated by G. Dauli. Milan: Istituto di Propaganda Libraria, 1952.
*L'Innocenza di Padre Brown [The Innocence of Father Brown]*. Translated by G. Dauli. Milan: Istituto di Propaganda Libraria, 1952.

*L'Incredulità di Padre Brown [The Incredulity of Father Brown].* Translated by M. I. Guintavalle. Balsamo: Edizioni Paoline, 1953.
*Un Prete Detective Padre Brown.* Translated by G. Dauli, M. I. Guintavalle, E. di Carli. Milan: Editrice A.A.S., 1956. [Contains *L'Innocenza di Padre Brown, L'Incredulità di Padre Brown, La Sagezza di Padre Brown,* and *Il Segreto di Father Brown*]

Japanese

*Aoi Jujika* ['The Blue Cross' from *The Innocence of Father Brown*]. Translated by Genpu Asano. Tokyo: Hakubunkan, 1922.
*Brown Kitan* [Selected Father Brown stories]. Translated by Sanjugo Naoki. Tokyo: Heibonsha, 1930.
*Brown Shinpu no Muchi [The Innocence of Father Brown].* Translated by Toshiro Murasaki. Tokyo: Hayakawa Shobo, 1955.
*Brown Shinpu [Father Brown:* selected Father Brown stories]. Translated by Tsuneari Fukuda: Tokyo: Sogensha, 1956.
*Brown Shinpu no Kaigi [The Incredulity of Father Brown].* Translated by Toshiro Murasaki. Tokyo: Hayakawa Shobo, 1956.
*Brown Shinpu no Chie [The Wisdom of Father Brown].* Translated by Toshiro Murasaki. Tokyo: Hayakawa Shobo, 1957.
*Brown Shinpu no Himitsu [The Secret of Father Brown].* Translated by Toshiro Murasaki. Tokyo: Hayakawa Shobo, 1957.
*Brown Shinpu no Shubun [The Scandal of Father Brown].* Translated by Toshiro Murasaki. Tokyo: Hayakawa Shobo, 1957.
*Brown Shinpu no Doshin [The Innocence of Father Brown].* Translated by Tsuneari Fukuda and Yasuo Nakamura. Tokyo: Sogen Shinsha, 1959.
*Brown Shinpu no Fushin [The Incredulity of Father Brown].* Translated by Tsuneari Fukuda and Yasuo Nakamura. Tokyo: Sogen Shinsha, 1960.
*Brown Shinpu no Chie [The Wisdom of Father Brown].* Translated by Tsuneari Fukuda and Yasuo Nakamura. Tokyo: Sogen Shinsha, 1960.
*Brown Shinpu no Himitsu [The Secret of Father Brown].* Translatd by Tsuneari Fukuda and Yasuo Nakamura. Tokyo: Sogen Shinsha, 1961.
*Brown Shinpu Monogatari [The Father Brown Stories].* Translated by Nishijiro Tanaka. Tokyo: Chuo Koron Sha, 1962.
*Brown Shinpu Tanpen Shu* [Selected Father Brown stories]. Translated by Toyoitsu Miyanishi. Tokyo: Toto Shobo, 1963.
*Brown Shinpu no Himitsu [The Secret of Father Brown].* Translated by Minoru Hashiguchi. Tokyo: Shinchosa, 1964.

Polish

*Niewinnosc ojca Browna [The Innocence of Father Brown].* Translated by Ziemilska. Warsaw, Rój, 1927.
*Grzechy ksiecia Saradine [The Innocence of Father Brown,* continued]. Translated by Ziemilska. Warsaw: Rój, 1928.
*O madrosci ojca Browna [The Wisdom of Father Brown].* Translated by Jósefa Zydlerowa. Warsaw: Rój, 1928.
*Tajemnica ojca Browna [The Secret of Father Brown].* Translated by Jósefa Zydlerowa. Warsaw: Rój, 1928.

*Niedowiarstwo ksidza Browna [The Incredulity of Father Brown]*. Translated by Adam Cehak-Stodor and Anna Szottowa. Poznan: Ksiegarnia sw. Wojciecha, 1929.
*Niebieski krzyz* ['The Blue Cross' from *The Innocence of Father Brown*]. Translated by E. Arthurton-Barker and N. Reh. Duns: Caldra House, 1947. [Bi-lingual edition]
*Prygody ksiedza Browna [Adventures of Father Brown*: selection of 18 Father Brown stories]. Translated by Tadeusz Jan Dehnel. Warsaw: Pax, 1958.
*Zlamana szabla* ['The Sign of the Broken Sword' from *The Innocence of Father Brown* and other Father Brown stories]. Translated by Tadeusz Jan Dehnel. Warsaw: KIW, 1968.

Portuguese

*The Wisdom of Father Brown*. Lisbon: Libraria Cruz, 1945.
*The Incredulity of Father Brown*. Lisbon: Libraria Cruz, 1945.
*A Inocenzia do Padre Brown [The Innocence of Father Brown]*. Translated by E. A. Cunha. Rio de Janeiro: Record, 1973.

Russian

*The Innocence of Father Brown*. Translated by V. Krymar. Berlin: 'Argus', 1923.
*The Incredulity of Father Brown*. Translated by E. Roks. Tallin: Estgosizdat, 1958.
*Stories* [Selection of 15 Father Brown stories]. Edited by A. Gavrilova. Foreword by A. Yelistratova. Moscow: State Publishing House, 1958.
*Selected Stories* [Selection of 8 Father Brown stories]. Edited by Elena Gusava. Moscow: Progress, 1960. [English text with Russian notes and glossary]

Spanish

*La Sabiduria del Padre Brown [The Wisdom of Father Brown]*. Translated by A. Nadal. Barcelona: Biblioteca Oro, 1936.
*La Incredulidad del Padre Brown [The Incredulity of Father Brown]*. Translated by I. Abello de Lamarca. Barcelona: Editorial Tartessos, 1942.
*El Candor del Padre Brown [The Innocence of Father Brown]*. Translated by A. Reyes. Barcelona: José Janés, 1946.
*El Escandalo del Padre Brown [The Scandal of Father Brown]*. Translated by F. G. Taujis. Barcelona: José Janés. 1946.
*La Sabiduria del Padre Brown [The Wisdom of Father Brown]*. Barcelona: José Janés, 1946.
*El Secreto del Padre Brown [The Secret of Father Brown]*. Barcelona: José Janés, 1946.
*La Incredulidad del Padre Brown [The Incredulity of Father Brown]*. Barcelona: José Janés, 1946.
*Father Brown Stories* [12 stories from *The Wisdom of Father Brown* in separate uniform editions]. Translated by Maria Antonio Oyuela de Grant. Buenos Aires: Editorial la Isla, 1956 and later.

Norwegian

*Fader Brown og hans oplevelser [The Innocence of Father Brown].* Translated by
Hans Jonstang. Oslo: Aschehoug, 1916.
*Den uskyldige Fader Brown* (9 Father Brown stories]. Selected, with an Intro-
duction and Bibliography, by Nils Nordberg. Translated by Per Th.
Edwardssen and Axel Amlie. Oslo: Gyldendal, 1973.

Swedish

*Den menlöse Fader Brown [The Innocence of Father Brown].* Translated by H.
Flygare. Stockholm: Gebers, 1912.
*Fader Browns visdom [The Wisdom of Father Brown].* Translated by H. Flygare.
Stockholm: Gebers, 1921.
*Fader Browns hemlighet [The Secret of Father Brown].* Translated by Kate
Hildén. Stockholm: Holger Schildt, 1930.
*Father Brown* [20 Father Brown stories]. Translated by T. Zetterholm.
Stockholm: Albatross, Norstedt, 1950.
*Den öövertraffade Fader Brown* [11 Father Brown stories]. Translated by
H. Flygare, K. Hildén, *et al.* Stockholm: Tiden, 1965.

BOOKS AND CHAPTERS IN BOOKS ABOUT FATHER BROWN

Ball, John ed. *The Mystery Story.* Harmondsworth, Middlesex, England: Penguin Books, 1978, pp. 95–96 (in Otto Penzler, 'The Amateur Detectives');
pp. 4, 19, 20, 111, 153, 175, 202, 300, 339, 341, 387–88, 390.
Bargainnier, Earl, ed. *A Baker's Dozen: Thirteen Englishmen of Mystery.* Bowl-
ing Green, Ohio: Bowling Green State University Popular Press, 1983.
Barker, Dudley. *G. K. Chesterton: A Biography.* London: Constable, 1973,
pp. 194–97, 205, 253–54, 259, 266–67 ('The Blue Cross'—his best).
Barnes, Melvyn. *Best Detective Fiction.* London: Clive Bingley; Hamden,
Conn.: Linnet Books, 1975, p. 33.
Barzun, Jacques, and Wendell Hertig Taylor. *A Catalogue of Crime.* New
York [etc.]: Harper & Row, 1971, Items No. 139–40, 490, 1571, 1925,
2135, 2316, 2319–20, 2322–23, 2350, 2361, 2405–12, 2569, 2642, 2728,
2735, 2750, 2765, 2778, 2784, 2795, 2798, 2875, 2899, 2904, 2914, 2920,
2921–26, 2955, 2967, 3008.
Benvenuti, Stefano, and Gianni Rizzoni. *The Whodunit: An Informal History of
Detective Fiction.* Translated by Anthony Eyre. New York: Collier Books;
London: Collier Macmillan Publishers, 1979, pp. 14, 37–39, 42, 56, 88,
92, 112, 144, 186, 189, 192, 199.
Bond, Raymond T. Introduction to *Father Brown Mystery Stories.* New York:
Dodd, Mead, 1962.
Boyd, Ian. *The Novels of G. K. Chesterton: A Study in Art and Propaganda.* New
York: Barnes & Noble; London: Paul Elek Ltd., 1975, pp. 139, 218, 221.
Bruce, Leo [Rupert Crift-Cooke]. *Case for Three Detectives.* Chicago: Acad-
emy Chicago Limited, 1980. [Parody of three detectives, Lord Peter
Wimsey, Hercule Poirot, and Father Brown (under the name of Mon-
signor Smith)]

Canovan, Margaret. *G. K. Chesterton: Radical Populist*. New York and London: Harcourt Brace Jovanovich, 1977, pp. 7–8, 155, 156, 166.

Chesterton, Mrs Cecil. *The Chestertons*. London: Chapman & Hall Ltd., 1941, p. 298.

Chesterton, G. K. *Autobiography*. New York: Sheed and Ward, 1936, pp. 332–40; London: Hutchinson, 1949, pp. 321–22. [Father Brown is based on Father John O'Connor, but not his physical appearance]

Clipper, Lawrence. *G. K. Chesterton*. New York: Twayne Publishers, Inc., 1974, pp. 121–25 ('Father Brown'), 62, 105, 126, 143.

D'Haussy, Christiane. *La vision du monde chez G. K. Chesterton*. Etudes Anglaises 77. Paris: Didier-Erudition, 1981?, pp. 48, 63, 72, 80, 81, 82, 109, 165, 185, 210, 211, 212, 234, 243.

Gilbert, Elliot L., ed. *The World of Mystery Fiction*. Del Mar, Calif.: University Extension, University of California at San Diego, Publishers, Inc., 1978, pp. 199–216 ('The Oracle of the Dog'), xxi–xxii, 198.

Hagen, Ordean A. *Who Done It? A Guide to Detective, Mystery and Suspense Fiction*. New York: R. R. Bowker Company, 1969, pp. 72, 431, 456, 509.

Haycraft, Howard. *Murder for Pleasure: The Life and Times of the Dectective Story*. New York and London: D. Appleton-Century Company, Inc., 1941, pp. 43, 74–77, 226, 227, 242, 304.

—— ed. *The Art of the Mystery Story: A Collection of Critical Essays*. New York: Simon and Schuster, 1946, pp. 3–6 (G. K. Chesterton, 'A Defence of Detective Stories'), 2, 4, 23, 50, 51, 61, 67, 68, 69, 82, 84, 102, 106, 107, 116, 132, 138, 194, 197, 209, 281, 288, 408, 412, 414, 457, 463, 479, 481, 499.

Hicks, Christopher. *The Mind of Chesterton*. Coral Gables: University of Miami Press; London [etc.]: Hollis & Carter, 1970, pp. 179–83, 243.

Hunter, Lynette. *G. K. Chesterton: Explorations in Allegory*. London [etc.]: The Macmillan Press Ltd., 1979, pp. 134–35, 140–58, 162.

Keating, H. R. F., ed. *Whodunit? A Guide to Crime, Suspense and Spy Fiction*. London: Shuckburgh Reynolds Ltd.; New York [etc.]: Van Nostrand Reinhold Company, 1982, pp. 29, 52, 71, 123, 136 ('Chesterton, G. K.'), 258 ('Brown, Father'), 270.

Kenner, Hugh. *Paradox in Chesterton*. Introduction by Herbert Marshall McLuhan. New York: Sheed and Ward, 1947, pp. 129–30.

Knox, Ronald, Introduction to *Father Brown: Selected Stories* by G. K. Chesterton. World's Classics No. 547. London: Oxford University Press, 1955. Reprinted in R. A. Knox, *Literary Distractions* (London: Sheed and Ward, 1958) as 'Father Brown'.

La Cour, Tage, and Harold Mordensen. *The Murder Book: An Ilustrated History of the Detective Story*. Translated by Roy Duffell. London: George Allen & Unwin Ltd., 1971. [Originally published as *Mordbogen* in Copenhagen in 1969, it contains two chapters on 'The Wisdom of Father Brown' and 'Father Brown in Films']

Murch, A[lma] E[lizabeth]. *The Development of the Detective Novel*. London: Peter Owen Limited, 1958, pp. 9, 10, 14, 62, 75, 199–202, 229.

Nehaus, Volker. 'Father Brown und Rabbi Small'. In Beda Allemann, Erwin Kappen, and Dieter Gutzen, eds., *Teilnahme und Spiegelung: Fest-*

*schrift für Horst Rüdiger*. Berlin and New York: De Gruyter, 1975, pp. 548–69.

O'Connor, Monsignor John. *Father Brown on Chesterton*. London: Burns, Oates, & Washbourne; Toronto: S. J. Reginald Saunders, 1937.

Papančev, Georgi. 'Razkazite na Čestertăn' ('Chesterton's Short Stories'). In *Prostodušieto na octec Braun (The Innocence of Father Brown)*. Sofia: Narodna Mladež, 1977, pp. 181–83.

Parkes, David L. 'Chesterton, G. K.' In Kenneth Richardson, ed., *Twentieth Century Writing: A Guide to Contemporary Literature*. London [etc.]: Newnes Books, 1969, pp. 124–25.

Penzler, Otto, Chris Steinbrunner, and Marvin Lachman, eds. *Detectionary: A Biographical Dictionary of Leading Characters in Detective and Mystery Fiction*. Woodstock, N.Y.: The Overlook Press, 1977, pp. 12 ('Brown, Father'), 104 ('Flambeau'), 118 ('Valentin, Aristide'), 129 ('Blue Cross, The'), 177 ('Secret Garden, The').

Queen, Ellery. *Queen's Quorum: A History of the Detective-Crime Short Story as Recorded by the 106 Most Important Books Published in the Field Since 1845*. Boston: Little, Brown and Company, 1951, pp. v, 28, 60–61, 68, 98, 109, 114, 117. [*The Innocence of Father Brown* is No. 47 (see pp. 60–61)]

Robson, W. W. 'Father Brown and Others'. In John Sullivan, ed., *G. K. Chesterton: A Centenary Appraisal*. London: Paul Elek; New York: Barnes & Noble, 1974, pp. 58–72; see also pp. 13–14, 39, 49–50, 83, 91–92, 158, 178–179, 211, 213, 215, 224–25, 226, 227, 231–33, 234, 235.

Sister M. Carol, A. C. *G. K. Chesterton: The Dynamic Classicist*. Delhi, Veranasi, Patna: Motibal Banarsidass, 1971, pp. 163–71.

Starrett, Vincent. *Best Loved Books of the Twentieth Century*. New York: Bantam Books, 1955. 'The Innocence of Father Brown', pp. 33–35.

Steinbrunner, Chris, and Otto Penzler, eds. *Encyclopedia of Mystery and Detection*. New York [etc.]: McGraw-Hill Book Company, 1976, pp. 48–49 ('Brown, Father'), 82–83 ('Chesterton, G. K.').

Symons, Julian. *Mortal Consequences: A History—From the Detective Story to the Crime Novel*. New York: Schocken, 1973 (Harper and Row, 1972), pp. 62, 73, 78–81, 94, 104, 120, 121, 171.

Ward, Maisie. *Gilbert Keith Chesterton*. New York: Sheed and Ward, 1943, pp. 251–52, 277–78, 368, 547.

West, Julius. *G. K. Chesterton: A Critical Study*. London: Martin Secker, 1915, pp. 45–58, 74, 166.

Wills, Garry. *Chesterton: Man and Mask*. New York: Sheed and Ward, 1961. *Father Brown Omnibus*, pp. 121, 124–25, 164, 202, 229, 231; 'Detective Tales', pp. 122–25.

Winn, Dilys. *Murder Ink: The Mystery Reader's Companion*. New York: Workman Publishing, 1977, pp. 19, 187, 469, 488, 489.

ARTICLES ABOUT FATHER BROWN

Bramah, Ernest. 'Father Brown'. *G. K.'s Weekly*, 24 (8 October 1936), 84–85.

Cherno, Melvin. 'Father Brown and the Historian'. *The Chesterton Review*, 10 (1984), pp. 159–64.

Christopher, Joe R. 'Father Brown and American Detective Fiction'. *The Chesterton Review*, 10 (1984), pp. 213–16.

Fabritius, Rudolf. 'Das Bild des "Gentleman" in G. K. Chestertons Detektivgeschichte "The Queer Feet" '. *Die Neuren Sprachen*, 14 (1965), 376–81.

Gillespie, Robert. 'Detections: Borges and Father Brown'. *Novel*, 7 (Spring 1974), 220–30.

Green, Benny. 'Father of Father Brown'. *Sunday Telegraph* (London), 7 June 1974.

Greene, Douglas. 'A Mastery of Miracles: G. K. Chesterton and John Dickson Carr'. *The Chesterton Review*, 10 (1984), pp. 307–15.

Grist, Anthony. 'Father Brown and Kenneth More'. *The Chesterton Review*, 9 (February 1983), 85–87.

—— 'Kenneth More as Father Brown'. *The Chesterton Review*. 10 (1984), pp. 177–82.

Hayes, Aden W., and Khachig Tololyan. 'The Cross and the Compass: Patterns of Order in Chesterton and Borges'. *Hispanic Review*, 49 (Autumn 1981), 395–405. [The influence of 'The Blue Cross' on Borges]

Hays, R. W. 'Religion and the Detective Story'. *The Armchair Detective*, 8 (November 1974), 24–26.

—— 'The Private Life of Father Brown'. *The Armchair Detective*, 4 (April 1971), 135–39.

Lowndes, Robert A. W. 'G. K. Chesterton's Father Brown'. *The Armchair Detective*, 9 (1976), 184–38, 235.

Melin, Lars. 'Fader Browns kristen-kriminologiska manifest'. *Credo: Katolsk Tidskrift* (Uppsala), 46 (1965), 216–20.

Mulloy, John J. 'The Twilight or Daylight World of Father Brown? An Answer to Professor Scheick'. *The Chesterton Review*, 4 (1978), 316–18. [See William J. Scheick, below; William J. Scheick replies, pp. 318–20]

Norberg, Nils. 'Father Brown in Scandinavia'. *The Chesterton Review*, 10 (1984), pp. 198–202.

O'Connor, Monsignor John. Father Brown. 'G. K. Chesterton: Recognita Decennalia'. *Nineteenth Century and After*, 139 (June 1946), 301–7.

Penzler, Otto. 'Collecting Mystery Fiction: Father Brown'. *The Armchair Detective*, 16 (1983), pp. 248–50.

Petrie, Maria. 'Father Brown and Concavism: More About the Private Chesterton'. *Manchester Guardian*, 11 June 1955.

Purcell, Mark. 'Mystery Reviewer's Handbook: Father Brown'. *The Armchair Detective*, 6 (May 1973), 159. [Poem]

Reinsdorf, Walter. 'The Perception of Father Brown'. *The Chesterton Review*, 10 (1984), pp. 265–74.

Robson, W. W. 'G. K. Chesterton's "Father Brown" Stories'. *Southern Review*, n.s. 5 (Summer 1969), 611–29. Reprinted in John Sullivan, ed., *G. K. Chesterton: A Centenary Appraisal*. New York: Harper and Row, 1974.

Scheick, William J. 'The Twilight Harlequinade of Chesterton's Father Brown'. *The Chesterton Review*, 4 (1977–78), 104–14. Comments by readers, 4 (1978), pp. 316–20.

## ADDENDUM

by WILLIAM WHITE

(1986)

*The Father Brown Omnibus.* With a Preface, 'A Tremendous Trifle', by Auberon Waugh, and a Foreword by R. T. Bond. New York: Dodd, Mead and Company, 1983. xvii, 993 pp.

Boulton, Marjorie. 'Father Brown in Esperanto'. *The Chesterton Review*, 10 (1984), pp. 317–23.

Chesterton, G. K. ' "Father Brown" and the Donnington Affair'. *The Chesterton Review*, 7 (1981), pp. 21–35.

—— ' "Folk Song" '. *The Chesterton Review*, 10 (1984), p. 134. [Poem]

Christopher, Joe R. 'Chesterton, Father Brown, and the Detection Club'. *The Chesterton Review*, 10 (1984), 327–30.

Eberwein, Jane Donahue. 'The Priest and the Poets'. *The Chesterton Review*, 10 (1984), pp. 165–76.

Pemberton, Max. 'The Donnington Affair'. *The Chesterton Review*, 7 (1981), pp. 1–20.

Purcell, J. M. 'Father Brown and Floating Admirals: G. K. Chesterton and the Oldstyle Detective Story'. *The Chesterton Review*, 10 (1984), pp. 203–12.

White, Gertrude M. 'Mirror and Microcosm: Chesterton's Father Brown Stories'. *The Chesterton Review*, 10 (1984), pp. 183–97.

Woodcock, George. 'Chesterton G(ilbert) K(eith)'. In John M. Reilly, ed., *Twentieth-Century Crime and Mystery Writers*. New York: St. Martin's Press, 1980, pp. 293–9.

## BIBLIOGRAPHIC SUPPLEMENT

by MARTIN GARDNER

### ESSAYS BY CHESTERTON ON THE ART OF THE MYSTERY STORY

'A Defence of Detective Stories', in *The Defendant* (London: R. Brimley Johnson, 1914).

'The Domesticity of Detectives', in *The Uses of Diversity* (London: Methuen, 1920).

'How to Write a Detective Story', in *G. K.'s Weekly*, 17 October, 1925. Reprinted in *The Spice of Life*, Chesterton essays selected by Dorothy Collins (Beaconsfield: Darwen Finlayson, 1964), and in *The Chesterton Review*, 10 (1984), pp. 111–18.

'On Detective Novels', in *Generally Speaking* (London: Methuen, 1928).

'Detective Stories', in *G. K. C. as M. C.* (London: Methuen, 1929).

'Advice to Literary Murderers', in *The Tribune*, edited by D. Mackenzie (London: John Horn, 1930). Reprinted in *Ellery Queen's Mystery Magazine* (New York, July 1947).

'On Detective Story Writers', in *Come to Think of It* (London: Methuen, 1931).

'About Shockers', in *As I was Saying* (London: Methuen, 1936).
'Sherlock Holmes', in *A Handful of Authors* (London: Sheed and Ward, 1953).

BOOKS BY CHESTERTON CITED IN THE INTRODUCTION AND NOTES

Only first British editions are given, the titles alphabetized. In some cases American editions have slightly different titles.

*Alarms and Discursions* (Methuen, 1910)
*All is Grist* (Methuen, 1931)
*Autobiography* (Hutchinson, 1936)
*The Ball and the Cross* (Wells Gardner, Darton and Co., 1910)
*The Club of Queer Trades* (Harper and Brothers, 1905)
*The End of the Armistice* (Sheed and Ward, 1940)
*Fancies Versus Fads* (Methuen, 1923)
*Four Faultless Felons* (Cassell, 1930)
*George Bernard Shaw* (John Lane, 1909)
*Greybeards at Play* (R. Brimley Johnson, 1900)
*Manalive* (Thomas Nelson, 1912)
*The Man Who Knew Too Much* (Cassell, 1922)
*The Man Who Was Thursday* (Simpkins, Marshall, Hamilton, Kent and Co., 1908)
*The Napoleon of Notting Hill* (W. Graham Robertson, 1904)
*The New Jerusalem* (Hodder and Stoughton, 1920)
*Orthodoxy* (John Lane, 1908)
*The Paradoxes of Mr Pond* (Cassell, 1937)
*The Poet and the Lunatics* (Cassell, 1929)
*The Resurrection of Rome* (Hodder and Stoughton, 1930)
*The Thing* (Sheed and Ward, 1929)
*Tremendous Trifles* (Methuen, 1909)
*The Uses of Diversity* (Methuen, 1920)

BOOKS ABOUT CHESTERTON CITED IN THE INTRODUCTION
AND NOTES

Hollis, Christopher. *The Mind of Chesterton*. Florida: University of Miami Press, 1970.
O'Connor, John. *Father Brown on Chesterton*. London: Frederick Muller, 1957.
Ward, Maisie. *Gilbert Keith Chesterton*. New York: Sheed and Ward, 1943 (London, 1944).
—— *Return to Chesterton*. London: Sheed and Ward, 1952.

# INDEX TO THE ANNOTATION

Where relevant, the note number is given as well as the page number, so that 201n6, for example, refers to Note 6 on page 201.